RABBI ZALMAN
SCHACHTER-SHALOMI

MODERN SPIRITUAL MASTERS SERIES

RABBI ZALMAN SCHACHTER-SHALOMI

Essential Teachings

Selected, Introduced, and Annotated by

OR N. ROSE

and

NETANEL MILES-YÉPEZ

Maryknoll, New York 10545

ORBIS BOOKS
Maryknoll, New York 10545

Fathers and Brothers
MARYKNOLL™

Founded in 1970, Orbis Books endeavors to publish works that enlighten the mind, nourish the spirit, and challenge the conscience. The publishing arm of the Maryknoll Fathers and Brothers, Orbis seeks to explore the global dimensions of the Christian faith and mission, to invite dialogue with diverse cultures and religious traditions, and to serve the cause of reconciliation and peace. The books published reflect the views of their authors and do not represent the official position of the Maryknoll Society. To learn more about Maryknoll and Orbis Books, please visit our website at www.orbisbooks.com

Library of Congress Cataloging-in-Publication Data

Names: Schachter-Shalomi, Zalman, 1924-2014, author. | Rose, Or N., editor. | Miles-Yepez, Netanel, editor.
Title: Rabbi Zalman Schachter-Shalomi : essential teachings / selected, introduced, and annotated Or N. Rose and Netanel Miles-Yepez ; preface by Arthur Green ; closing reflections by Tirzah Firestone, Matthew Fox, and Judith Simmer-Brown.
Description: Maryknoll : Orbis Books, 2020. | Series: Modern spiritual masters | Includes bibliographical references and index.
Identifiers: LCCN 2019048197 (print) | LCCN 2019048198 (ebook) | ISBN 9781626983632 (paperback) | ISBN 9781608338276 (ebook)
Subjects: LCSH: Schachter-Shalomi, Zalman, 1924-2014. | Spiritual life—Judaism. | Jewish way of life. | Jewish renewal. | Hasidism. | Rabbis—United States—Biography. | United States—Biography.
Classification: LCC BM723 .S2946 2020 (print) | LCC BM723 (ebook) | DDC
  296.7—dc23
LC record available at https://lccn.loc.gov/2019048197
LC ebook record available at https://lccn.loc.gov/2019048198

*We dedicate this volume to Reb Zalman's children,
grandchildren, and great grandchildren.
May the words of our teacher's Torah be sweet on
the tongues of future generations.*

Acknowledgments

We are grateful to the following individuals and organizations for their assistance with and support for this project—*rav todot, shukran jazilan*, thank you!

Rebbetzin Eve Ilsen

Elana Schacter

Shalom Schacter

Batya Ellinoy, Joey Glick

Rabbi David Maayan

Hillary Floyd

Rabbi Sharon Cohen Anisfeld

Rabbi Ebn Leader

Rabbi Marcia Prager

Rabbi Daniel Siegel

Jamelah Zidan

Judith Rosenbaum, Ma'ayan Rosenbaum, Aviv Rosenbaum

Rabbi Neal and Carol Rose

Rabbi Arthur Green

Dr. Judith Simmer-Brown

Father Matthew Fox

Rabbi Tirzah Firestone

Yesod Foundation (Aaron Claman, Tirzah Firestone, David Friedman, Thomas Hast, and Bobbie Zelkind), with special thanks for permission to use the Yesod *mehorah* symbol throughout the book

Contents

Foreword

Avraham Yizhak
(Arthur) Green

When I was invited to write a foreword to this collection of teachings by my dear friend and mentor Reb Zalman, I immediately heard a question he taught me to ask decades ago: "How do you say that in Jewish?" (My Aunt Ruth, asking the same question, meant Yiddish when she said "Jewish," but Zalman meant something else.)

The word for title page in Hebrew is *sha'ar*, gateway. The word for foreword is *petihah*, opening. So, I am here to open for you the gateway to the teachings of Reb Zalman Schachter-Shalomi. That sounds simple and straightforward enough. The challenge with it, however, is that Reb Zalman was himself a consummate gate opener. In fact, right after I heard that he had passed away, I wrote to a few friends as follows:

> Zalman was all about prayer. So my first thought in talking about him here comes from *tefillah* (prayer), rather than a verse from Torah. It is a line we know well from the *Ne'ilah* service of Yom Kippur: "Open the gate for us, as it is being closed!"

Zalman opened the gates of Judaism for so many, giving special attention to people at the beginning of their journeys. He always taught and wrote accessibly, warmly welcoming people into the tradition. Of course, he didn't care who you were: Jewish; non-Jewish; committed Sufi; Christian monk or nun; Buddhist practitioner—everyone was welcome! He recognized how difficult a traditional Jewish mystical path could be for beginners, and he tried to change that. In a world undergoing dramatic change—a "paradigm shift," as he so often called it—he followed the example of the head of his spiritual lineage, Rabbi Shneur Zalman of Liadi (1745–1812). In writing his great mystical treatise, the *Tanya*, Rabbi Shneur Zalman asked himself, what are the things a seeker really needs to know, and how can I say them in a simple, direct, but devotionally stirring manner?

As it is being closed. Zalman felt the terrible loss caused to the Jewish spiritual tradition, as well as to the Jewish people brought about by the Holocaust, which he had barely escaped. In the early years—and I had the privilege of knowing and hearing him teach first in the late 1950s—he would speak often of the lost masters and teachings that had gone up in smoke, the ways of living and understanding God's service that we would need to recover or re-create, because they had been obliterated. Lineage was terribly important to him; it remained so when he saw it being called upon by various Indian and Eastern teachers who claimed unbroken chains of tradition. His heart ached over the closing of Jewish gateways that had been brought upon us by this terrible history, and he wanted to recover and reopen them.

In more recent years, Zalman became terribly concerned, like so many of us, with the fate of the planet and all who live upon it. Here the closing of the gate took on new and urgent meaning. How do we open the heart, the collective conscience of humanity, to bring us to change our destructive ways of living before the gate closes? Leading people toward the inner quest—including the recognition of the interconnection of all life—began to look like an essential tool for our survival. Zalman was standing by the gateway, seeking to hold it open.

But he also saw a closing of the gates that referred to an overly insular and sometimes xenophobic community of the pious that Jewish suffering and isolation had brought about. "Unless you are willing to be completely *frum*, pious and observant in the traditional sense, there is no entry for you." Zalman fought against this his whole life. He tried over many years to fashion a broadened and open-minded alternative to the HaBaD Hasidic path that had done so much for him.

He needed to do this because he saw the locking down of those gates as a tragedy for the tradition as well as for those souls who would be left outside. "We who stand within this tradition need them!" he would say. "Why are they such seekers?" he would ask. "Why are the ranks of every guru's followers in the world overloaded with Jews? Because of *ibbur neshamah* (the inhabitation of souls)," he would say. Those millions of souls slaughtered in the Holocaust, especially the children who had not yet found their spiritual paths in life, wander about the world, joining (or implanting themselves in) the souls of Jews in the next generation, longing for spiritual nourishment. "How *dare* we keep them out?"

I am one of those souls. Born in 1941, the year when Hitler's armies hurtled across what had been the Hasidic heartland, Zalman quite convinced me that I was the bearer of one—or more—of those lost souls. He helped open the gate for me, allowing me to feel like an insider to a tradition that in my family had nearly been lost. It is by God's grace that I am here nearly eighty years later, holding open this outermost gateway to this great gatekeeper's teachings. I welcome you to enter. I promise that you will not regret it.

Rabbi Zalman Schachter-Shalomi: A Life of Renewal

INTRODUCTION

According to legend (Babylonian Talmud, Gittin 6b), after the destruction of the second Temple, Rabbi Yohanan ben Zakkai led a small group of Jewish refugees to the town of Yavneh, where they set about rebuilding Judaism for the new realities they faced. Beginning in the mid-1960s, Rabbi Zalman Schachter (better known as Reb Zalman, a less formal title he preferred)[1] argued that it was time for Yavneh II, a deep rethinking of how to be (or do) Jewish today. Indeed, he believed that all religious traditions were in urgent need of updating in the face of dramatic shifts in world events, technology, and consciousness. As he saw it, there was no aspect of human life that was unaffected by such events as the Holocaust; Hiroshima and Nagasaki; the Civil Rights, Hippie, and Feminist Movements; and the moon landing. In light of these phenomena, it was humanity's task to consciously build a new world with a renewed understanding of the interconnection and interdependence of all being. This, he insisted, required bold religious and cultural adaptation.

---

1. He would add the name Shalomi (from *shalom*, peace) later in life to balance his family name, Schachter, which means kosher slaughterer in Yiddish, the family occupation for several generations. The name change was suggested to him by his Sufi friend and colleague, Pir Vilayat Inayat Khan. See *My Life in Jewish Renewal: A Memoir*, 182. The term *Reb* means Mr. or Sir in Yiddish (as opposed to rabbi or professor).

1

Because of his commitment to these views and his experimental nature, Reb Zalman was often a controversial figure in his lifetime, beloved by many and dismissed or reviled by others. His students and admirers saw him as a kind and accessible mentor, a creative interpreter of Kabbalah[2] and Hasidism,[3] and a visionary religious innovator. Those who opposed him felt that he had betrayed the values and standards of traditional *Yiddishkeit* (Jewish life) and was too easily influenced by shifting intellectual and cultural trends. However, this opposition diminished significantly in his later years, as many former skeptics and opponents came to appreciate his creativity, learnedness, and demonstrated effectiveness. As he aged, Reb Zalman also honed and steadied his approach to renewal, consolidating various of his experiments and working with colleagues and students to establish the Jewish Renewal Movement and related professional training programs. As part of his *harvest* process, he also (re)produced an array of writings, videos, and audio recordings, sharing his erudition and passion for the tradition, while continuing to call for thoughtful innovation. By the turn of the century, Reb Zalman was increasingly viewed as a significant bridge figure between Eastern European Hasidism and North American Jewish life—a Neo-Hasidic[4] sage and spiritual innovator. Today, Jews the world over wear the B'nai Or rainbow *tallit* (prayer shawl) he

---

2. Literally "that which has been received," this Hebrew term is used to refer to the Jewish mystical tradition as a whole and more technically to the flowering of Jewish mystical activity in medieval Western Europe (beginning c.1150). See Daniel C. Matt, *The Essential Kabbalah: The Heart of Jewish Mysticism* (San Francisco: HarperCollins, 1995).

3. *Hasidism* (from the Hebrew root word *hesed*, loving-kindness) is a term used for various Jewish pietistic groups throughout Jewish history. In this context, it refers to the Eastern European mystical revival movement that emerged in the late eighteenth-century and continues to flourish today. See *Hasidism: A New History*, edited by David Biale et al. (Princeton, NJ: Princeton University Press, 2018).

4. This term refers to twentieth and twenty-first century Jewish figures who draw on Hasidic teaching and tradition for religious and/or cultural inspiration but who are not part of a traditional Hasidic community. See

designed, make use of meditative exercises he introduced, and study mystical texts he translated or first shared with close students decades ago. Further, Jewish Renewal rabbis and teachers are at the forefront of contemporary Judaism and its encounter with the changing nature of North American and global society.[5] ALEPH: Alliance for Jewish Renewal, the organization he originally founded as B'nai Or Religious Fellowship, continues to serve the core of Jewish Renewal communities around the world; and OHALAH: The Association of Rabbis for Jewish Renewal, originally begun by rabbis personally ordained by him, meets every year for fellowship, learning, and the ordination of new clergy. While these organizations remain small in comparison to the major North American Jewish denominations, like the Reconstructionist Movement[6] before it, renewal has had an outsized influence on contemporary Jewish life.[7]

From the earliest days of his career, Reb Zalman was also continually involved in dialogue with leaders and practitioners of other spiritual paths, including Trappist monks, Sufi sheikhs, and Aboriginal healers. These forays into what was then largely forbidden territory led him to jokingly describe himself as a

---

Arthur Green and Ariel Evan Mayse, eds., *A New Hasidism: Roots and Branches* (Philadelphia: Jewish Publication Society, 2019) [two volumes].

5. See Shaul Magid, "Jewish Renewal Movement," in *Encyclopedia of Religion*, 2nd ed. (Detroit: Thompson-Gale, 2005), 7:4868–74. See also Magid's "Jewish Renewal: Toward a New American Judaism," in *Tikkun* 21, no. 1 (January/February 2006): 57–60.

6. Magid, "Jewish Renewal Movement." To learn about the Reconstructionist movement—now called "Reconstructing Judaism"—and its founding ideologue, Rabbi Mordecai Kaplan (1900–1983), see Rebecca T. Alpert and Jacob J. Staub, *Exploring Judaism: A Reconstructionist Approach* (Wyncote, PA: Reconstructionist Press, 2000); and Mel Scult, *The Radical American Judaism of Mordecai M. Kaplan* (Bloomington: Indiana University Press, 2013).

7. This is especially the case as it relates to Jewish prayer and ritual, including the use of *niggunim* (wordless melodies); silent meditation; chant (including in English); dance; and drumming. Reb Zalman and his students themselves have blended various Jewish traditions with practices (or spiritual technologies as he referred to them) adapted from other religions.

"spiritual peeping-Tom." But far from being a mere browser, Reb Zalman became deeply engaged in the theory and practice of these traditions, praying matins, performing *zikr*, and sitting in sweat lodges. This personal, hands-on approach to dialogue and learning led to friendships with an eclectic group of leaders and thinkers, including Father Thomas Merton (1915–68); Pir Vilayat Inayat Khan (1916–2004); Ram Dass(1931–2019); Ken Wilber; and the fourteenth Dalai Lama. It also led him to develop an "organismic" vision of the world's religions, with each tradition serving its own constituents and contributing to the vitality of creation as a whole.

LIFE SPECTRUM

On August 17, 1924, Meshullam Zalman Schachter was born in Zolkiew (Galicia) Poland, to Shlomo and Hayyah Gittel Schachter. Due to rising anti-Semitism, the Schachters moved with their young son to Vienna, Austria, in 1925. His parents were both from traditional Hasidic families associated with the Belz dynasty.[8] The couple, however, fashioned a more modern religious life for themselves and their offspring. This included educating their oldest son in religious and secular schools and youth groups, including socialist-Zionist and Orthodox anti-Zionist groups. Among young Zalman's passions were chemistry, German novels about the American old West, and music.[9] While his boyhood religious and educational experiences were somewhat dizzying, they helped him learn to hold a broad range of ideas and perspectives at an early age. This would be a hallmark of Reb Zalman's mature intellectual and spiritual life.

---

8. As the Hasidic movement spread throughout Eastern Europe, various charismatic preachers and teachers formed courts and dynasties that were subsequently led by their sons, other family members, or close disciples. One such dynasty was founded by Rabbi Shalom Rokeah (1783–1855) in the second decade of the nineteenth century in the town of Belz, located in eastern Galicia.

9. *My Life in Jewish Renewal*, 13–17.

In 1938, when he was just fourteen, his family (including three younger siblings) began a long and harrowing flight from Nazi oppression through Belgium, France, North Africa, and the Caribbean, until they finally landed in New York City in 1941. This painful journey involved time in two internment camps in Vichy, France. While Reb Zalman was an ebullient and future-oriented personality, this upheaval understandably threw the teenager into a crisis of faith. Perplexed by the depravity of the Nazis, the enthusiastic or tacit support of so many other Europeans (including former friends, teachers, and neighbors), and the seeming absence or indifference of God, the young man was angry and existentially adrift.

In 1939, while still in Belgium, Reb Zalman joined an unusual circle of HaBaD Hasidim[10] who cut and polished diamonds in Antwerp. Together, they worked and sang Hasidic *niggunim* (melodies), studied Jewish sacred texts, and discussed works of modern European philosophy and literature. This association not only served as a much-needed balm for young Zalman's soul but also opened him to a more mature engagement with Jewish spirituality and thought.[11] While most HaBaD groups are not involved in the study of non-Jewish textual materials like the Antwerp circle, the dynasty has a long history of intellectual rigor and sophisticated teachings on prayer and meditation.[12]

---

10. This well-known dynasty was founded by Rabbi Shneur Zalman (1745–1812) of Liadi in White Russia in 1775. HaBaD is an acronym for *Hokhmah* (Wisdom), *Binah* (Understanding), *Da'at* (Awareness), the intellectual–spiritual ideals of this sect (based on earlier Jewish mystical teachings). Lubavitch is the town where the founder's offspring established and grew the community for a century. The two names (one conceptual, the other geographical) are used in tandem or separately. Members of the contemporary movement often use the English spelling "Chabad." See Naftali Loewenthal, "Lubavitch Hasidism," *YIVO Encyclopedia of Jews in Eastern Europe* (2010), https://yivoencyclopedia.org/article.aspx/Lubavitch_Hasidism.

11. See "The Diamond-Cutter Hasidim" in Chapter 6 of this volume.

12. See "Chabad," in *Hasidism: A New History*, 125–36. See also Rachel Elior, *The Paradoxical Ascent to God: The Kabbalistic Theosophy*

It also places great emphasis on the inner development of the devotee (the Hasid), in addition to the role of the *rebbe* (Hasidic leader) as spiritual guide and intercessor.[13] A chance encounter with Rabbi Menahem Mendel Schneerson (1902–94), who would later become the seventh Lubavitcher rebbe, also deeply impressed young Zalman.[14] And so, after arriving in the United States with his family, working for a brief period, he enrolled in the HaBaD yeshiva (religious academy), Tomhei Temimim, in Brooklyn. The sixth Lubavitcher Rebbe, Rabbi Yosef Yitzhak Schneerson (1880–1950, Menahem Mendel's father-in-law), not only welcomed Reb Zalman into the HaBaD yeshiva but also arranged for the schooling of his younger siblings and helped his family find housing and set up a small furrier business in their apartment.[15]

Reb Zalman had great respect and love for his *rebbe*. In addition to the elder rabbi's acts of *hesed* (loving-kindness) toward many recent émigrés, Reb Yosef Yitzhak was a brave and determined man who had endured tremendous pain and suffering while leading his flock in Eastern Europe, including imprisonment by the Soviet government, the rising tide of Nazi persecution, and significant health issues.[16] Reb Zalman greatly admired

---

of Habad Hasidism, translated by Jeffrey M. Green (Albany: State University of New York Press, 1993); and Naftali Loewenthal, *Communicating the Infinite: The Emergence of the Habad School* (Chicago: University of Chicago Press, 1990).

13. From the outset of the movement, Hasidic *rebbes* (also called *tzaddikim*, righteous ones) were believed to be endowed with unusual spiritual power, including the ability to intercede with God on behalf of their community members. See Green and Mayse, *A New Hasidism: Roots*, 220–21, including the quotation from Reb Zalman about his attraction to HaBaD. See also Arthur Green, "The Zaddik as Axis Mundi in Later Judaism," *Journal of the American Academy of Religion*, 45, no. 3 (September 1977): 327–47.

14. See *My Life in Jewish Renewal*, 45–48.

15. Ibid., 53–62.

16. See Samuel Heilman, *Who Will Lead Us: Five Hasidic Dynasties in America* (Oakland: University of California Press, 2017), 228–37.

his mentor's combination of intellectual and emotional sophistication, his devotional intensity, and steadfast commitment to rebuilding traditional Judaism in his new homeland.[17] Beginning in the mid-1940s, the rebbe began sending out HaBaD rabbis and educators to kindle the hearts of young Jews in postwar America. The effort was shot through with messianic yearning, following the unfathomable losses suffered by the Jewish community in the *Shoah* (Destruction, Hebrew term for the Holocaust). Reb Zalman was deeply honored to be among the first members of this educational vanguard. Even before receiving rabbinic ordination from Tomhei Temimim in 1947, he began outreach and teaching work in New Haven, Connecticut.

In 1949, Reb Yosef Yitzhak sent Reb Zalman and another talented young rabbi, Shlomo Carlebach (1925–94), to visit Jewish students on college and university campuses. He and Carlebach were both well suited for this work, sharing with students the riches of traditional Jewish religious thought and practice with warmth and charisma. Knowing they had to meet these young folks "where they were," the rabbis used Hasidic music and storytelling to open their hearts and minds. At the same time, these young rabbis were deeply moved and influenced by the students they encountered, who helped initiate them into the emerging counterculture of the age. While Reb Zalman and Reb Shlomo (he, too, preferred to be addressed informally) began their outreach efforts as faithful HaBaD *shelihim* (emissaries, informal educators), over the next decade they would become leading figures in the development of Neo-Hasidic culture in North America, attracting Jewish seekers from across the denominational spectrum.[18]

---

17. *My Life in Jewish Renewal*, 53–56.

18. See Natan Ophir (Offenbacher), *Rabbi Shlomo Carlebach: Life, Mission, and Legacy* (Jerusalem, Israel: Urim Publications, 2014). After Carlebach's death, several women came forward with reports that he acted toward them in sexually inappropriate and/or abusive ways. Since that time, there has been extensive discussion in Jewish circles about how to deal with his legacy, including both the many positive contributions he made and his

Between 1952 and 1956, Reb Zalman served three small
pulpits in Massachusetts and New York (as well as working
as a kosher slaughterer). With a growing family and very limited funds available for HaBaD *shelihim* (the organizational
infrastructure was still quite small in those days) he had to
find gainful employment. While these were challenging professional experiences (he had little organizational or administrative
training), Reb Zalman deepened his understanding of the realities of North American Jewish life, and he began to meet and
work with non-Jewish clergy (mostly Protestants). Inspired by
several positive interfaith experiences and a growing desire to
work more extensively with Jewish college students, he enrolled
in an MA program in the Psychology of Religion, with a focus
on pastoral counseling, at Boston University (1955–56).[19] This
experience was both intellectually and spiritually eye opening,
as it was the first time Reb Zalman studied Christianity formally
or studied religion with non-Jewish faculty and fellow students.
Further, unlike in yeshiva, his graduate studies included the use
of modern historical–critical methods. Reb Zalman's most significant mentor at Boston University was the Reverend Howard
Thurman (1899–1981), Dean of Marsh Chapel, and a towering African American preacher, pastor, and writer.[20] The young
rabbi was deeply impressed by Thurman's creative pedagogic
methods, modern mystical vision (including his emphasis on

---

damaging behavior. See, for example, Sarah Imhoff, "Carlebach and the
Unheard Stories," *American Jewish History* 100, no. 4 (2016): 555–60;
Neshama Carlebach [Reb Shlomo's daughter], "My Sisters: I Hear You,"
http://blogs.timesofisrael.com/my-sisters-i-hear-you/; and Shaul Magid,
"Shlomo Carlebach: A Transnational Jew in Search of Himself," in Green
and Mayse, *A New Hasidism: Branches*, 339–56.

19. He did so with the permission of his *rebbe*, Rabbi Menachem Mendel Schneerson.

20. To learn more about Thurman, see Louis E. Smith, Jr., ed., *Howard
Thurman: Essential Writings* (Maryknoll, NY: Orbis Books, 2006). See also
Or N. Rose, "Howard Thurman's Mentorship of Zalman Schachter-Shal-
omi," in *Interreligious Studies: Dispatches from a Field*, edited by Hans
Gustafson (Waco, TX: Baylor University Press, 2020).

contemplative practice), and passionate commitment to interracial and interreligious dialogue; he lovingly referred to the
Christian minister as his "Black Rebbe."[21]

In 1956, Reb Zalman moved with his wife (Feigel Res-
nick, 1922–2002) and children to Winnipeg, Canada, where
he became the director of the University of Manitoba's B'nai
Brith Hillel Foundation for Jewish student life and a professor
of Judaic studies. Inspired by his time with Dean Thurman, he
implemented a variety of innovative religious and educational
projects, working closely with students both in the classroom
and in informal settings. With the blessing of the seventh
Lubavitcher rebbe, in 1958 he wrote and privately published
The First Step: A Primer of a Jewish Spiritual Life, one of the
first booklets on Jewish meditation in English. Lengthy excerpts
from this work were later published in the popular, do-it-yourself book, *The Jewish Catalog*.[22] This little meditation manual
would be read by a generation (or more) of North American
Jewish seekers and by individuals as diverse as President Zalman
Shazar (1889–1974) of Israel and the Christian monk and writer,
Thomas Merton. During this same time, Reb Zalman became
friendly with other Hillel professionals, scholars, and rabbis of
different denominations, increasingly traveling to speak, teach,
and lead retreats on campuses and in synagogues throughout
North America. In 1959, he made his first trip to Israel as part
of a contingent of Hillel directors. During his visit to the Holy

---

21. See "Trusting the Holy Spirit," describing Reb Zalman's first meet-
ings with Dean Thurman, in Chapter 7 of this volume. See also Shawn
Israel Zevit's brief reflection in *Wisdom from Reb Zalman: Embracing the
Jewish Spirit*, edited by Goldie Milgram and Shohama Weiner with Carola
de Vries Robles and Robert Esformes (New Rochelle, NY: Reclaiming
Judaism Press, 2018), 67–68.

22. Richard Siegel, Michael Strassfeld, and Sharon Strassfeld, *The Jewish Catalog: A Do-It-Yourself Kit* (Philadelphia: Jewish Publication Society,
1973), 296–318. The editors printed Reb Zalman's text as the concluding
chapter of the volume. The layout is designed to emphasize the contemplative nature of the piece, with fewer words and more white space on each
of the final pages.

Land Reb Zalman met, among others, the great scholar of Jewish mysticism, Gershom Scholem (1897–1982), the leading Jungian psychologist, Erich Neumann (1905–60), and the Jewish philosopher, Shemuel Hugo Bergman (1883–1975).[23] He also visited several Hasidic communities, including the new HaBaD settlement (Kfar Chabad, established in 1949) in the center of the country.

Over the next several years, Reb Zalman became deeply engaged in the study of Catholicism. He was particularly attracted to the mystical writings of such medieval figures as Meister Eckhart (c. 1260–c. 1328), Teresa of Avila (1515–82), and John of the Cross (1542–91), as well as the modern writers Jacques Maritain (1882–1973) and Thomas Merton. Reb Zalman also began to dialogue with Catholic religious leaders, intellectuals, and activists. He was especially moved by the devotional intensity of the monks and nuns he met, and their grappling with issues of authority, tradition, and modernity. These were challenges Reb Zalman was facing himself as an evolving Orthodox rabbi and seeker. While in Winnipeg, he befriended members of a local Trappist community, Our Lady of the Prairies, located on the outskirts of the city. In late 1960, he struck up a friendship with the aforementioned Merton, writing letters back and forth, and sharing published and unpublished books and articles. Reb Zalman also visited his spiritual *pen pal* a few times at Merton's monastery, Our Lady of Gethsemani, in Bardstown, Kentucky. The monk and the rabbi developed enough trust over the years

---

23. *My Life in Jewish Renewal*, 113–20. Reb Zalman mentions that he briefly contemplated emigrating to Israel to study with Scholem and Neumann. He also indicates that one of Bergmann's associates translated *The First Step* into Hebrew. Elsewhere, Reb Zalman credits Bergmann for drawing his attention to the writings of the Neo-Hasidic writer, Hillel Zeitlin (1888–1942), whose vision of a modern Jewish spiritual community would serve as an important model for him. See *Hasidic Spirituality for a New Era: The Religious Writings of Hillel Zeitlin*, selected, edited, and translated by Arthur Green; prayers introduced and translated by Joel Rosenberg; foreword by Zalman M. Schachter-Shalomi (Mahwah, NJ: Paulist Press, 2012). See also note 26.

to discuss a number of sensitive theological and personal matters. Their relationship was anchored in a shared passion for contemplative practice and spiritual development.[24]

In 1964, inspired by his Trappist colleagues, the recently discovered Dead Sea Scrolls,[25] and Eastern European Hasidism and Neo-Hasidism, Reb Zalman issued a call for the creation of an intentional Jewish community he called B'nai Or (Children of Light) and began experimenting with a small circle of students in Winnipeg.[26] While Reb Zalman's dream of building a full-time residential community never came to fruition, this experiment in Neo-Hasidic counterculture served as a model and precursor to both the Havurah and Jewish Renewal Movements.[27]

---

24. See "My Friend Thomas Merton" in Chapter 7 of this volume. See also "An Interview with Zalman Schachter-Shalomi," conducted by Edward Kaplan and Shaul Magid (November 19, 2001), in *Merton and Judaism: Holiness in Words*, edited by Beatrice Brodeur (Louisville, KY: Fons Vitae, 2003), 301–23.

25. Discovered in the middle of the twentieth century, the Dead Sea Scrolls date from the third century BCE (mid-Second Temple period) to the first century CE (before the destruction of the Second Temple in 70 CE). The most well-known texts among the Scrolls are the religious writings found in a series of eleven caves at Qumran. Reb Zalman was fascinated by the devotional intensity and communitarian idealism expressed in these sources; so much so, that he often referred to B'nai Or as "Qumran USA." See *My Life in Jewish Renewal*, 121–32. For an introduction to the Scrolls, visit the Leon Levy Dead Sea Scrolls Digital Library, https://www.deadseascrolls.org.il/home.

26. As mentioned above, another important influence on Reb Zalman's vision of B'nai Or was the Eastern European, Neo-Hasidic writer and journalist, Hillel Zeitlin (1888–1942). Zeitlin dreamed of creating a new spiritual movement inspired by Hasidic and modern socialist ideals. At the center of this movement, he envisioned a core group of devotees forming an intentional community he called Yavneh (drawing on the rabbinic legend we mentioned in the opening of this chapter). See Zeitlin's Yavneh documents (from the 1920s) in Green and Mayse, *A New Hasidism: Roots*, 15–32, 343–51; compare these with Reb Zalman's call for the establishment of B'nai Or (1964) in the same volume, 240–56, 388.

27. See Arthur Green, "Renewal and Havurah: American Movements, European Roots," in *Jewish Renaissance and Renewal in America: Essays*

During this time, Reb Zalman began a gradual move away from Orthodoxy, both ideological and practical. This was spurred by several factors, including his study of the history of religions; a deep appreciation for the wisdom of non-Jewish religious traditions; exposure to impressive non-Orthodox rabbis, academics, and Hillel professionals; and shifting attitudes toward sexuality and gender in contemporary North American culture. His move toward a liberal piety gained greater momentum in the late 1960s and early 1970s. In reflecting on his religious evolution, Reb Zalman would later describe it as a movement from restoration to renewal, a fundamental change from working for the restoration of traditional Eastern European Hasidism in North America to the renewal of contemporary Jewish life in open dialogue with a variety of religious and other wisdom (humanistic and scientific) traditions.

In 1968, Reb Zalman completed his Doctor of Hebrew Letters from Hebrew Union College in Cincinnati, writing a dissertation on Hasidic forms of counseling, reading these traditions in dialogue with modern forms of psychotherapy and pastoral care. The fruits of this project led to the eventual publication of two books: *Sparks of Light* (1983) and the larger, more scholarly volume, *Spiritual Intimacy* (1990). It was during this same phase of life that the Lubavitcher hierarchy effectively separated itself from Reb Zalman.[28] The most significant issue was his open and enthusiastic experimentation with psychedelic drugs. In the summer of 1963 he met Timothy Leary (1920–96) by chance while visiting an *ashram* in Cohasset, Massachusetts.[29] A week later, he engaged in an LSD trip with the Harvard researcher, finding the experience utterly transformative. He reported feeling

---

in Honor of Leah Levitz Fishbane, edited by Eitan P. Fishbane and Jonathan D. Sarna (Waltham, MA: Brandeis University Press, 2011), 145–64.

28. See Reb Zalman's account of this painful public affair in *My Life in Jewish Renewal*, 175–76.

29. Although Reb Zalman occasionally ascribed these events to the summer of 1962, archival research has clarified that they took place in August 1963.

a powerful sense of the unity of life and the inadequacy of all philosophical or theological mappings to capture this reality. He was so moved by this and subsequent hallucinogenic experiences that he wrote about and lectured on the topic. He dared ask if LSD trips could be compared to the "soul ascents" spoken of by the Ba'al Shem Tov (1700–1760)[30] and other mystical voyages. If so, why not make use of the drug sacramentally like other mind-expanding substances and techniques used by traditional seekers and adepts?[31]

Despite his painful falling out with HaBaD, Reb Zalman continued on as an independent Hasid, teaching and lecturing to diverse Jewish and interfaith audiences throughout North America. In 1968–69, he took a sabbatical from the University of Manitoba and spent the year as a postgraduate fellow at Brandeis University studying ancient Semitic languages. That same year, he served as an informal mentor and honorary participant in Havurat Shalom in Cambridge (and later Somerville), Massachusetts. His teaching and modeling inspired members of this impressive group, several of whom went on to play major roles in contemporary Jewish life. This included the group's founders, Rabbi Arthur Green and Kathy Green (1944–2017), as well as

---

30. Israel ben Eliezer, The Ba'al Shem Tov (Master of the Good Name), was a mystical healer, teacher, and prayer leader in the Ukrainian town of Mezibozh. His shamanic talents (including the use of divine names in incantations and amulets) attracted both common folk and members of the elite. Several of his associates and disciples formed the nascent Hasidic movement, crediting him as the inspiration for their activities. To this day, the BeShT (acronym for Ba'al Shem Tov) is viewed by Hasidim as the founding father of the movement and by Jews the world over as a major religious personality. See Moshe Rosman, "Ba'al Shem Tov," *YIVO Encyclopedia of Jews in Eastern Europe* (2010), https://www.yivoencyclopedia.org/article.aspx/Baal_Shem_Tov.

31. *My Life in Jewish Renewal*, 141–54. As noted there, this account was edited for a general audience. The original version (available through the Reb Zalman archive at the University of Colorado) includes many more Hebrew and Yiddish terns and allusions. See also Reb Zalman's essay, "Conscious Ascent of the Soul," in Ralph Metzner, ed., *The Ecstatic Adventure* (New York: Macmillan, 1968), 96–123.

the editors of the *Jewish Catalog*, Richard Siegel (1947–2018), Rabbi Michael Strassfeld, and Sharon Strassfeld.[32]

Reb Zalman's last several years in Winnipeg were difficult. In addition to his experimentation with LSD, in the mid-1960s he divorced his first wife (an arranged marriage), entered a short-lived marriage with a former employee from the University of Manitoba,[33] and continued to explore his fledgling identity as a countercultural spiritual figure. All of these changes created tension between Reb Zalman and members of the local Jewish establishment. When he arrived in this quiet midwestern city in the mid-1950s, he was a creative, but traditional HaBaD Hasid; over the course of a decade or so, he grew to become a much more independent and experimental—some would say radical—seeker and teacher.[34]

In the early 1970s, Reb Zalman continued to travel and speak, particularly enjoying his visits to the West Coast, where he imbibed the flowering Hippie culture in Northern California. This included a growing interest in the Human Potential Movement, Buddhism, Hinduism, and Islam. He developed relationships with members of the Universalist Sufi community in the Bay Area, leading to close friendships with Pir Moineddin

---

32. As Reb Zalman notes, the editors actually experimented with the design and contents of the Catalog in a course he taught at Brandeis that year and were influenced by his earlier informal educational work, including his time as a "religious environmentalist" at Camp Ramah in Connecticut. *My Life in Jewish Renewal*, 166–67 (see also "Bringing *Shabbos* to Life" in Chapter 4 of this volume). The book was modeled after the iconic *Whole Earth Catalog* (first published in 1968).

33. Complicating matters further, his second wife, Mary Lynn Patterson, was a convert to Judaism, and Reb Zalman was a *kohen* (from the priestly line rooted in the biblical figure of Aaron the High Priest); according to traditional Jewish law *kohanim* are not allowed to marry converts. See Babylonian Talmud, Yevamot 46a, https://www.sefaria.org/Yevamot.4 6a.1?lang=bi&with=all&lang2=en.

34. Interviews (July 5, 2018) with Rabbi Jerry Steinberg and Rabbi Neal Rose, both colleagues of Reb Zalman's at the University of Manitoba during this period.

Jablonski (1942–2001) and Pir Vilayat Inayat Khan. As a sign of his respect and admiration for Reb Zalman, Pir Vilayat initiated the rabbi as a *sheikh* in 1975.[35] This unusual ritual took place only one year after Reb Zalman ordained his first rabbi, Daniel Siegel, who went on to play a central role in the development of the Jewish Renewal Movement.[36] That same year (1974), Reb Zalman helped found the Aquarian Minyan in Berkeley, California, which was an important context for further Jewish liturgical innovation and community-building.

Married for a third time, to Elana Rappaport in 1975, Reb Zalman relocated to Philadelphia, where he became professor of Jewish Mysticism and Psychology of Religion at Temple University in Philadelphia. He would remain in that academic post until he took early retirement in 1987, when he was named professor emeritus. Reb Zalman also established a B'nai Or community, drawing on his experimentation in Canada. The Schachters' home in Mount Airy became a laboratory for Jewish and interreligious innovation, including prayer, study, and meditation. Faculty members and students from the Reconstructionist Rabbinical College (RRC) and other nearby religious and academic institutions were attracted to the neighborhood, leading it to become a hothouse of progressive Jewish life. Reb Zalman taught on a part-time basis at the RRC (where his friend Arthur Green served as dean and then president between 1984 and 1992) at different points in his years in Philadelphia, and several graduates of the school played key roles in the development of the national Jewish Renewal Movement. This included renaming the growing organization P'nai Or (Faces of Light) Religious

---

35. See Netanel Miles-Yépez, "Foreword: The Merging of Two Oceans," in Gregory Blann, *When Oceans Merge: The Contemporary Sufi and Hasidic Teachings of Pir Vilyat Inayat Khan and Rabbi Zalman Schachter-Shalomi* (Rhinebeck, NY: Adam Kadmon Books and Monkfish Publishing, 2019), xiii–xxxiv.

36. Reb Zalman's first female ordinee was Rabbi Lynn Gottlieb who received *semikhah* (ordination) in 1981. Rabbis Everett Gendler and Shlomo Carlebach were the other members of her ordination committee.

Fellowship in 1986 (at the urging of feminist colleagues), until it took the name ALEPH: Alliance for Jewish Renewal in 1993. Among Reb Zalman's close students and colleagues in Philadelphia was the writer and activist, Rabbi Arthur Waskow. In fact, Waskow's Shalom Center merged with P'nai Or to form ALEPH, formally bringing together the spiritual and activist arms of the Renewal Movement under one banner for over a decade.[37]

In 1984, Reb Zalman took a forty-day retreat at the Lama Foundation in New Mexico and emerged with a new teaching about spiritual eldering, which later developed into his popular book, *From Age-ing to Sage-ing*,[38] and the national Spiritual Eldering Institute. At the age of sixty he came to realize that he could no longer maintain the same frenetic pace at which he had lived for so many years. During this same period, Reb Zalman and his fourth wife, Eve Ilsen, established an adult education initiative called the Wisdom School, influenced by the work of their friend and colleague Dr. Jean Houston, a popular New Age author and leader in the Human Potential Movement.[39] This, too, served as an important laboratory for Reb Zalman's

---

37. While Reb Zalman taught and mentored a number of Jewish political activists, including Waskow and Rabbi Michael Lerner, founder of *Tikkun* magazine, he did not regularly engage in organizing campaigns or protests. He largely expressed his social and environmental concerns through liturgical and homiletical creativity, as well as his pastoral work. In this regard, he was similar to his mentor, Reverend Howard Thurman (who pastored such figures as Bayard Rustin, Rev. Dr. Martin Luther King, Jr., and Vernon Jordan). In 2007, ALEPH and the Shalom Center decoupled due to differences in political strategy, especially on how to address the Israeli-Palestinian conflict. Reb Zalman was, at that point, retired and living in Boulder, Colorado.

38. Zalman Schachter-Shalomi and Roger Miller, *From Age-ing to Sage-ing: A Revolutionary Approach to Growing Older* (New York: Warner Books, 1995).

39. See Jean Houston, *The Possible Human: A Course in Enhancing Your Physical, Mental, and Creative Abilities* (New York: Tarcher/Putnam, 1997). See also Jessica Grogan, *Encountering America: Humanistic Psychology, Sixties Culture, and the Shaping of the Modern Self* (New York: HarperCollins, 2013).

still-unfolding psychospiritual thought and life review.[40] These developments led Reb Zalman to gradually hand over the day-to-day work of building the Renewal Movement to students and colleagues. As part of this process, in 1990 Reb Zalman began working with Rabbi Marcia Prager (a graduate of RRC and privately ordained by Reb Zalman) to create more formal structures for the ordination of rabbis (and later other programs in Jewish leadership), eventually leading to the establishment of the ALEPH Ordination Program in 2002.[41]

In 1990, Reb Zalman participated in a historic meeting in Dharamsala, India, between the Dalai Lama and his senior associates and Jewish leaders from North America and Israel. The Tibetan leader, himself entering his golden years, urgently wanted to discuss how Jews had survived their exile for two thousand years. After fleeing the oppressive Chinese regime beginning in 1959, the Tibetan exile community was deeply concerned about the future of their people. How could they best shape a vibrant and lasting diasporic culture? This dialogue, and Reb Zalman's prominent role in it, became the focus of a best-selling book by Rodger Kamenetz called *The Jew in the Lotus*.[42] The book quickly became a catalyst for Jewish–Buddhist dialogue and the delicate issue of why so many American Jews were involved in Buddhist and Hindu spiritual life. It also helped raise Reb Zalman's profile as a gifted religious teacher and interreligious practitioner.

Within a few years, Reb Zalman was invited to take up the World Wisdom Chair at Naropa University (where he had

---

40. See Dana Densmore, *Reb Zalman Gathers Figs* (Santa Fe, NM: Green Lion Press, 2013), which is a study of Reb Zalman's teaching of various biblical texts in the Wisdom School retreats.

41. Email correspondence with Rabbi Marcia Prager, Director and Dean of Ordination Programs for ALEPH (September 17, 2019). See also https://aleph.org/history-of-the-aleph-ordination-program.

42. Rodger Kamenetz, *The Jew in the Lotus: A Poet's Rediscovery of Jewish Identity in Buddhist India* (San Francisco: HarperCollins, 1994). See, more recently, Kamentz's introduction to *Wisdom from Reb Zalman*, 13–21.

previously taught as visiting faculty in 1975), the only accred-
ited Buddhist-inspired university in the Western Hemisphere.
Naropa University (then the Naropa Institute) became Reb Zalman's new teaching home. By the time of his retirement in 2004,
he had influenced thousands of students and spiritual seekers
from different backgrounds and commitments. He also became
a beloved figure in the Boulder Jewish and interreligious communities, praying at several of the local synagogues (of different
affiliations), teaching and mentoring clergy, and participating
in various cultural and civic events. Reb Zalman (dubbed the
Cyber Rebbe in the 1990s) also made extensive use of digital
communication to teach and counsel people around the world.[43]

In 2004, Reb Zalman also participated in the Vancouver
Peace Summit, where he dialogued with Nobel laureates, the
Dalai Lama, and Bishop Desmond Tutu. That same year, he
cofounded the Inayati-Maimuni Order with his student and
coauthor, Netanel Miles-Yépez, reviving the medieval Sufi–Jewish teachings of Rabbi Avraham Maimuni[44] (1186–1237), and
bringing the Hasidic lineage of the Ba'al Shem Tov into dialogue
with the universal Sufi lineage of Hazrat Inayat Khan (1882–
1927).[45] The following year, Reb Zalman made a pilgrimage to
Eastern Europe with his youngest son, where they visited the
graves of several of the early Hasidic masters, including the Ba'al
Shem Tov. There, the aging rabbi prayed that the Neo-Hasidic

43. A futurist with a lifelong love for machinery, Reb Zalman regularly
tinkered with computers and related gadgets, and used digital metaphors
in his later teachings.

44. On this fascinating medieval figure, see Elisha Russ-Fishbane, *Judaism, Sufism, and the Pietists of Medieval Egypt: A Study of Abraham Maimonides and His Times* (Oxford: Oxford University Press, 2015).

45. See Miles-Yépez's reflection on this experience, in "Foreword: The
Merging of Two Oceans." Hazrat Inayat Khan was the founder of the lineage of universalist Sufism, as well as the Sufi Order (1918) and the Sufi
Movement (1923). He initially came to the West as an Indian classical
musician.

activities he and his students undertook would be grafted onto the Hasidic tree rooted in this legendary healer and leader.[46]

As Reb Zalman grew older, it became increasingly important to him and his students and supporters to both preserve and disseminate his many teachings. This led to an intensive period of writing, editing, and cataloging of his work. With the aid of several cowriters and editors, he published numerous works in English and Hebrew in the last two decades of his life. In 2012, he was awarded the National Jewish Book Award for *Davening: A Guide to Meaningful Jewish Prayer* (written with Joel Segel), and the University of Colorado (Boulder) established a multimedia archive and exhibit dedicated to his life and work.[47]

In 2012, Reb Zalman was also awarded an honorary doctorate from the Starr King School for the Ministry in Oakland, California, and gave a popular series of lectures on the "Emerging Cosmology" as a part of the school's inaugural symposium, "Living in the Differences."

In 2014, he was again awarded an honorary doctorate, this time by Hebrew College in Newton, Massachusetts.[48] Shortly thereafter, he traveled to Connecticut to lead a *Shavuot* (Feast of Weeks or Pentecost) retreat at the Isabella Freedman Jewish Retreat Center. After this retreat, he fell ill with pneumonia. He recovered sufficiently to return home to Boulder, Colorado, where he passed away peacefully in his sleep on Thursday, July 3, 2014. Reb Zalman was survived by his wife and teaching partner, Eve Ilsen, eleven children, and many grandchildren and great grandchildren.

---

46. See Reb Zalman's reflection on this experience in "Grafting to the Ba'al Shem Tov's Tree," in Chapter 6 of this volume.

47. https://archives.colorado.edu/repositories/2/resources/1661. Materials in the collection were previously gathered by Naropa and Temple Universities, with the support of the Reb Zalman Legacy Project of the Yesod Foundation.

48. Arthur Green is the founding dean of the Hebrew College Rabbinical School; several other members of its faculty and student body studied with or were mentored by Reb Zalman.

OVERVIEW OF THE BOOK

As editors we faced several challenges in assembling this volume. How were we to present the essential teachings of a spiritual polymath with broad and evolving interests to a diverse multi-faith readership? Compounding this matter was the challenge of presenting an oral master and associative thinker in writing. Like many of his Hasidic forbears, Reb Zalman felt more comfortable sharing his *Torah* in the presence of an audience, using his sharp mind, quick wit, and interpersonal sensitivity to connect with those he was addressing. Further, while he produced a rather large written corpus, the quality of his writing was uneven, and he worked with a number of different cowriters and editors over several decades. Given the diversity of the material and differences in style, how were we to find one cohesive voice to present?

In the end, we attempted to identify those ideas, stories, and lessons that were either foundational to, or most prominent in, his work. Further, we favored accessible and relatively brief texts or extracts that convey big ideas or that highlight unique aspects of Reb Zalman's thought and life journey. We also tended to choose pieces he produced or reproduced in the last decades of his life, when he spent increased time focusing on his written legacy.

To help the reader ground her exploration of a given topic, we begin each chapter with a thematic introduction and, in some cases, a few questions for reflection. We also include brief introductions to individual pieces that we thought might otherwise be difficult for the general reader to navigate. Finally, there are many footnotes throughout the volume, including suggestions for further reading, and a glossary of Aramaic, Hebrew, and Yiddish terms. Our objective is to provide a compelling introduction to Reb Zalman's core teachings, appealing to a variety of readers. We seek to present the insights of an imaginative and nonlinear religious thinker (who was *also* attracted to various mystical and psychological mappings), with a gift for synthesizing a broad range of sources and ideas. The eight chapters in this volume, therefore, focus on both the theoretical and practical dimensions of Reb Zalman's expansive vision for contemporary Jewish and spiritual life.

The first chapter, "Our Changing Relationship with God," is dedicated to an exploration of Reb Zalman's reflections on theology, including his advice to contemporary seekers who find God-talk to be frustratingly abstract or rigidly dogmatic. Rather than give up on the enterprise, he invites the reader to enter into the discussion humbly and creatively, knowing that it will always involve more questions than answers. Further, he encouraged the seeker to think of their own life experiences as a sacred source for such deliberations alongside those of past theologians, philosophers, and poets.[49] In so doing, Reb Zalman shares his own attempts to name the ineffable reality he experiences, with acute awareness of the limits of language and cognition.

Chapter 2, "The Spiritual Path and the Terrain of the Soul," features Reb Zalman's views on spiritual development, including his insights from both Jewish mystical and modern psychological sources. As a spiritual counselor and mentor, Reb Zalman had an abiding interest in helping guide people in the search for meaning and purpose, whether they were beginners or more advanced seekers. Throughout his career he worked to refine his

---

49. As previous scholars have noted, Reb Zalman's prioritization of subjective human experience and his suspicion of grand theological systems are characteristic of many postmodern thinkers. Scott Kommel Meyers offers a helpful summary of recent scholarly discussions about Reb Zalman's thought in the context of New Age and postmodern thought, as well as the influence of American pragmatism. See Scott Kommel Meyers, "Religion of Reason in the New Age: Zalman Schachter-Shalomi, Hermann Cohen, and Messianic Politics" (MA thesis, 2017), *Religious Studies Graduate Theses & Dissertations*, #45, 4–11, https://scholar.colorado.edu/rlst_gradetds/45. As Reb Zalman notes in various writings, he was also influenced in this regard by various Jewish mystical sources on the unique spiritual makeup of the individual (including the origin of one's soul). See, for example, Zalman Schachter-Shalomi, *Spiritual Intimacy* (Lanham, MD: Jason Aronson, Inc., 1990), 316–18.

craft as a contemporary *rebbe*, weaving together old world and New Age knowledge and practice.

In Chapter 3, "The Sacred Work of Prayer and Meditation," we turn to Reb Zalman's reflections on davvenology (*davven* is Yiddish for prayer) as he called it, including his teachings on the setting of intentions (*kavvanot*), musical selections, liturgical creativity, and different meditative techniques (ancient and modern) to be used during the traditional hours for prayer and at other times. Given the centrality of this subject to Reb Zalman's life and work, this chapter is among the longest in the collection.

Chapter 4 is an extension of this discussion about religious devotion, as Reb Zalman, like so many of his mentors, believed that one of the primary goals of *tefillah* (prayer in Hebrew) is to help the devotee live prayerfully, with devotional focus in the world. It is for this reason that we named this chapter "Sacred Living: Time, Space, Person," using the nomenclature of the ancient mystical tract, *Sefer Yetzirah* (Book of Formation) to explore Reb Zalman's insights on fashioning a holistic Jewish life.

In Chapter 5, entitled "Jewish Renewal and Paradigm Shift," we take a step back, as it were, to see how Reb Zalman understood his work as both an inheritor and an innovator. Beginning in the mid-1960s he began to feel the need to adapt and update the Jewish tradition based on the shifting tides of history, technology, and human consciousness. In addition to the several more theoretical pieces on Renewal, we also include a few concrete examples of his approach to Jewish life in the new (or emerging) paradigm. These pieces complement and bookend the selections on praxis in Chapter 4.

Chapter 6, "Hasidism and Neo-Hasidism," features Reb Zalman's reflections on his experiences with and understanding of the world of Eastern European Hasidism. This includes recollections from his days in HaBaD, interpretations of Hasidic homilies and tales, and his thoughts on the relationship between Hasidism and Neo-Hasidism. By exploring these texts, the reader can see how his formation as a *HaBaDnik* both shaped him as a religious devotee and moved him to develop his vision of Jewish Renewal. This involved a complicated process of embracing and wrestling with the teachings of his mystical forbears and the spiritual and social norms of contemporary Hasidic life.

While in Chapter 6 we turn inward to explore Reb Zalman's relationship to Hasidism, in Chapter 7, "Deep Ecumenism and the Interreligious Encounter," we move outward to chronicle his journey as an interfaith practitioner and leader with over fifty years of experience in the field. This includes several of Reb Zalman's stories (some of which read like Hasidic tales) about his encounters with people, texts, ideas, and rituals that helped shape (or reshape) him as a seeker and rabbi. Just as Reb Zalman's spiritual hunger led him to HaBaD as a teenager, so too did it lead the young HaBaD rabbi to search for wisdom in other religious traditions beginning in the mid-1940s. His interactions with non-Jewish holy men and women convinced him of the need for ongoing dialogue, study, shared ritual, and joint action in the world.

In the eighth and concluding chapter of the book we turn to Reb Zalman's pioneering work on "Spiritual Eldering." In these selections, the seasoned *rebbe* shares with us what it is like for him to grow old, and his insights about how one can thoughtfully embrace the challenges and possibilities of the "winter" months of one's life. This work is not only addressed to seniors but to *all* readers who wish to be more intentional in thinking about the human life cycle.

We are delighted to open and close this volume with personal reflections from four distinguished religious leaders and scholars, all of whom knew Reb Zalman well and interacted with him in different and overlapping contexts. Because he was such a warm and outgoing person, we felt compelled to include these testimonials alongside Reb Zalman's teachings and reflections. Given his passionate commitment both to Jewish renewal and interreligious dialogue, we invited writers from Jewish, Christian, and Buddhist communities.

Like many other creative and pioneering figures, Reb Zalman grew and changed significantly over his long and fertile career—sometimes gradually and sometimes in faster bursts. A charismatic and passionate teacher, he was able to tap into the needs and interests of a generation of seekers yearning for a creative shift in consciousness. His curiosity and creativity led him to explore an array of intellectual and spiritual sources and experiences. At the same time, he was deeply committed to utilizing and sharing the treasures of the Jewish tradition, reformatting them, when necessary, for contemporary use. In many ways, this was his particular genius, to build the spiritual technology of the future using the wisdom of the past.   —O. N. R. & N. M-Y

1

Our Changing Relationship with God

INTRODUCTION

Throughout his long and adventurous career, Reb Zalman spoke of his deeply felt, intuitive experience of Divinity, and of the difficulty of expressing this reality in clear and consistent terms. A self-identified mystic, shaped in particular by HaBaD thought, he taught that God is infinite, surrounding and filling[1] all of existence. That is to say, the Divine is the Spirit that undergirds and energizes all of life and is manifest in all facets of being. As such, God is at once immanent and transcendent, both shaping space and time, and moving through these dimensions. It is for this reason that we, as "limited" or "mortal" creatures—bound by space and time—struggle to articulate our theological positions. How could we, finite beings, possibly fathom infinity?

Reb Zalman regularly warns his readers not to become overly fixated on trying to unravel this mystery once and for all. He reminds us to take seriously the many statements in our religious traditions about the need for epistemological humility. At the same time, he is not a strict negative theologian. He believes

---

1. The Hebrew terms are *sovev* and *memaleh*. They appear in various mystical sources, including in the teachings of the first master of HaBaD, Rabbi Shneur Zalman of Liadi (1745–1812). See, for example, *Likku-tei Amarim—Tanya: Bi-Lingual Edition* (New York: Kehot, 1984), 2:7, 307–21.

that as meaning-seeking beings,[2] *we need to try and speak our truths, even if partial and fragmented. He thus invites the seeker to enter into the lush and thorny field of theology in an imaginative manner, doing so with playful seriousness. In attempting to construct his own theological language, he makes creative use of Kabbalistic and Hasidic materials, in addition to a range of other Jewish and non-Jewish sources. At the same time, he insists that the contemporary seeker glean judiciously from these texts in light of their own life experience. As evolving beings who are part of evolving traditions, we must work actively to update our theological software.*

One way in which he encouraged such creativity was to point out that throughout Jewish history our prophets, poets, philosophers, and mystics have spoken of God in very different ways, depending on the context in which they lived. To illustrate this point, he would map (heuristically) different theological epochs in the life of the Jewish people, beginning with the polytheistic roots of ancient Near-Eastern culture and including periods in which versions of theism or deism have dominated the theological landscape. The point of this and other similar schematic exercises—including his use of astrological symbols—was to help the seeker lean in to a renewed discussion of God, knowing that Jewish thinkers have been working on this creative project passionately and imperfectly for centuries.

In the last decades of his life, inspired in part by the Environmental and New Age Movements, Reb Zalman increasingly spoke of his own theological position as pantheistic. As he wrote in different contexts, he found this term most helpful in expressing his conviction that God is the one animating Spirit giving rise to and sustaining all of existence. While some Jewish (and other Western) mystics prefer the term panentheism to describe

---

2. He was fond of Rabbi Abraham Joshua Heschel's (1907–72) term *theotropic* to describe the human being. Just as plants (which are heliotropic) search for sunlight, so, too, do human beings search for the Ultimate. See Heschel's *God in Search of Man: A Philosophy of Judaism* (New York: Farrar, Straus and Giroux, 1955), 416.

reality, as it maintains a distinction (however subtle) between Creator and creation, Reb Zalman sees no reason for this distinction; to him, God is the one ultimate reality in which all of life flourishes—ein od Milvado, "There is none beside Him" (in the parlance of HaBaD thought, based on Deuteronomy 4:39). In the introduction to his book Wrapped in a Holy Flame, *he states emphatically that "God did not create the world; God became the world."³ Commenting on Schachter-Shalomi's theological vision, Marie-Josée Posen writes that God is the word he uses to articulate his belief that "the entire universe is one, conscious, interconnected entity."⁴ The word "conscious" is important here as it reflects Reb Zalman's understanding of a dynamic Spirit; a feeling and thinking Force actively seeking expression through the unfolding of life. It is for this reason that Shaul Magid describes Reb Zalman's worldview as a personalist pantheistic vision of reality.⁵*

Unlike other versions of pantheism in which God's personhood is effaced, Schachter-Shalomi often spoke of God as a Thou (using Martin Buber's terminology) with whom the human seeker can develop an intimate interpersonal relationship. When doing so, he also readily admits that it is very difficult to know

---

3. Zalman Schachter-Shalomi, *Wrapped in a Holy Flame: Teachings and Tales of The Hasidic Masters*, edited by Netanel M. Miles-Yépez (San Francisco: Jossey-Bass, 2003), 20.

4. Marie-Josée Posen, "Beyond New Age: Jewish Renewal's Reconstruction of Theological Meaning in the Teachings of Rabbi Z. Schachter-Shalomi," *Jewish Culture and History* 8, no. 3 (2006): 87–112.

5. See Magid's *American Post-Judaism: Identity and Renewal in a Postethnic Society* (Bloomington: Indiana University Press, 2013), especially chapters 2–5 and 8. His earlier three-part series in *Tikkun* Magazine (2005–6) is also important to the discussion. This includes, "Jewish Renewal: Toward a 'New' American Judaism," 21, no. 1 (January/February 2006): 57–60; "Jewish Renewal and the Holocaust: A Theological Response," 21, no. 2 (March/April 2006): 59–68; and "Jewish Renewal, American Spirituality, and Post-monotheistic Theology," 21, no. 3 (May/June 2006): 62–66. See also Magid's more recent essay, "Between Paradigm Shift and Jewish Renewal: The New Metaphysics of Jewish Renewal," *Tikkun* 30, no. 1 (Winter 2015): 11–15.

if this dialogical perspective is real (ontological) or born out of our human need for an Other (psychological) with whom we can relate as friend, lover, parent, or judge. In a disarming moment in the book Jewish with Feeling, *he states, "In those moments when we feel the need to send out appreciation, or thanks, or pleading, or sorrow, or rage—not to a specific human target but to the universe—we send it out to an Other." He continues by stating, "To that philosopher in our head—or among our friends, or our family—we can say, 'This is the God that I need right now. Cut me some slack. You can come back with your objections later.'"[6]*

Reb Zalman is perhaps best described in this context as a "pastoral" or "applied" theologian.[7] He did not aim to create a systematic presentation of his beliefs. In fact, there was a part of him that chafed against all such attempts because of the seeming futility of the enterprise—"Thought does not grasp You at all" (Tikkunei Zohar 17a)—and because he believed that in the modern period, Judaism and other religions had become overly rationalistic, leaving little room for intuition, imagination, and emotion. At the same time, he was a gifted intellectual and voracious reader who hungered to better understand the who, what, where, and why of God. This pursuit was rooted in experiences of joy and exaltation and of trauma and pain, including his family's harrowing escape from Nazi-occupied Europe in the late 1930s. Reb Zalman sought to develop the necessary conceptual apparatus to ground and orient his spiritual quest as a postmodern seeker. Further, as a Jewish pastor and teacher working with many young, intellectually inclined seekers, he felt a responsibility to help provide them with enough theological scaffolding to embark on their own journeys and flourish as spiritual and ethical beings. This required exploring pressing questions about

---

6. *Jewish with Feeling: A Guide to Meaningful Jewish Practice*, with Joel Segel (Woodstock, VT: Jewish Lights Publishing, 2013), 9.

7. See Magid, "Between Paradigm Shift and Jewish Renewal," as well as Reb Zalman's response, "Renewal Judaism: Building Closeness to God," *Tikkun* 30, no. 1 (2015): 11—16.

God, *humanity, and the nature of existence—challenging past perspectives when necessary.*

In this opening chapter, the reader will find a selection of Reb Zalman's writings on God drawn from several of his works (mostly from the last decade of his life). In the spirit of our teacher, we invite you to read these pieces slowly, reflect on the ideas and images, and ask if they resonate with your own experience and understanding. If so, what do you find most compelling? What agitates or provokes you? Why? How would you revise or augment what he has sketched in these lines? How much consistency does Reb Zalman offer? How much do you need?

THE WORD GOD

Which handful of letters in the history of the world has accumulated more baggage than these? Martin Buber (1878–1965), in his book *Eclipse of God*, tells the story of a philosopher, Buber's host in a university town to which he had been invited, who protested passionately at Buber's use of the word. "How can you bring yourself to say 'God'?" the old man demands. "What word of human speech is so misused, so defiled, so desecrated as this?"[8]

On the one hand, as the old saying goes, "Our extremity is God's opportunity." When tragedy strikes, or great joy befalls us, or even when we're at the peak of sexual ecstasy—whenever an experience has shattered the usual language we use to describe such things—we have dialed that hotline to the center of the universe and said, in innumerable languages: "God! Oh, God!"

Too often, though, as soon as we catch ourselves at it, we hang up, quick. "Did you say 'God'?" Our internal prosecuting attorney jumps up with a list of objections as long as your arm. "That angry old man in the sky, that far-off 'Other' who commands and keeps score and rewards and punishes? That

8. Martin Buber, *Eclipse of God: Studies in the Relation between Religion and Philosophy* (Princeton, NJ: Princeton University Press, 2016), 5.

God who stands by while innocents suffer, while children die of hunger every day? The God that the rabbis were always invoking: God commands this, God forbade that?" Most of us are still angry with the patriarchal, punitive God of our Hebrew schools and synagogues, prayer books and Bibles. We have so little stomach for this God business that we are barred from everything it brings in its wake.

Our internal prosecutor presses the case: "How do we even know this God exists? What shred of evidence do we have that this God is anything more than a projection of human thought, an illusion woven together from all the prayers . . . that our people have murmured and shouted and sung and recited over the centuries? How can I take this God seriously? How can I take seriously anything this 'God' is supposed to have 'said'? What meaning does prayer have—prayer to what? to whom?"

These are all great questions, and Jews have been wrestling with them for centuries. Theologians have devoted their lives to constructing answers and systems we can live with.

But . . . *theology is the afterthought of spiritual experience*, not the other way around. We are not trying to construct some top-down authoritative system, but to nourish the seeds of our own personal spiritual experience. We start with wonder, or with thankfulness, or yearning, or even rage, and we ask ourselves: Wonder or rage at what? Thankfulness toward what? Yearning for what? It was simple, searching questions like these that started our ancestors thinking in terms of "God." Torah, Talmud, Hebrew school—all that came later.

Has the word *God* gotten so tainted that we have to throw it away, and all the sacred technology that comes with it? Some have, and many more have tried. I myself would like to suggest that a term like *God* can still be very useful to us in nurturing spiritual experience in our lives. For *God* carries not only all the centuries of trouble and objections. It also, in its very plainness and starkness and mystery, can allow us to move forward and *transcend* all the arguments, to say, in effect, "We're aware of the problems and acknowledge them, but we don't want to let them stand in the way of our experience."

Judaism has a lot of very valuable spiritual tools built around the "God" concept . . . finding a way to live with a thought named "God," to make it meaningful to us—not by signing any belief statements, but by trying to imagine the entity that could be our partner in our "something out there" experiences—will give us much better access to those tools. We can then begin to explore them to see which might be helpful to us in our search for deeper and more meaningful lives.   —*Jewish with Feeling*, 6–8

THE GOD YOU DON'T BELIEVE IN

The Tibetan Buddhist lama Chögyam Trungpa (1939–1987), founder of Naropa University in Boulder, where I teach, told a group of us one day that his son had asked him, "Daddy, is there a God?"

"No," Trungpa told him.

"Phew," the little boy sighed. "I was scared there for a while!"

Trungpa was looking over at me, trying to bait me a little—he was known for provocative behavior. So, I looked back at him and said, "The god that you don't believe in, I don't believe in, either."

We all have images of God that the past has bequeathed to us, and sometimes these images get in the way. But these images are not God: they are just images of God. "God language" can be of great help to us in relating to the Infinite, but we should not confuse it with the real thing. If we are to have some hope of regaining the wonder that inspired our ancestors to invent the word, if we are to gain any possibility of having "God" be our vehicle and partner in our search for meaning, we need to clean the word up a bit in our own minds, to scrape off a few of the barnacles of ages.   —*Jewish with Feeling*, 8

OUR ROOT METAPHORS AND MASKS FOR GOD

Once, William James (1842–1910), the psychologist who wrote *Varieties of Religious Experience* (1902), came to a town in New England and asked one of the wardens of a church:

"Who is God for you? In front of what do you place yourself in prayer?"

The warden said, "An oblong blur."

He was talking to a New England transcendentalist who was not inclined to think in terms of a form. But while the head may know that there is no form, the heart needs a root metaphor. I can be in a monist in my head, but I can't be a monist in my heart. In my heart, I have to have an *other* whom I love. That is where I am in the *I-Thou* relationship.[9]

In the past, people used to think of God as a King. We say *Avinu Malkeinu*, "Our Father, Our King." Sometimes we speak of the *Shekhinah* as our Mother, and this is wonderful. But the one I have the best conversations with is the one who sits in the passenger seat when I'm driving—*my Friend*. I can talk to my friend. I don't have to hide. I am not opaque to God. I do not want to hide anything from God. I can't hide anything from God anyway; but I do not *want* to hide anything from God. I am transparent; but I also want to talk to God. Part of the divine grace is that God will wear any mask that will allow me to communicate.

H. G. Wells (1866–1946) wrote a novel called *The Invisible Man* (1897), which was later made into a movie. But the question was: how were they going to make an invisible man interesting on the screen? Their solution was to wrap him in something; you wouldn't see his body, but you would see whatever he was

---

9. *I and Thou* (*Ich und Du*, German) is the name of the classic theological text by Martin Buber (first published in 1923), in which he calls for the cultivation of intentional personal relationships with humankind, the rest of the natural world, and the Divine (the "Eternal Thou"). For an introduction to Buber's life and thought, see *The Martin Buber Reader: Essential Writings*, edited by Asher D. Bieman (New York: Palgrave Mac-Millan, 2002). See also "Martin Buber" (including the introduction by Samuel Berrin Shonkoff) in Arthur Green and Ariel Evan Mayse, eds., *A New Hasidism: Roots* (Philadelphia: Jewish Publication Society, 2019), 51–132, 353–64.

wearing, and this gave a visible shape to him. In the same way, we provide God with masks. Sometimes they are terrible and terrifying. But I prefer a more motherly God. Then there are other times when I need to have a romance with God. The Sufis often speak of God as the Beloved. Sometimes this is precisely how I need to address God. Our own mystics were full of the same imagery. They had a romance with God.[10]

When you say, "Who is it that you come before?," check out the images that allow you the most heartful exchange with God.

—*The Gates of Prayer*, 112–13

GAIA: A NEW FACE OF GOD

Metaphors are so important. The more abstract the truth we are trying to grasp, the more we must rely on our imaginations—our human capacity to create images—to understand it. Nowhere has this been truer than in our visions of God, for if the world's religions agree on one thing, it is that the infinite God is beyond our power to grasp. The Kabbalists, for example, were especially perplexed by the question of how the infinite becomes finite—of how creation leaped that seemingly insurmountable barrier, and how we finite beings might somehow reconnect to the infinite. They came up with many complex and beautiful metaphors. Some imagined the existence of worlds upon worlds, parallel worlds in which the divine became ever more concretely manifest. Some spoke of *sefirot*, spheres or aspects of God, interwoven in a Tree of Life that was rooted on the earthly plane and had its crown in the heavens.[11] Some spoke of *partzufim*, literally

---

10. This imagery is based on the long-standing Jewish interpretative tradition of the Song of Songs as an allegory for the relationship between God (as male lover) and Israel (as female lover). See, for example, Arthur Green, "The Song of Songs in early Jewish Mysticism," in *The Heart of the Matter: Studies in Jewish Mysticism and Theology* (Philadelphia: Jewish Publication Society, 2015), 101–18.

11. To learn more about the *sefirot*, see Arthur Green, *EHYEH: A Kabbalah for Tomorrow* (Woodstock, VT: Jewish Lights Publishing, 2003),

masks or faces, core images or names of God that embodied
male and female, aged and youth.[12] In each case they were looking for an interface, a means to connect with the infinite, which
would otherwise be so utterly beyond us.

I believe that Gaia (Greek goddess of the Earth),[13] the face of
our living planet, represents a newly emerging *partzuf* or face
of the ultimate core reality of the universe . . . All of a sudden,
we see phrases like "God is kind" or "God is merciful" in a new
light. Instead of seeing God as an all-powerful patriarch in the
sky, we can affirm that, yes, the universe is kind in the sense of
being hospitable to life. Yes, the universe is compassionate in the
sense that the Earth heals her children. In our new understanding, such phrases become metaphors for the essential qualities of
this planetary miracle we call life.

Does this mean that we replace the unknowable God with
the name and face of Gaia, the Greek Earth Goddess? No. The
God that I can know as an object of my mind is not God. The
second commandment teaches us that every form or notion I
have of God is an idol. But as our sages said, the Torah speaks to
us in human language [see Babylonian Talmud, Zevahim 108b].
Partzufim are not God, but they help us connect. They help us
charge up the God field, as it were. I don't always need to address
God on a trans-galactic scale. I can often be perfectly content to
address the inherent intelligence of the universe as revealed right
here on planet Earth.[14]   —*Jewish with Feeling*, 168–69

39–60. See Reb Zalman's application of this symbol system to ritual life
in the selection entitled "The Rainbow Prayer Shawl" later in this volume.

12. See Lawrence Fine's discussion of the *partzufim* and related matters
in "Chapter 4: Lurianic Myth," in *Physician of the Soul, Healer of the Cosmos: Isaac Luria and His Kabbalistic Fellowship* (Stanford, CA: Stanford
University Press, 2003), 124–49, specifically 138–41.

13. See Reb Zalman's discussion of the "Gaian Hypothesis," as developed by the chemist James Lovelock and microbiologist Lynn Margulis, in
Jewish with Feeling, 163–65.

14. The juxtaposition of Gaia and the "trans-galactic" God echoes
classical Jewish mystical teachings about the immanent (often depicted

WHAT FACE OF GOD DO YOU NEED?

What is the face of God that you long for in your deepest moments? Is it a friend you need? Or a comforter? A rock you can lean on when you are most besieged? A recipient of your joy and thanks? An address for your prayers for yourself or your loved ones?

Can you give that face of God a name? Try it. See what wells up inside you. Take a quiet moment or wait until some joy or sorrow opens your heart. Perhaps it will be a name from our tradition, perhaps something you make up. Whenever you feel the need to reach out, say that name. Repeat it over and over to yourself. Say it out loud if you can. Try it out on your tongue. Savor it. Open an account for yourself. Start making a connection. —*Jewish with Feeling*, 8

AN EMERGENT GOD

"If God is God, He is not good," wrote poet Archibald MacLeish (1892–1982) in *JB* (1958), his play in verse based on Job. "If God is good, He is not God." This weighty problem comes up in every serious discussion about the existence of God. Theodicy, the philosophers call it: the problem of God's justice. The world is so full of evil on every scale, from genocide to a single innocent child abused. How can we subscribe to a God that allows this? How can we talk of God's justice, far less God's mercy? On the other hand, how can we take seriously any idea of a God that doesn't encompass evil as well as good?

To this question, again, we have no airtight theological answer. We can only offer a few ways of thinking about the problem that might help to allow and perhaps deepen our subjective experience.

---

as female) and transcendent (often depicted as male) dimensions of the Divine. See Daniel C. Matt's introduction to *The Essential Kabbalah: The Heart of Jewish Mysticism* (San Francisco: HarperCollins, 1995), 1–19.

We are attached to the idea of a good God, just as we are attached to the idea of a good parent. We want God to love us, to cherish us, to protect us from harm. We can see how we might deserve some unpleasantness for our transgressions, if that's the way the universe really works, but those punishments should be fair. A God who abandons us is a deadbeat God, unworthy of our allegiance.

These attachments and expectations quickly shatter in the face of reality. We see the innocent suffering all the time. It is startling how often the expression "only the good die young" comes to pass, how often the best and most inspiring among us get stricken with cancer or die in an accident. WHY? we feel like shouting. "Why does that wonderful, gentle, righteous person have to die?" or "Why me?" or "Why my child?" Sooner or later some of us may feel, "If it's for this you created me, God, you could have saved yourself the trouble." Can you imagine how those who lived during the Holocaust may have said, as Job did, "Cursed is the day my mother conceived me" (3:3)?

We cannot possibly express genuine love of God or our fellow beings if we always put a lid on this kind of existential anger. If we do not express this anger, we turn it on ourselves. Just as you might send out thanks to the universe when you feel lucky or blessed, take the time to send out your rage as well. No one who hasn't taken a vigil for the night and had it out with God can get to the place where their love and faith become real . . .

The Hasidic master Rabbi Nahman of Bratzlav (1772–1810), no stranger to depression and disappointment, illness and untimely death, offered a startling response to living with the problem of evil.[15] He points to the liturgy of *Ne'ilah*, the final prayer of Yom Kippur, in which the pleading congregation invokes Abraham, Isaac, and Jacob in turn. "Abraham knew you from youth," we begin. The usual interpretation, of course, is

---

15. To learn more about this outstanding Hasidic figure, see Arthur Green, *Tormented Master: The Life and Spiritual Quest of Rabbi Nahman of Bratslav* (Woodstock, VT: Jewish Lights Publishing, 1992).

that Abraham, the progenitor of monotheism, embraced the idea of God when he was still a young man. But Rabbi Nahman reads the line as meaning, "Abraham knew you from *your* youth," as if to say, "We knew you from the beginning of human relationship with you, when you were still young in the God business." Nahman seems to recognize that God, too, is still learning. We are struggling together.

Rabbi Nahman was not the only one to consider this idea. The whole Torah—from the Garden of Eden to the Flood to Abraham to Moses and beyond—can make much more sense if we think of God as an emergent God, evolving hand in hand with humanity and creation.[16] Like many such pronouncements, Nahman's formulation would seem heretical if taken as absolute. On the experiential level, though, it helps us to understand and accept the evil in the world by imagining an Infinite that, at least as manifested in the human sphere, is learning and evolving along with us over time . . .

The question of theodicy can stop our spiritual conversation cold if we let it, but we should not. It's a useful question, like a bone a dog chews on from time to time in order to sharpen its teeth. It challenges our complacency. How much of the evil in the world are we responsible for? Is that cancer, that road death, that famine purely arbitrary, or did we contribute to it in some far-removed way? Without absolving God or the perpetrators, did we bear any responsibility at all for an event like September 11, or even (heresy of heresies) the Holocaust?[17] Theodicy can throw us back on ourselves that way.

---

16. For a helpful discussion of the notion that the biblical God matures over time, see Yochanan Muffs, *The Personhood of God: Biblical Theology, Human Faith, and the Divine Image* (Woodstock, VT: Jewish Lights, 2005), 59, 66–69. Reb Zalman also read the works of modern process theologians who speak of God and world in dynamic motion, following in the footstep of the mathematician and philosopher Alfred North Whitehead (1861–1947).

17. He actually raised this wrenching question explicitly in his teaching. See, for example, "Some Dawn Thoughts on the *Shoah*," reprinted

Theodicy teaches us, too, to avoid loading our concept of God with a positive charge in too simplistic a way. Swami Satchidananda (1914–2002), the yogic master, has a good way of saying it: "Don't make any appointments, you won't have dis-appointments." We make a certain appointment with the word god. God loves good and hates evil, God wants this and doesn't want that, God would not allow for such and such a thing to happen. We make God the steward of morality and build up expectations, expectations that sooner or later are bound to be shattered. If instead we strive to accept all sides of the equation, if we could get into a Möbius strip mentality in which both sides of the page, good and evil, are one and the same, then we start to get a real sense of that famous phrase from *Adon Olam*: "God is one, there is no other."[18]   —*Jewish with Feeling*, 22–26

GOD: WHAT PART OF SPEECH?

One problem with the word *God* is that it is a *noun*. Almost all of our names and appellations for God are nouns. You remember the simple definition of a noun as it was first given to us in grade school: a noun is the name of a person, place, or thing. By defining "God" exclusively as a noun, we "thingify" or objectify God in our minds, no matter how often we protest that God is free from all the properties of matter, beyond time and space, and so on. How can we begin to conceive of an Infinite Being, an

in *Paradigm Shift: From the Jewish Renewal Teachings of Reb Zalman Schachter-Shalomi*, edited by Ellen Singer (Northvale, NJ: Jason Aronson, 1993), 63–73.

18. *Adon Olam* ("Eternal Lord" or "Sovereign of the World") is a well-known, medieval Jewish hymn (*piyyut*) that is often included in *Shabbat* evening and/or morning services (and at other times). It speaks of God's utter uniqueness, existing beyond space and time—"without beginning or end. To learn more about it, see "*Adon Olam*," in *My People's Prayer Book: Traditional Prayers, Modern Commentaries—Volume 5, Birkhot Hashachar*, edited by Lawrence A. Hoffman (Woodstock, VT: Jewish Lights Publishing, 2001), 93–98.

Absolute All that is in no way a thing? We must expand beyond the language of nouns, of objects.

I have for many years encouraged my students to think of God as a *verb*. Imagining God in terms of action, of process, opens up new ways of connecting to the infinite. Take the expression "Infinite Being" in the previous paragraph. If we think of God as a process of Be-ing, of *is*-ing, of infinite existing, we open up new ways of relating. We can begin to imagine a "godding," a process that the universe is doing, has been doing, and will continue to do—at least on our scale of comprehension—forever. In the largest sense, we can say that as part of that universe we are "godding" in everything we do. In the more limited, human sense, we could wake up in the morning and consider how we might "god" most effectively today. . . .

Thinking of God as a verb has its limitations too, of course. English verbs have two forms. Transitive verbs have direct objects: *She gave me a book*. Intransitive verbs do not require a direct object: *She gave generously*. They can be active or passive: We *love* and *are loved*. I have for years encouraged my students to imagine the God verb as *interactive*, a form that barely exists in English. Imagine a flag waving in the wind, said Buddhist monk Thich Nhat Hanh. Without the wind the flag would not wave. Without the flag the wind could not do the waving. Flag and wind are inseparable at that moment: they are *interwaving*. In this perception we have no subject or object, no active or passive, no "each" and no "other," but rather a single and indivisible phenomenon. So it is with God and creation, the world and the process that underlies it, that *is* it. We get a more Zen-like, instantaneous flash . . . of the whole picture this way. God in our expanded understanding can be all parts of speech.

—*Jewish with Feeling*, 19–21

UNDERSTANDING FAITH

Judaism places far less emphasis on faith than other religions. We have always been a religion of deeds. Perform the *mitzvot*, the commandments, classical Judaism teaches, and faith will take care of itself. Most of us today don't operate that way. We need to feel an urge, an inner whispering, that says, "Follow, I will take you. If you want to be more awakened, follow this." That inner whispering is the beginning of faith.

Weighing the notion of faith as we would any other logical proposition can make us uneasy. Better is to simply try to imagine it. What might faith feel like?

Faith is what I call a mind-move, a radical shift in awareness. The expression "a leap of faith" is so true. Faith is not something we can arrive at by a careful, step-by-step process. It is not something we can square with our intellect. Faith does not make sense, nor does it feel safe. It is what takes us further after the questions that can be answered logically have been exhausted. To have faith we must let go. Faith is like swimming the backstroke, reaching above and behind us into an unknown you cannot see. Faith is like driving forward with only the rear-view mirror as a guide. Some might even reason their way to the place where there is a God. But the *quality*, the *essence*, the *whatness* of God—that we can only reach with the opening-up, the joyful surrender, that is faith. To experience faith even for a moment we must make a leap beyond intellect, beyond logic. A leap into the beyond.

A story is told of the Indian saint Ramakrishna (1836–1886), who stands in front of an image of the Hindu goddess Kali. "I have served you," he tells her, "and you have not answered me. I love you, I sing to you, I worship you, I adore you—and you have not manifested yourself to me. A life in which you don't bother to answer me is not worth living." And with that he grabs Kali's ritual dagger and is about to throw himself upon it—when at the very last moment the presence of Kali engulfs him.[19]

19. Mahendranath Gupta, *The Gospel of Sri Ramakrishna*, translated and edited by Swami Nikhilananda (New York: Ramakrishna-Vivekananda Center, 1942), 13–14. Reb Zalman seems to also be drawing on a second description that Ramakrishna offered of this formative ecstatic experience,

The point of this story, to me, is not some miraculous event. It is that only when Ramakrishna, after all that pleading and singing and worship and adoration, finally breaks through the last mental barrier and is ready to offer his very life—only then does Kali become real to him.

Even the great Jewish teachers have been mystified by the problem of faith. Once Reb Shneur Zalman of Liadi, founder of the Lubavitch movement, was musing aloud to one of his followers. "Moshe," he says to him, "*Nu*, tell me, what is God? What is soul, Moshe? What is faith?"

"Rebbe," the disciple says, "you're the master. *I* should tell *you*?"

"But what do you think, Moshe?" the Rebbe persists.

"I don't know!"

The Rebbe sighed. "I don't know either. But maintain we must, and affirm we must, that that which clearly exists and besides which nothing else clearly exists—that is God."

The Rebbe stroked his beard for a few minutes and thought some more. "And what is soul, Moshe? Soul is that being that knows with certainty that God exists and that besides God nothing else clearly exists.

"And faith, Moshe? Faith is the *way* the soul knows that God exists and that besides God nothing clearly exists."[20]

In our day we lack even this degree of certainty. We replace the Rebbe's "must" with questions. Can we, if only for fleeting moments, affirm an Ultimate Existence? Can we get in touch with that part of us that truly knows that dimension of existence?

---

which can be found in Swami Nihkilananda, *Life of Sri Ramakrishna* (Kolkata, India: Advaita Ashrama, 2011), 59–60.

20. Rabbi Shneur Zalman of Liadi, founder of HaBaD Hasidism, discusses this subject at length in his classic work, *Likkutei Amarim–Tanya*. See Norman Lamm's (editor) translation and comments on two selections from it in "Chapter 1: God and Providence," in *The Religious Thought of Hasidism: Text and Commentary* (Hoboken, NJ: Yeshiva University Press and Ktav Publishing House, 1999), 9–14 (texts 2, 3).

This story also teaches us that God is not some independent "out there" entity. God, soul, and faith—"the known, the knower, and the knowing"[21]—are inseparable. We are one.

—*Jewish with Feeling*, 27–29

BEYOND I AND THOU
(THE PRAYER OF THE MONIST)

Reb Zalman published slightly different versions of the following prayer, using both of the above titles. The version below can be found in Gate to the Heart, *but we also include here a brief introductory note on the prayer that he penned for the volume* All Breathing Life Adores Your Name: At the Interface between Poetry and Prayer (2011):

> The mind enjoys reaching towards unity. It can conceptually reach infinity in solitude. On the other hand, the heart needs to flow to a dialogical Presence. It needs to have the Other to face and to love and to embrace. The contemplative, who still wants to experience love and longing without relinquishing the unitive awareness will find this poem a heart-full expression of what the intellect knows, and the soul intuits.[22]

Reb Zalman adds that he sought to capture the intimacy between the oneness of "the individual person" and of "the divine person" by using an acrostic (following a ancient Jewish poetic convention) in which his name—MeSHuLaM ZaLMaN—is embraced by the Divine names Y-H-V-H and EHYH.[23]

---

21. This expression is taken from Maimonides' description of the Divine. See Mishneh Torah, *Laws of the Foundations of the Torah 2:10*, https://www.sefaria.org/Mishneh_Torah%2C_Foundations_of_the_Torah?lang=bi.

22. *All Breathing Life Adores Your Name*, 155.

23. In keeping with the unitive (or monist) orientation of the prayer, both of these biblical names come from the root for "being." See Arthur Green, "Introduction: *Ehyeh* as a Name of God," in *EHYEH: A Kabbalah for Tomorrow* (Woodstock, VT: Jewish Lights Publishing, 2003), 1–5.

Yah, my God, where are You?
   I call You as if from afar,
   But You, my Redeemer,
   Dwell in my heart,
   So close, and I know it not.
Here You are,
   Present in my innermost,
   And so too at the outermost edge,
   Both my Source and Goal!
Where my feelings rise,
   There You are, stirring me,
   Nesting in the womb
   Of my very urge.
Here in my eyes,
   You are the pupil,
   And I yearn so much
   To make of You
   The object of my sight.

My innards are pure,
   Your sanctuary in me,
   Sacred by Your Presence;
   But how I long to scour them,
   To make them worthy of the honor.
Show me how to host You,
   Here in my body!
   What a blessing!
   Your nestling in my heart,
Life of my life,
   You are with/in me
   So how can I meet You
   On the outside?
My song I would
   Address to You
   Were You beside me,
   And not hidden in this voice.

Zoned in the point of knowing,
    You hide in unseen splendor,
    Glorious as I seek Your Glory;
Lingering on Your threshold,
    My ego squats, claiming to be
    The legal tenant of Your home.
More I cannot con-fuse
    The two who shimmer
    As one I-Am-ness;
Never can I leave this labyrinth
    My self by myself.
    Help me sortie and free me;
    Then my prayer
    Will be pure
    For You.

Echo—
    Are You the call
    Or the answer?
    Even these words,
    Are they mine
    Or Yours?
Help and tell me,
    Love of my Heart,
    Are You not also
    The Love and the Heart?
Yah! God, adored One;
    I want to offer You
    A gift You will not spurn—
    Your will be mine—
    Is it not already so?
Holy solitude,
    All One Al-one,
    My sole One,
    My soul's One,
    My part(ner)

My wholly,
Holy Other,
One.
Amen.

—*Gate to the Heart,* 105–07[24]

---

24. The interested reader might wish to compare this prayer with some of the early Yiddish poetry of one of Reb Zalman's mentors, Abraham Joshua Heschel (1907–72). See Heschel's, *Human–God's Ineffable Name,* translated by Zalman Schachter-Shalomi (Boulder, CO: Albion-Andalus Inc., 2012). See, in particular, "I and You" (3–4) and "God Follows Me Everywhere" (21–22).

2

The Spiritual Path and the Terrain of the Soul

INTRODUCTION

Reb Zalman published his first booklet on Jewish contemplative practice privately in 1958. He entitled it the The First Step, *as it was designed for students and others new to this world of discourse and practice—seekers beginning their spiritual journeys. By the early 1960s, he had gained a reputation within HaBaD circles as a rabbi who could work with* far-out *types, sharing the riches of Jewish mysticism and spirituality with warmth and openness to their questions and doubts. By the early 1970s, he emerged as a pioneering figure in the burgeoning heterodox, Jewish countercultural movement, serving as a* rebbe *figure to many hippie seekers. Part of what fueled this work was meeting young Jews across the United States and Canada who were looking for spiritual sustenance in ashrams, zendos, and retreat centers, believing that Judaism had little to offer them. While Reb Zalman had great interest in and respect for other religious traditions, he also felt an abiding responsibility to help turn people on to Yiddishkeit (Judaism in Yiddish).[1] While he was no longer a conventional Hasid, he carried with him some of*

---

1. See, for example, Reb Zalman's comments in the introduction to his book, *Fragments of a Future Scroll: Hassidism for the Aquarian Age*, edited

the zeal from his early HaBaD days, now in a more universalist "Aquarian" key.[2]

As part of this effort, he felt compelled to share the mystical and meditative riches of the tradition with newcomers or returnees to Jewish life. He felt strongly that there were too many rationalist Jewish teachers who were embarrassed by these old-world sources (that include discussions of angels and demons, magical incantations, incarnation and resurrection), and traditional Jewish mystics who were unwilling to disclose their secrets to the unlearned. Young Jewish seekers were spiritually hungry, and Jewish teachers had a responsibility to nourish and nurture them. Otherwise, these people would continue to look elsewhere for sustenance and support.[3]

Over the decades, Reb Zalman taught countless numbers of Jewish and non-Jewish students and wrote a score of articles, pamphlets, and books about the Jewish spiritual journey from his unique vantage point as a postmodern mystic who was at home in both the old and new worlds. This included a unique synthesis of Hasidism and Kabbalah with ideas and insights from the fields of psychology, philosophy, the arts, and other religions.

In this chapter, the reader is invited to explore several of Reb Zalman's reflections on the spiritual journey, including teachings on the inner landscape of the human spirit. This includes a discussion of various stages and phases along the path (what the Hasidic masters refer to as madregot, rungs of consciousness and/or development) and his interpretations of core Jewish mystical concepts related to the multidimensional nature of the soul and the worlds in which it is conceived, sustained, and

---

by Philip Mandelkorn and Stephen Gerstman (Germantown, PA: Leaves of Grass Press, 1975), ix–xiv.

2. See Arthur Green's comment about the messianic impulse in Reb Zalman's thought (long after his years in HaBaD) in Arthur Green and Ariel Evan Mayse, eds., *A New Hasidism: Roots* (Philadelphia: Jewish Publication Society, 2019), 229.

3. See *Fragments of a Future Scroll*, ix–xiv.

challenged. As you read, consider if and how these teachings might be useful to you in your ongoing journey in relationship with self, other, nature, and Divinity. If you are familiar with other Jewish mystical works, other esoteric traditions, or psychological systems, you might compare and contrast these teachings with the texts before you. What is familiar? What is new or different? Is there anything that you wish to investigate further?

SPIRITUAL HUNGER

We all feel spiritually hungry at different times in our lives, and we feel that hunger in different ways. Sometimes it is an absence that we feel, an ache, a yearning for something beyond what we experience day to day. We need someone to talk to sometimes, an Other with whom we can share our innermost thoughts—not a spouse or a lover, a parent or a friend, not even a therapist, but someone who is closer to us than all of these. Someone to share those existential questions that besiege us in dark moments: Does my life have any real meaning? Does the way I behave or what happens to me really matter? Will the world be safe for my children? Someone to rage at: "Why me? Why is my life such a mess? Why are my kids (or my partner, or my boss) doing this to me? Why can't I make ends meet? Why am I ill? Why must a life be cut short before its time?" Someone to thank for the blessings in our lives, the superabundance of them or the few that remain to us: If you've had serious surgery, as I have, even something as simple as going to the bathroom without pain can bring on a feeling of, "Thank goodness, my body is working right today."

Sometimes it is a presence that beckons or calls to us, a presence that reveals itself to us in glimpses. The other day I was sitting down by a lake where I live as day turned into evening. It was summertime, the fish were jumping. A dog was swimming in the water. The geese and the next generation of goslings were making their way around. On the horizon the Rocky Mountains, washed in pink light, rose up to the sky. It was so beautiful to see. I could feel a Presence twinkling at me. "See, I'm right here. I am all this."

Perhaps you witnessed the birth of a child, or saw the new buds on the trees in spring, and felt the miracle of new life emerging in the world. Or maybe you stood at the deathbed of a loved one and thought you glimpsed their soul departing this world, leaving only their earthly shell behind. Sometimes it's a serendipity we experience, a crumb that life drops in our laps, a question answered *just like that*, a request granted out of the blue in a way that *couldn't* be just a coincidence—could it? Sometimes it's more extreme than that: a born-again mountaintop experience, a near-death or out-of-body experience, an epileptic aura, a vision of unity. Other times it feels like a warning from the universe, a stop sign that says to us, "You can't continue the way you've been going. You need to change your life before it's too late."

If you've ever felt the presence of—or yearning for—such a dimension to the world, you may have wondered: What is this feeling? What is it that I am experiencing? How can I connect to that more? How can I bring more beauty and connection and clarity into my daily life? And you may have wondered, too: Isn't such clarity and connection what religion is supposed to be about? Then why do I feel it so rarely in so-called "religious" settings?

These questions are at the heart of the spiritual search of so many in our time, and they are beautiful questions. For such wondrous or painful experiences are the very stuff of religion. They were the seeds from which all religions grew, the nutrients that sustained and renewed them over time. They are still what religion *should* be about. The problem is that our ancient faiths have become oververbalized and underexperienced. We talk too much and feel too little. —*Jewish with Feeling*, 3–5

THE SOUL'S WAKING

Years ago, when my daughter was young, she once asked me, "*Abba* (Daddy), when you're asleep you can wake up, right?"

"Right," I answered.

"So, when you're awake," she said, "can you wake up even more?"

That part of us that always seeks to awaken even more, I call *soul*. Judaism speaks of the soul as a spark of God. I like to think of the soul as a holographic snippet off the old block. Each spark, each snippet, contains the all.

There's a wonderful Jewish teaching about an angel that teaches us the entire Torah when we are in our mother's womb and then, just before we are born, taps us under the nose (which gives us that hollow above our lip), and we forget it all.[4] This memory loss, to me, bespeaks that tendency, that pull, that we all have toward a point of origin that we once knew but now must strive to recall. The image of forgetfulness in the story is crucial: forgetting something is not the same as never knowing it in the first place. Even those things that we seem to have forgotten completely are merely dormant, like a spore that has been planted within us, waiting for the proper conditions to germinate and grow.

This soul; this spore; this snippet off the holographic block; this teaching that each of us has learned and forgotten but that lurks deep in our memories—all these images point to an intricate dance between the God that is us, each individual creation, and the God that is All.

In the various dramas of our lives, we often forget the truth of our godliness and think of ourselves only as separate. In the early years of our development to adulthood and sometimes for long periods afterwards, this feels perfectly okay. Being an individual is fun. It is what we all strive towards as we mature. It feels in some very deep way like the right way to be. But sooner or later, as we get older, perhaps have children, start to sense our own mortality, we begin to feel that pull toward the All. At first we try to ignore it. We hear "I want" and we go to the fridge. Our soul wants so bad that we feel physical pain, so we reach

---

4. Babylonian Talmud, Niddah 30b, https://www.sefaria.org/Niddah .30b?lang=bi.

for a pill. We feel edgy and restless, so we plan a vacation, try to "get away." Years of distraction and estrangement later we are still feeling lonely in some profound way and lost.

But we are not cut off. In rare and fleeting moments of grace we feel a shot of love pouring into us, the creations, from the Creator. Hasidism teaches, furthermore, that the worldly delights with which we try so hard to assuage our spiritual hunger themselves contain a spark of holiness, for they echo the holy love we once knew before separation. The Ba'al Shem Tov (c. 1700–1760) . . . taught that our attraction to these delights is precisely what makes it possible for us to love God. If these worldly desires had not been etched into our bodies, we would never develop the sensitivity needed for spiritual being. Thus, the obstacles to what the Hasidim call *deveikut*, adhering to God, can serve as the very cement that adheres us to God.[5]

This frees us to delight in our individuality, the unique stamp of creation that each of us bears and embodies. The spark of delight in being separate, to the Ba'al Shem, resides in the intention and goal of the separation, which is to put our individuality at the service of union, of Oneness.[6] We whose hunger is

---

5. The early Hasidic masters speak of the need to acknowledge one's corporeal desires, and to uplift them in service of the Divine. By rechanneling this energy (rather than trying to ignore or hide from it), the devotee can come closer to God since *everything* (including these *lower* urges) is ultimately rooted in the Divine. See Louis Jacobs, "The Elevation of Strange Thoughts," in *Hasidic Prayer* (London: Littman Library of Jewish Civilization, 1972), 104–20, and notes 174–76. To learn more about the concept of *deveikut*, see "Clinging to God" in Chapter 3 of this volume.

6. This theme is explored in a popular story attributed to the Ba'al Shem Tov in which a wise king creates a set of illusory towers, walls, and gates through which his subjects must pass to meet him. At each passageway, the king places various riches from the kingdom. While different seekers pass through one or more of the gates, none of them make it to the king; they take the riches and leave. Only the king's son is able to see through the mirage and go directly to the king. The teaching ends with a favorite Hasidic citation from Isaiah 6:3: "God's glory fills the whole earth!" See a translation of this text (from the book *Keter Shem Tov*) and complementary Hasidic source in *God in All Moments: Mystical and Practical Spiritual*

unfulfilled feel the glimmerings of that intention but have not yet found a way to carry it out.

So we dance, God the Creator and God the created. We separate, come close, and separate again. The quest is, in a sense, about how we might more consciously join that dance—and how we as partners might start to lead rather than follow, to develop more sure-footed moves of our own.

This is no easy matter. It's all very well to say that our goal as spiritual beings is to put ourselves at the service of union, but what does that really mean? How do we go about it? More pointedly, how do we go about it without losing our individuality and in the context of our daily lives?

—*Jewish with Feeling*, 30–33

MOMENTS OF CLARITY

What are those moments in your own life when you felt the clarity of higher purpose? I remember the first time I came to Camp Starlight, Pennsylvania. That was where the B'nai B'rith camp was, and students from Hillel foundations would gather there the last week of the summer. I was about thirty years old at that time, a rabbi at a *shul* (synagogue) in New Bedford, Massachusetts. I saw how passionate and involved the Hillel students were, and I went out into the field and started to cry and pray to God, "*Ribbono shel Olom*, Master of the Universe, so much one can do with these young people! I hear Your call. Please, give me the opportunity to do it."

This is a "yes" born of an insight: Who am I? "God made us," a verse from Psalms declares. "We did not make ourselves" [Psalm 100:3]. I belong to God; I am nothing but an expression of God. On Yom Kippur we sing a hymn that says, "We are as clay in the Potter's hand." A host of other metaphors see us as an expression of godly intent "like the tiller in the Helmsman's hand, like a stone in the Mason's hand." My entire life

---

Wisdom from Hasidic Masters, edited and translated by Or Rose with Ebn D. Leader (Woodstock, VT: Jewish Lights Publishing, 2004), 36–37.

and everything I do are nothing but God "godding Godself" as Zalman. The best thing I can do, then, is to make my life a good ride for God, to consciously devote my actions to that purpose.

At first our "yes" may be hesitant: "OK, I'll do it." Over time though, as we keep responding, as we keep volunteering for whatever mission God has for us in the world, that "yes" takes on a promise of quality. It says, "Yes! I'll do it! But I so want to do it well. I want it to be noble, I want it to be beautiful." The kabbalist, Rabbi Moses Hayim Luzzatto (1707–1747), in his *Mesillat Yesharim* (Path of the Just), gave this goal a name: *sh'leimut ha-avodah*. The second word, *avodah*, means "work" or "service." *Sh'leimut* means "fullness," "wholeness," "completeness," "perfection." So *sh'leimut ha-avodah* captures our aspiration for a completeness or perfection in our service to God.

—*Davening*, 13–14

THE MYSTICAL APPROACH TO RELIGIOUS LIFE

If we were to make a distinction between the mystical and dogmatic elements in religious practice, the distinction would boil down to how much of the *experiential* element is present. Mystical doctrine claims that we can experience the Infinite *right now*, that beneath the surface of the obvious, there exists Divinity.

The dogmatic approach, on the other hand, doubts the possibility of experiencing God on this plane, and contents itself with belief in revealed principles, reasoned theology, outward observances, and ritual. Religious dogmatists see little purpose in looking below the surface for hidden meanings and experiences. Religious mystics, on the other hand, see little purpose in simply reciting prayer formulae and not looking beyond them.

People seem naturally drawn to one of these two positions: to the exoteric, focusing on outer behavior and ritual practice, or to the esoteric search for the inner experience.

In the Jewish tradition, the mystical body of knowledge is called *Kabbalah*, which literally means, "the Received." Kabbalah is [often] transmitted orally, with only the outlines being written down. This is in part to protect it from being used without guidance, and because the mystical experience doesn't translate very well from direct experience into indirect words.

There is a teaching in Kabbalah that tells of the original "vessels" created by God "in the beginning," which God filled to the brim with Divine light. The full force of light was too much for these vessels and they shattered, showering shards of vessel and sparks of light everywhere. Eventually, shells formed on the outside of these sparks of light, hiding the sparks within them; this is the basis of the material world we live in today.[7]

The Hasidic masters taught that these sparks of divinity reside in everything, animate and inanimate, and that each of us has it in our power to redeem the imprisoned sparks and send them back up to their divine Source, to rejoin Divinity. [They also teach] . . . that this release and reunion of sparks is accomplished by every holy act.[8]

What defines such an act is *not* only the outer prescriptions of behavior in the Jewish tradition, but also what we are doing on the inner plane. When we are offering the outer act of love, obedience and service, that is only the shell of it. On the inner level, we are sorting out sparks, offering them up, creating a *tikkun*, a "fix" or "rectification" for the original catastrophe of the shattering.[9]

---

7. The teaching of the "shattering of the vessels" is one of the major contributions of the revered sixteenth-century mystic, Rabbi Isaac Luria (1534–72). See Lawrence Fine, *Physician of the Soul, Healer of the Cosmos: Isaac Luria and His Kabbalistic Fellowship* (Stanford, CA: Stanford University Press, 2003), 134–38. See also the excerpt from his disciple Rabbi Hayyim Vital's (1542–1620) *Likkutim Hadashim*, entitled "*Tsimtsum* and *Shevirah*: Withdrawal and Shattering," in Daniel C. Matt, *The Essential Kabbalah: The Heart of Jewish Mysticism* (San Francisco: HarperCollins, 1995), 94–95, and the explanatory notes, 195–96.

8. See the teaching from *Tzava'at Ha-RYBaSh* (#109) entitled "Holy Sparks," in *God in All Moments*, 54–55.

9. See Arthur Green, "Tikkun Olam," in *These Are the Words: A Vocabulary of Jewish Spiritual Life* (Woodstock, VT: Jewish Lights Publishing, 2000), 174–75.

That, at least, is the classical formulation. From another point of view, there was never a catastrophe; only a loving, intentional, and creative act. The fact that things are not totally symmetrical creates the possibility, the imbalance that allows for this particular reality. The "fall" from the Garden of Eden, then, was not a fall at all; it was a "set-up" to allow the human being to individuate, to become a self-conscious, individual being.

—*Gate to the Heart*, 6–7

STAGES ON THE PATH

Spiritual progress is often charted in linear stages, though the actual experience of these is usually more dynamic and organically unique to the individual seeker. However, a linear progression is useful for teaching, so I like to speak of five such stages.

The first is the rung of *Love*, fueled by the neophyte's enthusiasm. Optimistic, grateful for new light and growing joy, it overlooks the difficulties ahead. But many are caught in a loop here, moving from one path to another on the same level, all in order to continue enjoying the thrill of newness and the sweet emotion of discovery. Fortunately, the newness wears off and the thrill eventually evaporates. It necessarily ends in order to propel movement to the next stage.

The rung of *Power* is the level of mastery of the medium, the technique. At this stage of rigorous discipline, one develops a new center of gravity, a place of personal power, inspired by an initial understanding of the inner light through focused mastery of the medium. At this stage, one has to be careful not to get caught up in a practice of ascetic-athletics and over-strictness, which is often accompanied by intolerance of "weaker" others.

Having found the limitations of the rung of Power, we ascend to the rung of *Beauty*, a level in which symbols are highly charged and new depths of meaning suggest themselves in emotional creativity. Here, at the gate of Beauty, the various dramas between the soul and her Source are revealed. Here, God is the Parent, the Friend, or the Beloved in the life drama.

One eventually moves on to the rung of *Community*, where the harmonious collectivity of all souls is the highest concern. Having enjoyed the levels of creativity in the previous stages, we question whether this creativity is in itself of any benefit to others:

> Does the Earth get healed by it?
> Do exiles get released through it?
> Is the pool of knowledge enhanced by it?
> Are those people who need to work and dream and share together, working, dreaming and sharing together?

But this level of integration cannot occur until one has had the experience of the various games and names and roles of self and God within the rung of Beauty.

By God's grace, we are then called to the rung of *Union*. Union is an achievement that is beyond our efforts, and is of a reality that is, beyond our usual considerations, already present. That is to say, where the very identity of the soul with the Beloved, of God with the person, is already a fact. The realization of Union is what occurs on this rung, not the unchanging existence of Union. Periodic reflection on this truth is spiritual medicine for depression at any stage of practice.

In our daily meditations, we pray to the Divine who fills the world, and fills our hearts, and moves us from rung to rung, until we arrive at where we have always been. And then we take another step so that the soul can come to encompass the vastness of the knowable as well as the unknowable.[10]

—*Gate to the Heart*, 4–6

THE SOUL'S FLAW

A word must be said about our "blind-spot," the way in which we conceal our true self from ourselves and conceal this act of

---

10. This teaching is based on Dr. Karl Stern's adaptation of Freud's five stages of psychosexual development. See Reb Zalman's account of meeting Dr. Stern (1906–75) and exploring this schema with him in *My Life in Jewish Renewal*, 101–02.

concealment. This blind-spot is highly charged, and even as we catch a glimpse of it, it recedes, provoking all sorts of avoidant behaviors. However, if it is confronted and contained it ultimately yields its secret and strength.

Sometimes, I like to talk about this as the soul's flaw. For every soul—*though truly a part of God's holy perfection*—is possessed of a "flaw." This flaw is not unlike the flaw in an opal, which creates its special "fire," its charm and attraction. The only difference between the fire and the flaw in the opal is in the refraction of light. Likewise, the soul's flaw can be a vice, or in different light, a virtue. The soul's main task is to work *on* and *with* that flaw.[11]

The particular soul trait, which attracts people to it and sparks something in them, is the same trait that is thought of as a flaw. Only, when it appears as a flaw, the special light in it has gone and, because of a shift in time and circumstances, the flaw remains unadorned. This flaw and its unique fire are two sides of the same configuration of the soul.

Very few people have the ability to stay aware of their blind-spots. Even if they experience moments of awareness, they quickly vanish. One of the most crucial issues in the examination of one's conscience is the search for the awareness of one's basic flaw and fire.

There is no way to get away from the problems caused by the flaw. It takes great vigilance to learn to move the flaw into the right light where the fire in it begins to show. Often, it takes courageous work with a spiritual guide or friend to begin to reveal it and discern its outlines; but, in the end, only the person in whom it dwells can ultimately deal with it.

The flaw insinuates itself into every facet of our lives; and unfortunately, it is our failures—which are often so close to

---

11. This image calls to mind Rabbi Nahman of Bratzlav's story (originally published in the back matter of *Sippurei Ma'asiot*) about the artisan who crafts a chandelier made entirely from the "flaws" of other craftspeople. See Reb Zalman and Rabbi Daniel Siegel's translation of this brief tale in *Credo of a Modern Kabbalist*, 313–15.

our successes—that tell us most about it. Moreover, the flaw is multi-leveled, so that even when one manages to control it in behavior, it shows itself again on the plane of feeling. And even if controlled there, it will continue to manifest on the plane of thought. Thus, it is a lifelong relationship of struggle and revelation.

—*Gate to the Heart*, 87–88

LEVELS OF THE SOUL

In the following text, Reb Zalman explores the Jewish mystical description (prominent in HaBaD thought) of the soul as containing five levels or gradations. This connects with the image of the soul as a "holographic snippet" in the text above entitled "The Soul's Waking," as it points to the multitextured nature of this divine essence. Reb Zalman found this mapping very helpful in exploring different facets of the self or ways of being and knowing.

Our discussion of the stages of practice and the meaning of mysticism must be combined with an understanding (and experience) of the levels of the soul. The lowest of the five levels, according to the Kabbalah, is called *nefesh* and corresponds to the aspect of action. The other levels, in ascending order, are *ru'ah*, *neshamah*, *hayyah* and *yehidah*. *Ru'ah* is the feeling level, and *neshamah* is the intellective. *Hayyah* and *yehidah* are beyond the verbal and discursive mind, but may be considered, respectively, as the levels of life beyond our understanding and the primary monad of self in eternal union with God.

The Zohar says, "Each is given a *nefesh*. If one so merits (by refining oneself), one is granted *ru'ah*, etc." So we start out with *nefesh*, and refine the soul from there through each of the other four levels by means of intention and meditation.[12]

—*Gate to the Heart*, 7–11

---

12. An idea encountered frequently in the *Zohar*. See, for example, *Zohar* I:205b-206a, available in Daniel C. Matt's annotated translation, *The Zohar: Pritzker Edition* (Stanford, CA: Stanford University Press, 2006), 3:262–64. This is a good illustration of Reb Zalman's attempts to

THE HUMAN–SOUL COMPLEX

When we speak about a person, we mean the concatenation of body and these five orders of soul. As the attunement and attention vary from level to level, or where we focus at a particular time, that is the part of the soul that is then manifest. If I am involved in athletics, I'm most likely attuned to *nefesh*, and my *nefesh* is in an active state. If I listen to a piece of music, or attend a drama, then my *ru'ah* is most likely involved, while my *nefesh* is in a quiescent state. When meditating on ideas, I'm attuned primarily to *neshamah*, and not to other parts of my being.

Now, though we speak of these levels distinctly, they are of course inter-dependent. This is what we mean by the phenomenon of the *Merkavah*, "Chariot," so often spoken of in Kabbalah.[13] Even while I'm in meditation, or contemplating with *neshamah*, I need the assistance of *ru'ah* and *nefesh*, as well as the body. So my *neshamah* is riding in the *ru'ah* of an awakened heart, which is riding in the *nefesh* of an awakened energy-field, which is riding on the *guf* of an awakened body. In this kind of chariot, one vehicle is invested in another.

Further, I cannot say that the rider in the chariot is the *neshamah*, because even it is being driven by something that rides higher, the *hayyah*. And *hayyah* itself is being energized and focalized into existence by the specificity of that *yehidah*, which is the individuated aspect of the Infinite.

Here is an example that illustrates the dynamic interplay of the levels of soul: There is a compliment that nobody has given me before, but that I feel I deeply deserve. Of all the compliments I've ever received, all of them are chaff in comparison to

---

engage contemporary seekers—Jewish and non-Jewish alike—in a process of significant spiritual discovery and growth, often understood by past mystics, including the authors of the *Zohar*, to be available only to learned, upright, male Jewish adepts.

13. This tradition is based on the prophet Ezekiel's vision of God riding in a chariot across the sky (1:1–28). This text inspired the *Merkavah* mystics beginning in the early centuries of the Common Era, as well as subsequent groups of aspirants.

this one I have not yet received. It is the important one. Then somebody gives me this compliment and I begin to cry. Why am I crying? What has happened?

What has happened is not just that affect has felt pleasure in the compliment, but that *hayyah*, that part of myself for which I do the deepest things in my life, has suddenly found recognition of its intention and let go. The melting that takes place at such a moment is *hayyah* melting through the dimension of *ru'ah*, and the purpose of my life is given a moment of fulfillment. All the trouble it has taken to get here seems to have been rewarded. It was worth it.

That peak experience affirming that "it was worth it," is what's called, "Seeing your world in your lifetime" (Babylonian Talmud, Tractate Shabbat 17a). This is getting *Olam ha-Ba*, the "Coming World," in *this* world, and the striving is over at that moment. That excites *yehidah*. And if we can stay with this in the heart, not "clinging" to it, but staying with it and breathing into it further, suddenly we see it not from the point of view of the recipient, but from the point of view of the Divine Grantor. And my identity is for that moment with the Divine, saying, "My child, today I have begotten you; this was the purpose of eternity" [Psalm 2:7].   —*Gate to the Heart*, 11–13

THE FOUR WORLDS

Another mystical schema that Reb Zalman made regular use of in his teaching (particularly when working on prayer) was the Four Worlds. Like the five levels of soul, these four rungs are traditionally organized in vertical fashion, moving, in ascending order, from the physical plane to ethereality. In fact, mystics often use these two mappings interactively (along with the ten sefirot) *to chart the dynamic journey of the human being in relation to God and creation. The worlds are, in ascending order:* Assiyah, *the world of doing;* Yetzirah, *the world of feeling;* Beriyah, *the world of knowing; and* Atzilut, *the world of being.*

Within Jewish mysticism, these inner spaces are represented by the letters of the Divine Name, *Y-H-V-H*: the *Yod* representing *Atzilut*; the *Heh* representing *Beriyah*; the *Vav* representing *Yetzirah*; and the lower *Heh* representing *Assiyah*. When these letters are stacked one on top of the other like the worlds (instead of side-by-side), they look like the figure of a human being. This suggests that we are made in the image of God (see Genesis 1:27).

—Gate to the Heart, 13

BRINGING THE WORLDS DOWN TO EARTH

Whenever we talk about the Four Worlds of Kabbalah, it sounds like we are going into spiritual places, far away. But it is not really so far away from us. It all has to do with how we are engaging them, here and now. To make this clearer, I once wrote some simple lyrics to a melody that my friend, Reb Shlomo Carlebach, composed long ago:

> *Lord I want to do for you;*
> *Lord I want to feel for you;*
> *Lord I want to know for you;*
> *Lord I want to be for you.*
>
> *You are action;*
> *You are feeling;*
> *You are knowledge;*
> *You are being.*
>
> *You are action;*
> *You are feeling;*

You are knowledge;
You just are.

This is a way of understanding how we relate to the Four Worlds. When you look at spirituality from that perspective, you get a sense that this is where we are all the time. We are in *action*, in *feeling*, in *knowing*, in *being*, and these are not things that have to do with "other worlds." These are all a part of our here and now . . . that is where we need all this the most, in the everyday. How do you stay "spiritual" when you are shopping, or when you are doing the dishes, or when you are taking the kids to school? Unless we install spirituality into our ordinary lives, it will not help us much.[14]

There is a wonderful line in the daily *davvenen* (prayer) that says: "The holy ones praise you every day." But I read it as, "Those who are holy *in the everyday* praise You."[15] The real praise for God is not the holiness that people have in their holy places, but in the everyday.   —*The Gates of Prayer*, 95–96

---

14. While in this piece Reb Zalman focuses on the use of the Four Worlds model in everyday life, he also regularly used it in his teaching on prayer (based on his learning and experience in HaBaD), grafting it to different parts of the *Shaharit* (Morning) service. It has become an important structure for many renewal prayer groups. The interested reader can explore this interface in Reb Zalman's book, *Davening: A Guide to Meaningful Jewish Prayer*, written with Joel Segel (Woodstock, VT: Jewish Lights Publishing, 2012), 58–84.

15. In fine rabbinic fashion, Reb Zalman here takes advantage of the flexibility of Hebrew grammar to bring fresh meaning to a well-known liturgical verse that might otherwise be read inattentively. He makes similar interpretive moves in two texts included later in this volume: "Who Am I to Give Blessing," and "Bringing *Shabbos* to Life."

3

The Sacred Work of Prayer and Meditation

INTRODUCTION

In eulogizing Reb Zalman, Rabbi Arthur Green describes his longtime friend and mentor as a quintessential ba'al tefillah.[1] *While this term is usually rendered as a* prayer leader, *Green uses it in this case more expansively to point to Schachter-Shalomi's virtuosity as a teacher and model of intentional, heartfelt, and joyous prayer. Throughout his life, Reb Zalman had a passion for* tefillah *or* davvenen *(prayer in Hebrew and Yiddish), believing that it was essential to cultivating the human spirit, helping one live a life in service of God. This was one of the key teachings of the founders of Eastern European Hasidism.[2] In fact, part of what drew him to HaBaD was its sophisticated approach to prayer and meditation, including careful attention to one's intention and state of mind before, during, and after engaging in these sacred activities. He often spoke with reverence about*

---

1. See Green's opening remarks in "Some Words on the Words of Prayer," in *Worlds of Jewish Prayer: A Festschrift in Honor of Rabbi Zalman M. Schachter-Shalomi*, edited by Shohama Harris Weiner and Jonathan Omer-Man (Northvale, NJ: Jason Aronson, 1993), 71. Appropriately, Green renders the word *ba'al tefillah* as *prayer master* in this context.

2. See *My Life in Jewish Renewal*, 60.

*his experiences praying in the presence of the sixth Lubavitcher
Rebbe, Rabbi Yosef Yitzhak Schneersohn, whose sincerity, intensity, and steadfastness young Zalman found deeply inspiring.[3]
He also spoke with great respect and appreciation for other mentors and peers in Lubavitch who helped him develop a nuanced
approach to* avodat ha-lev *(service of the heart, prayer).*

*From the time he began working as a HaBaD emissary in
New Haven, Connecticut, until his final years in Boulder, Colorado, Reb Zalman was deeply immersed in the work of "davvenology," as he referred to it. This included attention both to
form and substance, including music, breath work, posture,
wording, pacing, lighting, and other dimensions, both internal
and external.*

*One concrete example of this integrated approach is the
now-famous rainbow* tallit *(prayer shawl) that he fashioned
in 1961. It was inspired by his study of rabbinic and mystical
sources, combined with a deep appreciation for religious aesthetics. At the time, the vast majority of prayer shawls were black
and white; none were multicolored and laden with mystical symbolism. Since designing that first rainbow tallit over sixty-five
years ago, there has been a wave of creative and colorful design
work done with tallitot (plural of tallit), often by artists who are
unaware of Reb Zalman's pioneering project.*

*Reb Zalman's prayer journey also led him to engage in signif-
icant exploration of the devotional practices of other religious
and spiritual traditions—West and East. This included chanting psalms with Trappists, reciting* zikr *(remembrance exercise)
with Sufis, and sitting in sweat lodges with Indigenous people. A
self-described empiricist (and spiritual peeping Tom, as he often
quipped), Reb Zalman was always on the lookout for techniques
and insights that might expand the mind and open the heart.
He was also interested in exploring if, and how, elements of
these rituals could be incorporated meaningfully into a Jewish*

---

3. See "*Rebbe*-Talk: A Conversation with Reb Zalman" in Chapter 6
of this volume.

context. *He was also not shy about recommending ways for non-Jewish practitioners to learn from and thoughtfully adapt Jewish rituals.*[4]

Reb Zalman's influence on contemporary Jewish prayer and meditation is profound. He helped countless Jewish seekers discover the richness of the siddur *(prayer book); the sacred logic of the daily, weekly, and seasonal blessings and services; and exoteric and esoteric teachings on various aspects of Jewish worship. This included, of course, sharing an array of Hasidic and Kabbalistic concepts and practices with many people who would otherwise have difficulty accessing these resources. This was fueled, in part, by an urgent desire to help young Jews see that Judaism possessed powerful spiritual resources that were not commonly shared in mainstream contexts. Just as Buddhism and Hinduism have rich contemplative and ecstatic exercises, so does Judaism. As a refugee from Nazi-occupied Europe, he also felt an abiding sense of responsibility to share the wisdom of Jewish spiritual traditions that had been snuffed out or severely fragmented in the wreckage of the Holocaust.*[5]

Reb Zalman also regularly engaged people in discussion about the need to blend tradition and innovation. Following

---

4. For example, while participating in a historic meeting between Jewish and Tibetan Buddhist leaders in Dharamsala, India, in 1991, he suggested to the Dalai Lama and his associates that they make creative use of the Passover *seder* as a model for an embodied, intergenerational exploration of the themes of exile and redemption. See Reb Zalman's brief reflection on the encounter in "Universalism and Particularism: The Dalai Lama," in Chapter 7 of this volume, as well as Rodger Kamenetz's account of the journey in *The Jew in the Lotus: A Poet's Rediscovery of Jewish Identity in Buddhist India* (San Francisco: HarperCollins, 1994).

5. One of Reb Zalman's early postwar dreams was to have members of his B'nai Or community study and lead one another in the prayer modes of lost or imperiled Jewish communities in Europe and other far-flung locations (Cochin, Baghdad, etc.). See *My Life in Jewish Renewal*, 129. Even after he moved on from his *restorationist* phase (c. 1946–66), he viewed himself as a bridge figure, knowing that so many traditional spiritual leaders had been murdered by the Nazis.

in the footsteps of his teacher, Howard Thurman, he encour-
aged his students to maintain an experimental mind-set when it
came to prayer and meditation (and all of religious life, for that
matter), asking how these practices could help one come closer
to God and live more harmoniously within God's creation. As
a person who loved Jewish tradition and was concerned about
issues of continuity, he was not interested in simply jettisoning
existing practices, but rather asking if and how they might be
adapted to make them more meaningful for a new generation.
This, he argued, required an ongoing process of discernment
(birur, in Hasidic parlance)—individual and communal—about
how best to fashion a life of holiness in the here and now. It was
this sensibility that animated his entire Jewish renewal project.

THE POETRY OF THE SOUL

If you have ever tasted an apple plucked right off a New England
tree, you will know the difference between a supermarket apple
and a real apple. A supermarket apple has been washed, waxed,
refrigerated. Vital parts of its chemistry have ebbed away. But an
apple plucked from the mother tree—a *mehayyeh* (enlivening or
refreshing). Tastes like a living apple!

Prayer is the same. Many who live their lives as Jews, even
many who pray every day, live on a wrapped and refrigerated
version of prayer. We go to synagogue dutifully enough. We
rise when we should rise, sit when we should sit. We read and
sing along with the cantor and answer "Amen" in all the right
places. We may even rattle through the prayers with ease. We
sacrifice vitality for shelf-life, and the *neshamah* (soul) can taste
the difference.

True prayer is a bursting forth of the soul to God. What can
be more natural and more human than turning to God's listen-
ing presence with our thanks and our burdens? Prayer is one
of the simplest and easiest of practices. It's always right there.
The act of speaking directly to God, of opening our hearts to
God's response, is one of the ultimate mystical experiences. Like

great art and great music, prayer brings out the poetry of soul. Some of our most beautiful writings can be found in the pages of prayer.

Without true prayer, on the other hand, a very deep yearning that we have goes unanswered. We try to satisfy that hunger for God in other ways. We mistake the yearnings of soul for the cravings of body. We feed them with food and drink, drugs and sex, money and power, but these things just inflame our appetite further. We might seek higher things, intellectual pursuits, or artistic accomplishments. Even these do not touch us in that loneliest of places, the place that longs to be filled with God. That's why prayer, to me, is not a luxury but a necessity, a safeguard for our survival and our sanity.   —*Davening*, xi–xii

A ROOM TOO FULL OF PRAYER

An old story tells of the Ba'al Shem Tov coming to a synagogue and turning back at the door, unable to enter. Too many prayers inside, he said.

"But Master," asked his disciples, "surely a room full of prayer is a good thing?"

"But all the prayers are stuck there in the building," the Ba'al Shem answered. "None of them are going up to Heaven."[6]

You might get this feeling today. Clergy and congregants together might be dutifully singing and reciting—but somehow the prayer has no wings. You still feel uninspired. Maybe you've known the peace that can sometimes follow real prayer. Maybe you have prayed until you were drained and exhausted, for yourself or for someone you love. Maybe you've been there when a room full of people have managed to leave their individual preoccupations behind and are singing and swaying and making a joyful noise unto the Lord [Psalm 100]. If you've been blessed

---

6. A version of this story, entitled "The Crowded House of Prayer," can be found in Martin Buber's *Tales of the Hasidim*, translated by Olga Marx (New York: Schocken Books, 1991), 73.

with such an experience, then you may have some sense of what the Ba'al Shem Tov meant. Sometimes we're transformed, and sometimes we're not.

That's why we talk about *kavvanah*.

Jewish prayer begins with *kavvanah*. To *davven* (pray) with *kavvanah* means to pray with focus, intention, meaning. It means praying from the heart, rather than prayer centered solely in the mind.   —*Davening*, 5

DOING THE DIVINE THING

What does the word *davvenen* mean? Well, if you go into a *heymishe shul*, a warm and friendly synagogue of the traditional type, and ask what the people are doing there, they will say that they are *davvenen*. The word covers so many things: it is both deeply engaged prayer and worship, and also just what you do when you put on a *tallit*, a prayer shawl, and sway back and forth, lifting your voice in prayer.

Though the origins of the word are unclear, I believe it comes from the Latin, *divinum*, "to do the divine thing." This is true of a number of words in the Jewish lexicon. For instance, after you have eaten, you *bentsh*, or say the grace after the meal. This is derived from the Latin, *benedictio*, to say the "benediction," the "good word."

When I speak about *davvenen*, I am talking about an inner process that goes far beyond ordinary prayer and worship; it is something that encompasses one's entire spiritual life. My sense is that a person can recognize that one who is *davvenen* is actually in touch with God—even when they are walking in the street, they are nevertheless connected to God and *davvenen*. It is a constant element in their lives.

When we talk about *davvenen*, one of the things it brings to mind is what we want to achieve in it. If you ask people who are good in *davvenen*, they will tell you, "I want to be in *deveikut* with God; I want to have *deveikut*."   —*The Gates of Prayer*, 19–20

CLINGING TO GOD

The root of the word *deveikut* is *d-b-k*, which connects it to a whole family of Hebrew words that have something to do with "sticking," "glue," "adhering," "being close to," "being connected in a cozy way."

When I shift one letter of the root and make it *h-b-k*, we get Hebrew words that mean, "hug" or "embrace." And if we make it *a-b-k*, we get "wrestling," as in the biblical moment when our father Jacob [wrestled] with the angel [Genesis 32:25].

But when we are talking about *deveikut* in *davvenen*, the idea is that of "sticking" or "adhering" to God, a devotional "clinging." It has a sense of saying, "What can I bring to You, God? I love you so much; I want to give you all that I can." What can I give you [Psalm 116:12]?

The word also has a social meaning. If I want to be deeply connected to my teacher, my *rebbe*, I might ask, "How can I be in *deveikut* with you, my teacher?" I am trying to imitate and emulate my teacher. This is not a cheap imitation, something *ersatz*. This is imitation in the sense in which Thomas à Kempis (1380–1471) used it in his classic work, *The Imitation of Christ*, of *following*, *emulating*, and *tuning-in* . . .

There is a wonderful story about Gershom Scholem (1897–1982), the great academic scholar of Kabbalah. When he first came to Israel, he wanted to study with an authentic kabbalist. He asked one of the teachers of Kabbalah in Jerusalem, "In what way would you teach me?" The kabbalist answered, "The only way in which I will teach you is if, for the next two years, you will not ask me questions."[7]

---

7. See Gershom Scholem, *On the Kabbalah and Its Symbolism*, translated by Ralph Manheim (New York: Schocken Books, 1996), 87–117; and Boaz Huss, "Ask No Questions: Gershom Scholem and the Study of Contemporary Jewish Mysticism," *Modern Judaism* 25, no. 2 (May 2005): 141–58.

You see, if Scholem were asking questions in order to fit what he was learning into his own academic system, he would never learn what the kabbalist was trying to teach him. He would simply hold on to the previous matrix of the learning. So it isn't only the content, but the attitude, the approach to the text, the attunement to the holiness inherent in it. That is a most important thing, for *deveikut* is like emulating the other.

Sometimes the rabbis of the Talmud ask, "How can one be close to God if God is infinite?"[8] And they answered, "Find one of the divine modes and emulate that mode"[9]—"Just as God is kind and gracious, so you should become kind and gracious; just as God is compassionate and merciful, so you become compassionate and merciful" [Babylonian Talmud, Shabbat 133b]. In this way, I stretch myself to fit the divine template . . . Do you get that? "Cleave to God's modes!" I measure myself in God's view and decide to shape myself according to that template. This is a part of *deveikut*.   —*The Gates of Prayer*, 20–22

STEERING OUR MINDS

Our Jewish path to inner awareness begins with *kavvanah*. Our meditative lives as Jews could not be complete without it, for it is the steering wheel of all inner consciousness work. Our inner search for *kavvanah* might at first be satisfied with a momentary boost of intention. Ultimately, though, we want our *kavvanah* to be transformational. We seek a complete realignment of the soul, *mesirat nefesh*, a handing over of the soul to God's work.[10] We wish to become the very intention and *kavvanah* of God.

---

8. This teaching is based on Babylonian Talmud, Ketubot 111b, which reads (more literally): "But is it possible to cleave to the Divine Presence (*Shekhinah*)? Is it not written: 'For the Lord your God is a devouring fire' (Deuteronomy 4:24)?" See https://www.sefaria.org/Ketubot.111b?lang=bi.

9. See Babylonian Talmud, Sotah 14a, which is frequently cited by Hasidic preachers in combination with the text in the previous note. See https://www.sefaria.org/Sotah.14a?lang=bi.

10. The term *mesirat nefesh* has a long history in Jewish thought, including physical and spiritual self-sacrifice. In its most extreme form, it

Kavvanah gives meaning to our rituals of marriage and birth
and death. It inspires us to perform a *mitzvah* on a more conscious and ultimately more rewarding level. *Kavvanah* lies at the
heart of Jewish devotional life. That one word encompasses an
entire body of inner work necessary to live consciously in the
presence of God.   —*Davening*, 6

THE FREEZE-DRIED PRAYER BOOK

Now, what about the prayer book, the *siddur?* I want to say, the
siddur needs "cooking." The liturgy in the prayer book is really
"freeze-dried prayer."

What do I mean by that?

Well, you can simply read the words of the prayer book, of
course, but don't you wonder sometimes, "Who wrote these
words?" You have to realize that someone actually wrote down
and expressed what they had experienced in prayer as a prayer!
Or someone else wrote it down for them . . .

Imagine you are hungry. You come for lunch and I serve you
freeze-dried or dehydrated soup!

I say, "Eat!"

Looking perplexed at the dehydrated soup, you say, "Perhaps
you could add a little hot water to it?"

That is exactly the situation with the prayer book. Feelings
are the "hot water" you have to add to the dehydrated experience of the *siddur*.

All prayer that is devoid of feeling feels unanswered, because
it was not really asked. King David says, "My heart says it is for
You that I am looking" [Psalm 27:8]. If the heart has not said
that, I will not feel that it has actually gotten to God's heart to be
answered. That is a very important part of this then, to get into
the heart.[11]   —*The Gates of Prayer*, 4–5

---

refers to martyrdom. See, for example, Babylonian Talmud, Sanhedrin 74a,
https://www.sefaria.org/Sanhedrin.74a?lang=bi.

11. This brings to mind the statement made by various Muslim and
Jewish writers, "Words that come from the heart enter the heart." The

BEING ALONE WITH GOD

Hitbodedut is making a place in which I can disconnect from my social connections and other sensations. All I want to do in that place is contemplate. Today, it is the Bratzlaver Hasidim [followers of Rebbe Nahman of Bratzlav] who use this word the most, but it actually has a long and venerable history, going back to the time of Elijah and Elisha, and even further back to the time of Samuel the prophet[12]. . . Later on, we find that the authors of the Dead Sea Scrolls were doing similar things: sitting in silence and solitude and doing their contemplation. At that time, people would go into the desert and sit in a cave in order not to be distracted by externals. From there it was the flight of the *one* to the *One*. [See the closing words of Plotinus's *The Enneads*.]

If you were to ask the hermit, "What are you doing?" The hermit would say, "I am dwelling here in solitude." If you asked, "How can you bear to be alone?" They would respond: "How could I be alone? God is with me; I am *not* alone." That element of being in such a connection with God was called *hitbodedut*. Nowadays, most praying is done with prayer books. What's the problem with that? It is a problem if a person thinks that reciting *Ashrei*[13] from the *siddur* (prayer book) is what constitutes a

---

Hasidic masters make frequent use of it in their teaching. See the interpretation of this adage in *Tzava'at HaRYBaSh: The Testament of Rabbi Israel Baal Shem Tov*, translated by Jacob Immanuel Schochet (New York: Kehot, 1998), 57. In the context of prayer, of course, all one can do is intend to have her words enter God's "heart."

12. Elijah often went to be alone with God (e.g., 1 Kings 18:3, 19:3), and frequently describes himself as "alone" (*levad*, the root of *hitbodedut*), 1 Kings 18:22, 19:10. Various commentators associated Samuel, and later Elisha, with groups of aspiring prophets, whose practices included *hitbodedut*. See, for example, Maimonides, Mishneh Torah, Foundations of Torah, 7:4.

13. The *Ashrei* prayer is traditionally recited three times daily: twice during the morning service (*Shaharit*) and once during the afternoon service (*Minhah*). One can find Reb Zalman's interpretive translation of this prayer in *Sh'ma: A Concise Weekly Siddur for Praying in English* (Boulder, CO: Albion-Andalus, 2010), 16–17.

relationship with God. What if we never had a prayer book? All we need to be aware of is that we know that we are getting the attention of God, and God will listen to what we have to say.

Oy! How I would go to the essentials at this point! I would say, "Dear God, I need Your energy and Your strength and Your wisdom!" I would begin to talk in this direct way, pouring out my heart to God. Often, I switch to Yiddish. My Yiddish expresses my heart-feeling for God better than my English.[14] And when I am talking to God in this way, the tears begin to flow, because I am so involved in the words I am offering before the living God, and am certain that I am not just talking to the wall!

Reb Nahman of Bratzlav would encourage his disciples to go out into the woods at night when no one could hear them and pray in this way.[15]   —*The Gates of Prayer*, 25–26

CONTEMPLATION AND SITUATIONAL THINKING

Another subtle and powerful technique of meditation or contemplation is called *hitbonenut* or self-understanding.[16] It is a technique that comes from the HaBaD school of Hasidism, and which can be done in the course of one's daily prayers or separate from them. In it, one thoroughly explores a spiritual concept, filling one's awareness with it until it brings about a change in one's life.

---

14. Here Reb Zalman is, in fact, following Rebbe Nahman's instruction to carry out the practice of *hitbodedut* in one's mother tongue (and not in Hebrew, "the holy tongue") in order to allow for heartfelt expression before God. See the compilation of teachings on *hitbodedut* from Rebbe Nahman entitled *Outpouring of the Soul*, translated by Rabbi Aryeh Kaplan (Jerusalem, Israel: Breslov Research Institute, 1980), 20–22.

15. Rabbi Herbert Weiner offers a moving description of his experience engaging in *hitbodedut* with Bratzlavers on the outskirts of Jerusalem in the 1960s in his memoir, *9½ Mystics: The Kabbala Today* (New York: Simon & Schuster, 1997), 197–226.

16. While often rendered as "contemplation" in English, Reb Zalman is emphasizing that the word *hitbonenut* is the reflexive verb form of the word *binah*, "understanding," in Hebrew.

At first, we think about the idea or concept in an objective way, attempting to understand it intellectually, down to its very last detail. But when we have finished filling out the concept and have mastered the thought-sequence in all its rich detail, we then move into the dimension of *situational-thinking*.[17] That is to say, we must re-invest the conceptual material with a "real-life" context.

This situational mode of thought is called *ada'ata d'nafshei*, "soul-knowledge"[18] . . . and fills us with an immediate emotional awareness that provokes us to action. For example, we might understand what it means in general for someone to inherit a large sum of money, considering the situation and all its various ramifications, such as the personal, social, and societal effects of a sudden acquisition of capital. But now imagine *you* are the *actual* beneficiary, right now, in this moment . . . finding yourself filled with emotion that begets a corresponding response in behavior. From this, you can immediately see just how vital *ada'ata d'nafshei* thinking can be to your meditation.

—*Gate to the Heart*, 18–19

JEWISH MEDITATION

What are the especially *Jewish* dimensions that we need to include in meditation? In the past, I have been a vocal critic of so-called "Jewish meditation" that just seemed to be *Vipassana* (Buddhist-style meditation) with *shmaltz* [fat, a superficial layer of ethnic or religious symbolism] on it. Doing Buddhist meditation in a *tallit*, in a prayer shawl doesn't make it Jewish. But doing it in the presence of God at least adds a Jewish dimension to it.

---

17. As he notes elsewhere, Reb Zalman adapted this term from Abraham Joshua Heschel. See Heschel's *God in Search of Man* (New York: Farrar, Straus and Giroux, 1955), 5–6.

18. In Jewish legal discourse this term indicates that a person carries out an action for his own benefit. See, for example, Babylonian Talmud, Shabbat 19a, https://www.sefaria.org/Shabbat.19a?lang=bi.

Imagine I am doing *Vipassana* meditation, quieting the mind and watching the breath—*I calm myself, and I am paying attention to what arises.* Most of the time, people sit down on the cushion and close themselves off—"I don't want to know about anything else; I don't want to let anything in." But that is not conducive to entering a state that is characterized by alpha or theta brain waves, because you are too tightly wound; nor is it the Buddhist ideal. It needs to breathe; it needs to be open.

Now, if you are Jewish, this openness is to God. And when thoughts and feelings arise in your meditation, you can release them to God: "God, here comes anger again . . . Here comes lust . . . Here comes boredom." It is not that I am simply acknowledging these things and releasing them into the ether; I am releasing them to God. It is a process that is open to a higher dimension, and I make a window for God to look into me as I'm meditating.

Now why should you want to bother with meditation in the first place? Because I think it is a *mitzvah*. It is a *mitzvah* to place oneself in the presence of God. It is a *mitzvah* to work on moral transformation.[19]   —*The Gates of Prayer*, 45–46

THE PRAYER SHAWL

Tradition has given us the *tallit*, the prayer shawl, a blanket for our aura, providing us with a safe space in which we can be cozy with God. These feelings of comfort are similar to those of the child who wants to bring everyone together under one blanket, so that the whole family can share the warmth.

But the *tallit* is also the four-cornered garment whose fringes, or *tzitzit*, are meant to remind us of the 613 *mitzvot* (commandments).[20] The *tzitzit* are, as Reb Arthur Waskow has so beautifully

---

19. See the comment by Rabbi Moses Isserles (1530-72) on the importance of God-consciousness in his first gloss on the classic code of Jewish law, the *Shulkhan Arukh*.

20. In Numbers 15:37–41 God instructs the Israelites to attach *tzitzit*, fringes on to the corners of their garments as a physical reminder of their covenant with the Divine. It is common in traditional Jewish circles to refer to the full range of Jewish sacred obligations as the "613 *mitzvot*" (based

put it, "the bleed-off of the field into the environment."[21] Recognizing this, my friend, the artist, Menahem Alexenberg, has also built a school in Yeruham (southern Israel), from the four corners of which hang heavy rope *tzitzit* that run into the sand! This is a way of saying, "Yes, I am safe here; I am grounded in this environment."

—*Gate to the Heart*, 75

THE RAINBOW PRAYER SHAWL

In the following selection, Reb Zalman explains how he envisioned the multicolored tallit *he created in 1961. As he notes, he was inspired by the rabbinic image of God donning a light-filled prayer shawl. This then led the young rabbi to think about the Kabbalistic mapping of the ten* sefirot, *the primal emanations and attributes of the Divine. In this imaginative medieval portrait of God's inner life and creative process, each of the* sefirot *is associated with a different color. Reb Zalman used a version of this mystical color scheme to envision his rainbow* tallit. *Just as the Divine is wrapped in light (the full spectrum), so too is the human soul, as it is a microcosm of the Creator. By wrapping ourselves in the rainbow* tallit, *we are invited to meditate on the qualities we wish to bring forth through our prayers and actions in the world.*

---

on the teaching of Rabbi Simlai in the Babylonian Talmud, Makkot 23b, https://www.sefaria.org/Makkot.23b?lang=bi). See also Ronald L. Eisenberg, "Enumeration of the Mitzvot," in *The JPS Guide to Jewish Traditions* (Philadelphia: Jewish Publication Society, 2004) 515–16. Therefore, looking at the fringes (and kissing them while reciting the verses from Numbers as part of the daily *Shema*) is a way to recall one's relationship to God and Torah.

21. For a sampling of Rabbi Waskow's many writings on prayer (including *tzitzit*), and related issues of spirituality and social and environmental justice, visit the Shalom Center website, https://theshalomcenter.org/treasury/8. Waskow worked closely with Reb Zalman for several decades.

"How did God create light? God wrapped God's self in a *tallit* and began to shine" (Genesis Rabbah 3:4).[22]

It was this *midrash* that inspired me to design the now well-known rainbow striped B'nai Or Tallit, each color of which represents one of the *sefirot*, or divine emanations, through which God's energy becomes manifest in the world.[23]

The *atarah*—the embroidered strip at the neck of the *tallit*—represents *keter*, the "crown," the source of God-energy, which flows into *hokhmah* and *binah*, represented by the white of the *tallit* itself. These three "upper" *sefirot* represent divine energy beyond human comprehension.

From there, the energy flows into the "lower seven" *sefirot*. Each of these corresponds to some aspect of the Divine, and to one of the days of creation.

The purple stripes represent *hesed*, "loving-kindness," and the first day of creation, *bereshit*. The deep purple stripe suggests ultra-violet light emerging from total darkness. The lighter purple stripe, with some white mixed in it, symbolizes the light becoming visible. This stripe is very wide because the nature of *hesed* is broad and sweeping. Thus, it needs strong black lines to contain it.

The next stripe is *tekhelet* blue, representing *gevurah*, "rigor," and the second day of creation when the sky, the blue fluids above, were separated from the blue sea-waters below.

---

22. As Reb Zalman notes elsewhere, he was further inspired by the images of God's light and enfolding presence in Psalm 104:1–2 and 36:8–11, which are both commonly recited before putting on the *tallit* each morning for prayer. See also "Putting on the Tallit," in *My People's Prayer Book: Traditional Prayers, Modern Commentaries—Volume 5, Birkhot Hashachar*, edited by Lawrence Hoffman (Woodstock, VT: Jewish Lights Publishing, 2001), 55–66.

23. For an in-depth introduction to the ten *sefirot*, see Arthur Green, *EHYEH: A Kabbalah for Tomorrow* (Woodstock, VT: Jewish Lights Publishing, 2003), 39–60. The reader might wish to review Reb Zalman's reflection with the chart of *sefirot* in hand; see the diagrams in *EHYEH* on 40, 48, 58.

Following the creation story, the third stripe is green like chlorophyll, representing *tiferet*, "beauty," and the creation of vegetation. God said, "It is good" (Genesis 1:10, 12) twice on the third day, so there are two green stripes with the white light of *keter* coming through the middle. *Tiferet* needs a vessel, so there are black lines containing it.

The yellow stripe represents *netzah*, "victory," and the fourth day, when the moon, stars and sun—a yellow star—were created.

Next is the orange stripe, representing *hod*, "glory," and the fifth day when the fish, reptiles, birds, and insects were created. Because these are all egg-laying animals, the stripe is the color of egg-yolk.

There is a close relationship between *netzah* and *hod*, with different kabbalistic systems interpreting them in different ways. There is no glory *(hod)* without victory *(netzah)*.

The sixth stripe is red and represents *yesod*, "foundation," and the sixth day of creation when the warm-blooded animals were created. As chlorophyll is the blood of plants, hemoglobin is the blood of animals, so the stripe is blood red. *Yesod* also represents sexuality and needs strong black lines to contain it.

The final stripe represents *malkhut*, "sovereignty," and the creation of human beings from humus, earth. This stripe is brown because all living things come from earth and return to earth when they die.

As I mentioned, the black lines and white stripes have meaning. The black lines border those *sefirot* which need strong boundaries to contain their energy. But, some of the *sefirot*, like *gevurah* and *malkhut* do not need the lines, because they are themselves containers.   —*Gate to the Heart*, 75–77

FIND YOURSELF IN THE PRAYER

Here are some suggestions for entering into a psalm or prayer. If you *davven* alone, wrap yourself in a *tallit*, or "prayer shawl," and begin to read the psalm slowly with chant and expression. Make the sound beautiful and rich, the body posture an accompaniment to the words, the face in harmony with the words to be spoken. Then, close your eyes and visualize the scene surrounding the words, and placing yourself in King David's palace, recite them as he might have when he first composed them.[24]

Do you find yourself in the prayer? Or, in the case of one of the psalms, are you really exhorting all creation to praise God [see Psalm 148]? Are you the sky and the sun and the moon praising? Are you the flora and fauna? Are you the kings or queens of the earth, the old people and children? With each *halleluyah* simulate that praising creature in some way. Are you just out of Egypt, redeemed by God, led dry-shod through the split sea [see Exodus 15]? Treat the text as a model for adoration. Each time you mention the music of an instrument [see Psalm 150], become that instrument; hear it on the inside and offer the consciousness of the sound to God.[25]   —*Gate to the Heart*, 50–51

GATHERING TOGETHER

Where do we meet for prayer? In the *shul*. I like the word *shul* better than temple or synagogue. *Shul*, or "school," implies that we are always learning. What do you study in a *shul*? The *siddur* or prayer book, which is an *aid-memoire*, a way to keep you on track so that you might not lose your place while ascending the sacred ladder.

---

24. One way in which Reb Zalman helped people to engage more personally in prayer was by inviting them to envision themselves as a biblical figure uttering a prayer preserved in the traditional liturgy. "Can you imagine yourself as Abraham, Hannah, or King David, calling out in joy or sorrow with these words?" In such cases, he was not concerned with historical–critical questions about the authorship of the text—did King David actually compose this psalm? Rather, he hoped that such imaginal exercises would stir a person's heart and help her see how the prayer book, when infused with emotion, could be used as a tool for personal expression and connection with past liturgists and worshippers.

25. All of the images Reb Zalman mentions in this brief paragraph are part of the *Pesukei d'Zimra* ("Verses of Praise"), the second section of the *Shaharit* (Morning) service. To learn more about this prayer rubric, see Reb Zalman's *Davening*, 96–103.

Now when you are praying in a *shul*, you want to have a *minyan*, a prayer quorum. The Jewish desire to pray in a communal way is based upon a belief that, when ten people are gathered together in a *minyan*, they form one field, which allows the holy *Shekhinah*, the Divine Presence, to manifest.[26]

Traditionally, a *minyan* consists of ten men; but in Jewish Renewal [and other egalitarian *minyanim*] we count ten human beings, ten committed Jews.

As I said, it is believed that there is a greater manifestation of the Divine Presence when ten or more people are gathered together for prayer. But I want to suggest still another meaning for why we wish to *davven* with a *minyan*. Sometimes I am not fully present. But the likelihood is that someone else is fully present even when I am not. Thus, the *minyan* supports me in my *davvenen* even if I lose awareness in the middle.

—*The Gates of Prayer*, 33–34

PRAYING FOR THE YOU IN ME

Praying in a *minyan* is praying in community. You never walk into a *shul* without looking around. You want to see who is there. This, too, can be a challenge. The likelihood is that I may have some judgment on people. In HaBaD we would follow the morning blessings with a *kavvanah* from Lurianic Kabbalah: "I take upon myself the commandment to love my neighbor as myself" [based on Leviticus 19:18]. This gave us an intentionality with which to proceed. I can say, "Dear God, whatever jealousies and resentments I might harbor in my heart, please remove this judgment from me." In that first look around I want to be able to say, and mean it in my heart, "You, and you, and you—all of you—may your *davvening* this day achieve the

---

26. See Babylonian Talmud, Berakhot 6a (based on Psalm 82:1), https://www.sefaria.org/Berakhot.6a?lang=bi. This image is developed significantly in Jewish mystical sources, which identify *Shekhinah* as the feminine, indwelling divine Presence. See Green's *EHYEH*, 55–58.

highest possibility; may it bring you to the highest realization."
By opening that up for them, I open it up for myself too.[27]

Reb Pinhas of Koretz (1726–91), the great Hasidic master,
wondered how we can pray for other people to become better.
Are we not depriving that person of their choice and free will?
The answer, he says, is that we are all part of each other. You
are in me, and I am in you. Praying for the "you in me" to be
better—the "you" that resides in my heart—somehow helps the
"me in you" to do something good for you, and the "you in you"
to become better.[28] This is not a moral vision but an *organismic*
vision. On a prayerful level, we are all part of each other and of
the greater whole. So, look around and open yourself to *ahavat
ha-beriyot*, "love of your fellow creatures."[29]

—*Davening*, 144

WHO AM I TO GIVE BLESSINGS?

Every one of us has inherited from Abraham, our first Jewish
ancestor, the power to give blessings. When God first appears
to Abram (he was not yet renamed Abraham) and tells him to
leave his birthplace and go to the land that God shall show him,
God makes Abram a few promises in return: "I will make you
a great nation, and I will bless you and make your name great,
and you shall be a blessing. And," God continues, "*avarkhah
mevar'khekha*" [Genesis 12:2–3]. The usual way to translate
these two words is "I will bless those who bless you." But we can
also understand it as "I will bless those whom *you* will bless."

The question of blessing is simple. Can we say, "God bless
you," and mean it? I don't wait for people to sneeze before I
say that. It's more than a habit; when I'm in a warm-hearted

---

27. Like his Hasidic forebears, Reb Zalman includes this intention in
his prayer book, *Sh'ma': A Concise Weekday Siddur for Praying in English*,
edited by Netanel Miles-Yépez (Boulder, CO: Albion-Andalus, 2012) 12.

28. See "The Totality of Souls" in Chapter 6 of this volume.

29. See Pirkei Avot 1:12, https://www.sefaria.org/Pirkei_Avot.1.12
?lang=bi.

relationship with somebody, it's a necessity. I have a feeling in my heart that needs to find release in blessing.

A blessing is a special kind of prayer. Blessing another person requires that we summon all the *hesed* (loving-kindness) we can muster at that moment—all the gentleness and compassion, all the shared humanity and connectedness. In Yiddish we called this *farginnen*. There's no one-word translation for this in English; it means the opposite of begrudging, to truly want the best for that person. That's what we do when we bless someone: we wish the person well in the most active sense. We pray for their wellbeing . . .

So, the act of blessing invites you to become transparent, to become a channel. *Berakhah*, the Hebrew word for blessing, resonates in different ways. Some . . . hear [in it] a relationship with the root *b-r-k*, meaning, "knee" [Sefer Bahir 4]. Blessing God . . . is like going down on our knees in supplication. The letters of *berakhah*, blessing, are also identical to those of *b'reikhah*, "pool" [Genesis Rabbah 39:11]. Imagine a reservoir of blessing, waiting for the person on some high level. All it needs is someone to be the pipe, the conduit, to draw the blessing down to this plane.[30]   —*Davening*, 155, 157

SINGING TO GOD (EVEN OFF KEY!)

Once at a weeklong conference and workshop on higher spirituality, I led a group of people in a ritual which called for parading around the room in a circle while we invited the stars, the

---

30. The *rebbe* is often described as such a "channel" in classical Hasidic sources. See, for example, Samuel H. Dresner's translation of an early teaching on the subject attributed to the Ba'al Shem Tov (based on Babylonian Talmud Berakhot 17b) in *The Zaddik: The Doctrine of the Zaddik According to the Writings of Rabbi Yaakov Yosef of Polnoy* (New York: Schocken Books, 1960), 125–29. Here, Reb Zalman democratizes this concept (as earlier Hasidic masters did in some cases) and invites us all to serve as channels of blessing. For a contemporary guide to Jewish blessing, see Marcia Prager, *The Path of Blessing: Experiencing the Energy and Abundance of the Divine* (Woodstock, VT: Jewish Lights Publishing, 1998).

trees, the clouds, the birds, and all the other natural beings to sing praises to God [Psalm 148]. At first there was some tentativeness, some self-consciousness, but by the time we got to the clouds, everyone was singing. As it usually does, this exercise released a great deal of energy. Before it was over, all of us were not only singing, we were singing with joy and delight.

After the workshop a man came up to me and said, "Something happened to me once when I was a boy in music class. We were singing, and the teacher walked by and listened to me. She made a sour face; then she leaned over and whispered, 'You just move your lips. You'll be a silent one.' And since that day, I have never sung. That was thirty-five years ago. Today was the first time I sang since then. When we began singing the halleluyahs [from the Book of Psalms] and everybody joined in, I found myself opening up. I was singing before I knew it. All of a sudden, I found that I could."

As I listened to this man, I knew he was talking not only about singing with his mouth, but about soul singing. He was talking of worship and ecstasy, the healing glow you feel when you are in harmony with the universe . . .

Once the Ba'al Shem Tov was praying on Yom Kippur with a group of Hasidim. Normally, the Ba'al Shem Tov's prayers rose to Heaven like flocks of birds, but on this day everything seemed constrained. It was as if the souls of all those present were held down by chains of doubt, like the man who could not sing.

Despite great efforts, no prayers took flight. The Ba'al Shem Tov strained, hoping to break through and make contact, to reach an *at-one-ment*. But nothing happened.

In the group was a father and his young son. The father was an upright man, but the son had shown little interest in prayer or other traditional forms. He usually spent his time watching his father's small flock on the hills and meadows. While he watched over them, it was his habit to play on a small whistle, which he always carried in his pocket.

As the tension mounted in the *shul*, all eyes were on the Ba'al Shem Tov at prayer. The boy got caught up in the effort and wanted to help. Instinctively, he reached for his whistle. His father tried to stop him, but the boy pulled the whistle out of his pocket, brought it to his lips, and blew a piercing note. TWEET!

The father was deeply embarrassed. Everyone turned to the boy with scowls on their faces. Everyone except the Ba'al Shem Tov, for at that moment the chains which had shackled prayer were suddenly snapped. Free of restraint, the Ba'al Shem Tov's prayers rose up like swallows and flew straight to God. The Ba'al Shem Tov turned to the people, his face radiant with joy, and said, "Don't reprimand the boy. It was the song of his whistle that carried our prayer up to Heaven."[31]

Nobody had ever heard of blowing a whistle during the Yom Kippur prayer, but the boy did it and the Ba'al Shem Tov approved. It was appropriate because it was a pure offering. In a completely natural, unselfconscious way, the boy offered up his best intentions. He released his song like a bird, without a thought about permission, and the song was sweet to God.

—*First Steps to a New Jewish Spirit*, 67–68, 70–71

THE PALACES OF MELODY AND REPENTANCE

A *niggun* is a wordless prayer, a melody that a Hasid sings to get closer to God. In the Old Country, if a *hazan* [cantor] was too much in love with the sound of his own voice, they would say, "That *hazan* is a fool. He frequents the palace of *neginah* [melody, as in *niggun*], which is right next door to the palace of *teshuvah* [repentance, return to God]—and yet he never goes in!"

At HaBaD we had a saying: "Every locksmith has a master key with which to open many doors. *Neginah* is such a key, for it can unlock all doors." Why? Because a *niggun* sung in the proper way is like doing *teshuvah*, like a moment of true repentance

---

31. A version of this popular tale appears under the heading "The Little Whistle," in Martin Buber's *Tales of the Hasidim*, translated by Olga Marx (New York: Schocken Books, 1991), 69–70.

and turning to God. The wellsprings of *niggun* and *teshuvah* are the simple yearnings of the heart that we all share.

Not long ago, I was teaching at a Reform synagogue in Calgary on *Shabbos* morning. "Tell me," I began, "do you sometimes have the feeling that you ought to be better? Do you wish that you could be different, higher, wiser? Closer to God?"

People nodded.

"Let's take a moment to get in touch with that feeling," I said. "Now, I'd like you to say, '*Oy.*' Just like that, from that place of aspiration: '*Oy, Oy, Oy.*'" So the people did that, and there were some heartfelt *Oy*'s! Then I said, "You know what? We just have done a little *teshuvah.*"

Because that's what it is. That sense of longing, that sense that "*Oy*, if only I were better, if only I could be in a greater place—not from some crippling sense of guilt, like Woody Allen, but because we love God, we want to be closer to God—that's *teshuvah*. At that point, because the palace of *neginah* and the palace of *teshuvah* are side-by-side, we are ready to sing.[32]

—*Davening*, 29–30

A THANK YOU PRAYER

Thank You, God of Eternity,
for the great wonder of Your creation,
for the earth, the stars, the sun, and the moon,
and the beauty of Your universe,
with which in Your great kindness You have blessed me.
Thank You for granting me life, in all its richness,
for its brilliant moments of joy,
which allow me to soar as the birds,
and even for its anguish and pain,
which somehow seem to precipitate inner growth and
   change.
For all these things, God, I am grateful.

---

32. See "The *Niggun* and the Texture of Time," in Chapter 4 of this volume.

But thank You, especially, God, in Your abundant love,[33]
for having chosen to make me a human being,
blessed among all the fruits of Your creation,
with a mind to reason and seek truth and justice;
with a soul which can feel pain, ecstasy, and compassion,
and has the freedom to choose life and goodness
over cruelty and destruction;
and with a heart which can love and care,
and reach out to touch the hearts of my brothers and sisters,
as together we walk through the years of our lives.
                    —*All Breathing Life Adores Your Name*, 132

33. This expression is taken from the opening words of the *Ahavah Rabbah* prayer, which is recited (among Ashkenazic Jews) immediately before the *Shema* during the morning service. This text speaks of God's "great" or "abounding love" for the community of Israel as manifest through the gifts of Torah (Jewish religious teaching writ large) and the *mitzvot* ("commandments," sacred practices). In the *Shema*, the human worshiper responds by declaring her love to the Divine and commitment to Jewish learning and observance. See Lawrence A. Hoffman, *The Sh'ma and Its Blessings* (Woodstock, VT: Jewish Lights Publishing, 1997), 67–82.

4

Sacred Living: Time, Space, Person

INTRODUCTION

In Sefer Yetzirah *(Book of Formation), one of the oldest extant Jewish mystical texts (dating from the early centuries of the Common Era), the anonymous author speaks of three intersecting dimensions of reality:* Olam *(Space),* Shanah *(Time), and* Nefesh *(Inner Life). In shaping this chapter, we have used these categories (beginning with Time and then proceeding to Space) to organize Reb Zalman's teachings on what one might call holistic Jewish living. He regularly used this and other mystical mappings (sefirot, olamot, soul levels) to help people reflect on the rich layers of human experience, inviting us to examine (and deconstruct, if necessary) our habitual thought and behavioral patterns, asking how we might restructure our lives guided by Jewish wisdom.[1]*

In undertaking his decades-long project of Jewish renewal, Reb Zalman repeatedly asked what he called a functional question: what are the teachings and practices from the great storehouse of Judaism that are most helpful to us in living today meaningfully in relation to God, humankind, and the rest of the natural order? Reb Zalman was at once a person who was deeply

---

1. See, for example, his discussion of this tripartite division in his book *Credo of a Modern Kabbalist*, written with Rabbi Daniel Siegel, 223–26.

attached to tradition but who also felt an urgent need to ask if our inherited ideas and practices needed alteration (whether subtle or dramatic) in order to continue to be effective tools for human flourishing. When, where, and why was a given ritual or statute introduced? How did it serve our forebears? Does it continue to help us become more thoughtful, compassionate, and responsible beings?

This chapter opens with several reflections on organic time, as this was a major concern of Reb Zalman as a person living in an age of rapid technological advancement (including the development of increasingly lethal military machinery) in which time is often commodified—too often measured in terms of productivity and financial gain. Like his mentor, Abraham Joshua Heschel,[2] he believed Judaism offered important correctives to this imbalance through such practices as daily prayer (aligning with the natural rhythms of light and darkness), the Sabbath, and the calendar and life cycle. This also dovetailed with his ecological and societal concerns, and the need for people to learn to live in greater harmony with the earth and with one another. One example of this sensibility is his pioneering work on eco-kashrut *(a term he coined in the late-1970s), calling for an expansive definition of traditional* kashrut *that includes environmental and social justice considerations.[3]*

Related to the issues mentioned above, we have also included in this chapter pieces on the body, and the need to care for our physical selves. This includes reflections on work and rest, eating and exercise, and sanctifying our sexual relations. These teachings reflect Reb Zalman's commitment to a holistic vision of the

---

2. See Heschel's classic work, *The Sabbath* (New York: Farrar, Straus, and Giroux, 1951).

3. Here, too, Heschel was an important model, as he asked provocative questions about the relationship between Jewish ritual practice and contemporary ethics. For example, in an anecdote relayed by Susannah Heschel, he asked his seminary students, "Are nuclear weapons kosher?" See *Abraham Joshua Heschel: Essential Writings*, selected and edited by Susannah Heschel (Maryknoll, NY: Orbis Books, 2011), 34–35.

human being, and the need to move beyond a religious world-view in which the body must be subdued (or even punished) in order to free the spirit. Instead, he proposes an integrated approach in which a person engages her body and spirit in the quest for holiness. In presenting his views on this issue, he often turns to teachings from the Ba'al Shem Tov and other early Hasidic masters who grappled with the role of asceticism in the Jewish pietistic tradition.[4]

COMMODITY TIME AND ORGANIC TIME

We do strange things to time. We invent games in which we stop and start time at our pleasure: *Time in! Time out!* When some of us go to work, we punch a time clock. Between "important" events, we *kill time*. When somebody breaks the law, we punish him by making him *serve time*. Television gives us the *Six O'clock News*, the *Eleven O'clock News*, the *Today Show*, the *Tonight Show*, the *Tomorrow Show*. And TV also gives us *prime time*. This is how we measure and evaluate time now. We have bought a concept of time as a standardized commodity, and the price we pay is consciousness. What we lose in the exchange is organic time. And the more we lose touch with organic time, the more automated we become.

Commodity time is good for industries, banking, business, and television, but it's not good for living life. In order to survive the regimen of nine-to-five time, we need the counter regimen of organic time, which changes texture with the turning of our planet. Corporate convenience cannot set the clock by which life is lived. Life is lived in organic time; it runs on the ebb and tide of forces which exist in the universe.

Time as commodity is out of phase with time as it flows in nature. The Jewish notion is to bring these two aspects of time into sync with each other. Judaism says: Sunrise . . . sunset. Six days and the *Shabbat*. New moon, full moon. Equinox and

---

4. See *Hasidism: A New History*, edited by David Biale et al. (Princeton, NJ: Princeton University Press, 2018), 174–79.

solstice. The full moon of the vernal equinox is Passover. The full moon of the autumnal equinox is *Sukkot* (the Feast of Tabernacles). The last phase of the moon in the last phase of the sun is Hanukkah.

These holidays come at their organic time, coinciding with the realities in nature. Looking from a larger perspective within the Jewish calendar, we can see patterns of one year, a seven-year cycle, ending in a sabbatical year, and then seven seven-year cycles, ending in a Jubilee Year. "Six years shall you sow your field, and six years you shall prune your vineyard and gather in its fruit. But the seventh year shall be a *shabbat* of solemn rest for the land, a *shabbat* for the Lord: you shall neither sow your field nor prune your vineyard . . . And you shall count seven *shabbatot* of years, seven times seven years . . . And you shall hallow the fiftieth year and proclaim liberty throughout all the land to all its inhabitants: it shall be a jubilee for you; and you shall return every man to his possession, and you shall return every man to his family" (Leviticus 25:23–25). As a result of these patterns, we are constantly involved in an incredible rhythm of rhythms, the pulsing life of the universe.

The rhythm of organic time is inherent in all life. It is not something that is only outside of us; it is within us on all levels of our beings. Inside us there is also an ebb and tide during day and night. And there are the rhythms of digestion that go on all the time; and the faster rhythms of pulse and heartbeat; and the still faster rhythms of exchanges that take place in the lungs; and the rapid interactions within the capillaries; and finally, there are the ultrafast rhythms that take place in the nervous system and in the brain. And on the molecular and sub-molecular levels, rhythms occur in angstrom wave lengths, with millions of reversals per second.

Organic time is actually humming inside us. It is one of the voices of God. Rabbi Nahman of Bratzlav called it "the voice of my Beloved" [Song of Songs 5:2]—the pulse. "If you want to know God," he said, "you need only listen to God's voice within. You need never be lonely for the Divine or out of touch with

God's inner spirit; you can always touch your pulse and say, 'Oh, there You are.'"[5]   *—First Steps to a New Jewish Spirit*, 1–3

ONCE UPON A TIME

Mircea Eliade (1907–1986), the great scholar of comparative religion, used to speak of this concept with the phrase, *in illo tempore*, "at that time." When you tell a story today, and you say, "Once upon a time," you are actually repeating the introduction that was first given in Latin when the priest would read from the Gospels. The priests would say, *in illo tempore*, and then would teach how Jesus went and did thus and such. It is a reference to mythic time.[6]

Now, if you really live with a liturgical calendar, you live *in illo tempore*, in mythic time. Therefore, every Passover, Jews go out of Egypt. Every *Shavuot* (Feast of Weeks or Pentecost), Jews receive the Torah. Every Christmas, Jesus is born. That is part of living *in illo tempore*. Our yearly celebrations are the ways in which we sanctify and mark time. After the Temple was destroyed, Jews no longer had that holy place to visit and find God. So where could Jews look for God, if not there? In the ten days between Rosh Ha-Shanah and Yom Kippur. In other words: not in *space*, but in *time*.[7]

I once heard a story about an Orthodox Christian family preparing for the penitential fast of Lent. A woman described a ritual in which all her family stood in a circle and each person asked forgiveness of the other. She said, "I looked at my daughter then and thought of all the times I had treated her unfairly

5. See Rebbe Nahman's *Likkutei Moharan*, Volume 1, Lesson 160, edited and translated by Moshe Mykoff, annotated by Chaim Kramer (Jerusalem, Israel: Breslov Research Institute, 1999), 10:268–69.

6. See Eliade, *The Sacred and the Profane*, translated by Willard R. Trask (New York: Harcourt, Brace, and World, 1959), 68–113.

7. Babylonian Talmud, Yevamot 49b: "'Seek the Lord where he may be found' (Isaiah 55:6) . . . Rabbah bar Avuah said: 'These are the ten days between Rosh Hashanah and Yom Kippur,'" https://www.sefaria.org/Yevamot.49b?lang=bi.

. . . how I had treated her as less than a full human being, simply because I was busy and she was young. I had all kinds of excuses, but it wasn't right." So she asked her daughter's forgiveness, and her daughter was so moved that she, too, asked for her mother's forgiveness.

In Judaism, we sometimes do something like this at a wedding, prior to going up to the canopy. We ask siblings and parents and children to forgive one another so that everyone can go into the ceremony with a clean slate [See Babylonian Talmud, Yevamot 63a]. But why was this Christian family asking for forgiveness at that time? Because it was Lent; they were in the penitential season of preparing for Easter. Because if you are Christian, and you want to have God "arise" in you, to have a "resurrection" in you, you had better prepare for it. Likewise, for Jews, this is happening between Rosh Ha-Shanah and Yom Kippur.

In Judaism, it is difficult to speak of God as being incarnate in the flesh,[8] but we can speak of God as being incarnate in time. Yom Kippur is the clearest God-time that we have on our calendar. There are twenty-six hours of Yom Kippur, reflecting the fact that the divine name, Y-H-V-H, is numerically equivalent to twenty-six.[9] By adding an hour before and an hour after, we enrich Yom Kippur with "extra time," as it were.[10] And this is how God shows up in time for us.

---

8. Shaul Magid explores the subject of "incarnational thinking" in various Hasidic sources in his monograph, *Hasidism Incarnate: Hasidism, Christianity, and the Construction of Modern Judaism* (Stanford, CA: Stanford University Press, 2014).

9. Reb Zalman is using the ancient interpretive method known as *gematria* (perhaps from the Greek word for geometry) in which each Hebrew letter is represented by a number (*aleph* = 1, *bet* = 2, etc.). There are several variations to this system, which are used widely by Jewish mystics. In our case, the number 26 is reached as follows: Y=10, H=5, V=6, H=5.

10. The ancient sages teach that it is a *mitzvah* to "add" time to Yom Kippur. See, Babylonian Talmud, Rosh Hashanah 9a, https://www.sefaria.org/Rosh_Hashanah.9a?lang=bi.

There is a famous painting by Jean-François Millet, called "*L'Angelus*," of a man and woman standing in the middle of a field and praying. Next to the man is a pitchfork, and at the woman's feet is a basket of potatoes. In the background is a church steeple in which a bell is ringing at a time when the angels are singing in heaven. So when the man and woman hear the bell, even in the middle of their work, he takes his hat off and they both adopt an attitude of prayer to join with the angels in the adoration of God. It is the same in Islamic countries when one hears the muezzin's call, "Prayer is better than sleep! God is greater! There is no god but God!" In the *shtetl* (village), Jews used to have the equivalent of muezzin before the High Holidays. A man with a wooden mallet would go around the settlement banging on doors in the early hours, saying, "Time to wake for the penitential prayers!" The bells, the call to prayer, and the knocking were all ways to wake us up, to help us be conscious of God at a particular time, so that this time would be, as it were, filled with God!

—*Wrapped in a Holy Flame*, Introduction

ORGANIC TIMES FOR PRAYER

In the following two pieces, Reb Zalman advocates for the renewal of prayer in rhythm with the daily cycle of light and darkness. While he does not mention the three daily services— Shaharit *(Morning),* Minhah *(Afternoon), and* Ma'ariv *(Evening)—in these selections, he invites the reader (however distant from conventional practice) to explore the potential power of utilizing these prayer rubrics to locate herself within creation, to reawaken to the holistic nature of life.*

Every day we need to re-experience the moment in which we realized that we are integral to the universe, that we are part of it, not a separate entity only passing through. The Psalms tell us this: "You are my child. Today I have begotten you" [Psalm 2:7]. When we re-experience this great awareness, we are regenerated. We need to reconnect with it every day, if only for a moment—it reestablishes our natural place in the order of the universe. When this connection happens, we are filled again with light, acceptance, and *at-one-ment*. For it to happen, we have to make time. Our ability to connect with the universe is especially strong at dawn and dusk, sunrise and sunset . . . This is how you can strengthen your connection with organic time.

The special quality of dawn and dusk doesn't have to be taught. All of creation knows about it—the birds and beasts in the forest; the creatures of the sea, who rise and fall to different levels of the ocean; in the city, even the pigeons coo at daybreak. The classic symbol of responding to dawn is the rooster crowing. He puffs himself up, throws his head back, and sings cock-a-doodle-do! It is such an important image of how to react to organic time that we Jews have made it the first of the morning blessings in the prayer book: "Blessed are You, *Adonai*, Cosmic Majesty, for having given the rooster discrimination to know the difference between day and night."[11]

—*First Steps to a New Jewish Spirit*, 5–6

A MINI-SABBATH AT WORK

Commodity time is the price we pay for organic time. In order to earn a living, this is the bargain you strike: you give your employer work, in return for which they give you money. While you are working, your time belongs to your employer, and it's used to create *commodities* of one sort or another for them. A question arises out of this situation: what is your moral obligation to your employer (what constitutes an honest day's work?) and what is the best way to fulfill it? In one sense, your obligation is met by accepting the convention of commodity time and acting accordingly while you are at work. The best way to do

---

11. Just as *Shaharit* opens with references to daylight, the opening blessing of *Ma'ariv* speaks of God "arranging the stars," and "rolling light away from darkness and darkness from light." See Reb Zalman's translation of this prayer at the *Open Siddur Project*, https://opensiddur.org/prayers/solilunar/everyday/nighttime/evening/maariv-aravim-translated-by-rabbi-zalman-schachter-shalomi-zl/.

this, however, and the most productive for your employer, is to step out of commodity time once or twice during the work day to recharge yourself with a hit of organic time. This improves both your sanity and efficiency. Imagine that it is early or mid-afternoon. You've already eaten your lunch and digested it. There's a pile of work on your desk, but your energy is low and perhaps you're even feeling a little drowsy. It's time for a coffee break, a chocolate bar, or a handful of nut-raisin-seed mix. This is a common occurrence; it happens to most people at around the same time of the afternoon. It's the reason that management approved of the afternoon coffee break—it improves workers' efficiency. But there's a better way to do that.

If you can, instead of having a coffee or candy break, find a quiet space where you can sit down, and make *Shabbat* for ten minutes by allowing your mind to leave the world of *doing* and enter the world of *being*. Your body is aching for this—crying out, "Please let me rest a little bit." I suggest that you spend your afternoon break as a kind of meditation, a moment to say your afternoon prayers. It doesn't need to be long. Ten minutes is really enough. It's better than anything else, and your effectiveness will improve immediately . . .

Now is the time to make yourself truly comfortable. Exhale and take a deep breath which fills your lungs to their capacity. Then exhale again; let it all out until your lungs feel empty. Inhale again, and with the next exhalation, visualize yourself leaning back, back, back, and falling into night. Visualize all the tiredness of your body coming out like a wave, engulfing you, and you yielding to it. Another breath. You slow your pulse even further. At this point you yield wholly to that urge that wants to be rid of work and obligation. Let it encompass you so completely that all that exists is your limp weight on top of the chair leaning against the desk.

Don't forget to breathe. Take another breath. All right. Now you're there. You've fallen into a very relaxed, sleepy state, and one of your favorite images from daydreams or previous meditations comes up again, sustaining and energizing you. Or you relive a peak experience, one of those moments when you *saw*, *felt*, and *understood* some aspect of your life and its place in the order of the world. Look at that peak experience. Now, in the deepest enjoyment of it, open yourself up again to that verification which comes from the center of the universe. You belong. You are loved. You're integral. You're reborn. You're being nourished. You're growing further.

At this point you're filled with gratefulness. You breathe in once again and with the next breath you feel a zing in the air and you've already turned one hundred and eighty degrees from sunset toward sunrise. Now you're facing a new day and the future. With each breath, you breathe all the way to your toes, then into the bottom of your spine. Your whole body begins to rise, reaching toward what is to come. And here you enter the sunrise, and you open up your concerns for this afternoon, for the rest of the work shift, for the evening you will spend with your family. With each breath you take, you become more and more alert and intent. You're opening your eyes. You're visualizing your tasks slowly, with ease and focus. You see all the pieces that must fit together and all the steps you have to take. You send out a thank-you to the universe. You look around the room, see all the people in their places, and you acknowledge them. The other person across the room who knows what you have been doing acknowledges you, too.   —*First Steps to a New Jewish Spirit*, 7–10

THE SABBATH DANCE

It is Friday night and my thoughts are turned toward *Shabbat*. A wave of forgiveness flows through me and I feel a sense of well-being for all the creatures in the universe. This is an expansive feeling, part of the sense of God's plenty that arrives with the coming of *Shabbat*.

On the eve of *Shabbat*, the Jewish home is filled with the aromas of God's cornucopia, telling of an abundance that is greater than all our needs, real or imagined. This sense of God's abundance is luxurious. Despite the urgency of preparing for *Shabbat*, it relaxes me. I feel loved and cared for, and my usual workday worries begin to fall away. Even the deepest knots loosen up.

Friday afternoon is a mixture of opposites, a give and take between the tension of preparing for *Shabbat* and the deep relaxation of being in it. The preparations are like a dance; we develop a rhythm and work up a fine sweat, but it is the sweat of pleasure, not of hard work.

Like most dances, the preparing-for-*Shabbat* dance is best done with other people. The household hums with satisfaction as all the members go about their tasks of getting ready. We bump into each other as the pace quickens, but we do not mind. We smile at each other in our shared concern—we are comrades, partners, lovers. —*First Steps to a New Jewish Spirit*, 81–82

A BIT OF THE COMING WORLD

We say that *Shabbat* is *me'ein Olam ha-Ba*, "a bit of the Coming World."[12] We take from the messianic future and invest in the present. Reb Pinhas of Koretz saw the Ba'al Shem Tov as the messianic light condensed and sent to keep us from fainting (from hardship and persecution). Likewise, every *Shabbat* a bit of the future is condensed and brought into the present. *Shabbat* is not for living in the past, "driving by the rear-view mirror." It calls for seeing differently. One dreams of the future in terms of the trends of today, though some of these have not yet come to discernment. In the soul exists the ability to visualize perfections that have not yet been manifested in this world—the spark of the Divine in us is not bound by the restrictions of time and space. On higher levels, in dimensions many times the power of ours, there are many more points of contiguity. This is what allows one to visit a time not yet come—the *Olam ha-Ba*—and to see visions there. Bringing them back to this set of dimensions, we can begin to initiate here the processes that will lead

---

12. See Babylonian Talmud, Berakhot 57b, https://www.sefaria.org/Berakhot.57b?lang=bi, and Genesis Rabbah 17:5, https://www.sefaria.org/Bereishit_Rabbah.17.5?lang=bi.

to the greater fulfillment. This indeed is the *Shabbat* and weekday cycle. On *Shabbat*, we envision as-yet-unrealized futures, and after *havdalah* (brief service of "separation") at the close of *Shabbat*, we begin to move toward the realization-phases that are linked with the weekdays, anchored in the here and now.   —*Gate to the Heart*, 94–95

BRINGING *SHABBOS* TO LIFE

The deep psychological and spiritual insight of *Shabbos* is one of our tradition's great treasures. Our modern contributions are flexibility and creativity, which I believe are more important at this point than the rigidity around *Shabbos* that the tradition can sometimes display. We need to bring a process of experimentation to augment the wisdom of *halakhah* [Jewish law]. In the Saturday morning *kiddush* we say, "Let the Children of Israel keep the *Shabbos* for generations." Creating a *Shabbos*, in other words—and creating a *Shabbos* that our next generation will want to pass on to their children—is *in our hands*. There are all sorts of ways to bring our practice of *Shabbos* alive. Engage as many senses as you can.

Clothing. When we divest ourselves of our weekly garments, the kabbalists taught, we should intend to cast from ourselves the otherness in which we dwell most of the time. When we put on our *Shabbos* garments we then draw upon ourselves an additional level of holiness.[13]

The lawyer or broker who wears jeans on the Sabbath is making a statement about resting. He has taken off his professional role and donned clothes in which he can loaf at his ease. Others might put on special garb to enhance the delight of heart, mind, and soul . . .

---

13. See Elliott Ginsberg, *The Sabbath in Classical Kabbalah* (Albany, NY: State University of New York Press, 1989), 231–42 (and accompanying notes).

Food. A favorite song sings of the "quail and fish" consumed on *Shabbos*[14]—even though the *shtetl* poor could probably afford nothing of the kind. We might choose to give our stomachs a Sabbath from processed foods by way of celebration, to enjoy a day of uncooked fruits and vegetables and juices during the summer months. Health permitting, this would certainly be a great time to indulge in that dessert we've been denying ourselves all week.

Shabbos is a time of plenty. As you raise the food to your lips, try to feel as if God were feeding you directly, or as if you yourself were feeding the *Shabbos* bride. Our souls, in their superabundance that we receive on this day, become the *Shabbos* bride at that point.[15]

Fragrances. The Jews of Yemen and other Sephardim (Jews of the Middle East and North Africa) had the custom to prepare fragrant flowers and herbs for *Shabbos* . . . I once held the post of "religious environmentalist" at Camp Ramah, a camp run by the Conservative movement in Connecticut. One of my goals was to transmit to the kids some of the sensory, non-verbal values and experiences that go into the adjective *shabbosdik* [befitting the Sabbath]. Every Friday, for example, as the kids were dressing for *Shabbat* and the special Friday night meal was cooking in the kitchen, we would take all the fans we had and set them up to blow the smell of the food all over the camp, to permeate the air with the anticipation of *Shabbat*. I felt that linking non-verbal experiences to the social and other pleasures of *Shabbat* would store these experiences in a much deeper place than just verbal explanations, a place that would attract them back to these experiences later in life.

---

14. Part of the chorus to *Mah Yedidut* (How beloved!), a popular *Shabbat* table song. A transliteration and translation are available online at http://siddur.org/transliterations/shabbat-second-meal/mah-yedidut.

15. On the association of the *Shabbat* Bride with the *Shekhinah*, and Her intimate relationship to the Community of Israel and to individual souls, see ibid., chapters 1–2.

Music and other media. The traditional Friday night prayer for welcoming the Sabbath is full of references to song. Psalm 95: "Come, let us sing to God. . . let us call out songs of praise." Psalm 92: "A song for the Sabbath day. It is good to thank God, to sing the praise of your name . . . Upon ten-stringed instrument and lyre, with singing accompanied by harp." Rabbinic law prohibits the playing of even non-electronic instruments on *Shabbos* for arcane reasons.[16] But a person who loves playing music but is not a professional musician, who only on *Shabbos* can find the time to sit down—maybe with friends—and offer a song or a tune in honor of *Shabbos*, is celebrating the day in a way that the liturgy itself suggests. Taking the time to listen to the symphony we never have time for during the week, and to listen with the express purpose of welcoming and enjoying the Sabbath and transcending the everyday, is to me a quintessentially *shabbosdik* activity. Best of all is to make all our preparations for such activities ahead of time, so that all we have to do on *Shabbos* is to soak it in and enjoy . . .

There are a whole series of movies, albums, and other things that could be shared. Imagine sitting with the kids and watching a comedy like *Frisco Kid*, about a Polish rabbi (Gene Wilder) in the Wild West! We need not resort to any media at all: dancing and singing are part of the traditional repertoire, especially among Hasidim.

And so, of course, is silence.

Bath. Taking a bath or shower before *Shabbos* to wash the week out of our hair has a special significance. In very religious circles adults would go to immerse themselves in the *mikveh* or ritual bath on Friday afternoon. This immersion, the *Zohar* tells us, makes visible the additional aura that *Shabbos* bestows

---

16. See Reb Zalman's discussion of music on *Shabbat*, including his criticism of the traditional prohibitions against the use of instruments, in Rabbi Zalman Schachter-Shalomi and Rabbi Daniel Siegel, *Integral Halachah*, 76–79.

on us.[17] Simply washing our face with both hands, kabbalists believed, revealed the image of God that the week normally obscures in our visage. Not everyone has time to immerse themselves in some way before *Shabbos*, however. On *Shabbos*, too, we can imagine family members gathering in a hot tub, sharing their week, clearing away any *shmutz* that has accumulated in the air, forgiving each other and relaxing with each other, washing away the week.

Sex. Tradition makes no secret of it: sex on *Shabbos* is a *mitzvah*. A loving couple who make sure to take their time enacting our union with the *Shekhinah*, the feminine face of God,[18] and doing so lavishly and tenderly, are celebrating *Shabbat* in the most wonderful way . . .

Other soul-nourishing activities. Save up for *Shabbos* those activities that pamper your soul. If you enjoy gardening for its own sake, rather than regard it as a chore you'd just as soon delegate to someone else; if you're enjoying spending time with your plants rather than working on a crop with which to feed your family, then gardening is a *shabbosdik* activity for you. If you're a computer programmer by trade but a potter at heart, and if setting aside some *Shabbos* time each week would allow

---

17. On the Kabbalistic transformation of the older rabbinic practice of bathing before *Shabbat* into a spiritual rite of immersion in a *mikveh*, see Ginsburg, *The Sabbath in the Classical Kabbalah*, 224–31.

18. In general, engaging in permitted sexual relations is viewed as a *mitzvah* in classical Judaism. The Babylonian Talmud, Ketubot 62b, https://www.sefaria.org/Ketubot.62b?lang=bi, emphasizes that *Shabbat* night is the ideal time to perform this *mitzvah*. For a helpful introduction to the subject of sex in Judaism, see *Jewish Voices, Jewish Choices: Sex and Intimacy*, edited by Elliot N. Dorff and Danya Ruttenberg (Philadelphia: Jewish Publication Society, 2001). The notion that holy relations *below* (among human beings) can engage the indwelling divine Presence and stimulate Her union with the masculine dimensions *above* (within the Divine self) is emphasized in Kabbalistic sources. See, for example, *Zohar* I:12b–13a, available in Daniel C. Matt's annotated translation, *The Zohar: Pritzker Edition* (Stanford, CA: Stanford University Press, 2004), 1:87–89.

you to enjoy sitting down at the potter's wheel, then pottery is a *shabbosdik* activity for you[19]. . .

Spiritual gains should not come at emotional expense. Trying any new activity can rock the family boat at first. Discuss these issues beforehand to prepare the ground and start small. Go at a pace that everyone can handle. Developing re-ensoulment skills takes time.   —*Jewish with Feeling*, 57–62

THE *NIGGUN* AND THE TEXTURE OF TIME

My mentor, Abraham Joshua Heschel used to say that a *niggun* is "a tune flowing in search of its own unattainable end," because when you come to the end of the melody, you start it all over again.[20] Like my friend Reb Shlomo Carlebach used to say, "A *niggun* is never finished." Once it ends, you want to go back and sing it over and over again.

There are several kinds of *niggunim*, depending on the circumstances in which they are sung. Most often you find *niggunim* around a festive table where they are spoken of as *zemirot* [songs]. Since the *niggun* is itself wordless, people have sometimes attached lyrics to them which match the feel of the melody. The melody may also be sung in different ways which betray different ethnic influences. Sometimes the *niggun* itself has a Russian flavor, or a Hungarian flavor. We sing these around the table because a dinner table is considered an altar in Judaism [Babylonian Talmud, Menahot 97a], and around the altar the

---

19. Traditional *halakhists* regard both gardening and pottery as prohibited on *Shabbat* because these activities are considered forms of labor (and *Shabbat* is a day of rest). Reb Zalman, however, following his method of *psycho-halakhah*, seeks to clarify "first principles, and then redefine the specifics in their light." The key question for him in this case is how to make *Shabbat* a joyous day, since experiencing *ta'anug* (delight) on the Sabbath is a core Jewish value. See Reb Zalman's discussion of this matter in *Integral Halachah*, 75–76.

20. Abraham Joshua Heschel, *The Earth Is the Lord's: The Inner World of a Jew in Eastern Europe* (Woodstock, VT: Jewish Lights Publishing, 2001), 15.

Levites used to sing during the offering of the sacrifices. If a meal is served on *Shabbat* or *yontif*, a holiday, you will always find people singing table hymns, which we call *tish niggunim*, or "table melodies."

Now imagine that *Shabbat* is ending, and we no longer have any artificial light in our little *shtiebl*, or prayer house. The only light is coming from the *ner tamid* [eternal light] on top of the holy ark. We are sitting around the table at *shalosh se'udot*, the third meal. The food is not what is important at this meal; it is the mood which says, "*Oy! Shabbat* will soon be over!" From where will we take the holy energy that we need during the week? From these beautiful melodies, full of longing. So much yearning comes out in them. You simply sing these melodies together and there is no need for talking. Then there wells up in people a sense of longing which can tune one's spirituality for the whole week.

My criticism of a lot of modern spirituality is that there is no longing in the method. So many teachers of spirituality work with self-satisfied people who are saying, "Now I am going to meditate." It is often missing the ingredient that asks—"How will I become what I need to become? How will I serve in the way in which I need to serve?" The *niggunim* that "ask" these questions are what you call *ga'agu'im*, "longing" *niggunim*, and they are very beautiful. They create the shared sacred model for us by raising an unspoken prayer.

If people think that we are merely singing melodies, they are wrong. If I am singing the Tzemah Tzedek's[21] *deveikut niggun* ("cleaving" melody) words cannot even approach what I am saying about "How I long to be how *You* would want me to be, God" without words in the *niggun*. These are the unspoken prayers of contemplative *niggunim*.

There are also some *niggunim* that are based on traditional modes. For instance, if I begin to sing a High Holiday tune for the evening prayer, in my imagination I hear it as if it were

---

21. Rabbi Menachem Mendel Schneersohn (1789–1866), the third Lubavitcher Rebbe (the second to lead in the town of Lubavitch).

played by an orchestra. I can hear the brass and the fanfare as if proclaiming a welcome to the Divine Sovereign into our midst. This is what we do on Rosh Ha-Shanah night. But we are not the first to sing this melody. If I look into the genetic line of that melody, it would take me to my father and grandfather, my great-grandfather, and well beyond; for all of my Ashkenazic [Central and Eastern European] ancestors used this melody on Rosh Ha-Shanah night.

This repetition through the generations has created what Rupert Sheldrake calls a "morphogenetic field."[22] When I enter into that field, I move from "commodity time" to "sacred time." I move into the vibration of Rosh Ha-Shanah when I sing this melody with *kavvanah* and energy. Therefore, these modes are powerful stimulants. We call them *nussah* [style or mode]. They are clues to the worshiper on how to fine-tune his or her inner being.

Imagine it is a *Shabbat* before the new moon, and you are saying that prayer for the new moon, the prayer which begins with the words, "May it be thy will Lord our God to renew for us the coming month and grant us life and health." The cantor begins the prayer with a pleading recital. The worshipers want to be included in what the cantor is praying for, so they afford the cantor a harmonious chord in a minor key, and the cantor weaves this pleading prayer around their sound. From time to time you might even hear a sob to punctuate the pleading.

The *nussah* melodies are ways to entrain us in specific ways of being.   —*The Gates of Prayer*, 29–31

22. Sheldrake, a biochemist by training, applied his theory of "morphogenetic fields" (which has been challenged widely in the contemporary scientific community) to explain the existence of enduring and evolving patterns of thought and behavior in religious and culture communities.

WHY DO WE KISS THE TORAH?

What we kiss is the outer covering[23] of what inside is a path, an opening, a way of reconnecting to . . . the light that God created on the first day of creation. On that day God said, "Let there be light and there was light" (Genesis 1:3); and on the fourth day, God created the sun and the moon (1:14–15). Rashi (1040–1105)[24] then asks a question in the name of the rabbis who came before him: "What happened to the light that was created on the first day?" Quoting the Talmud (Babylonian Talmud, Tractate Hagigah 12a), he answers that God saw that it would not be fitting for wicked people to have use of this light, and so it was hidden away for the righteous to have in the future. This is because this light is described as allowing a person to see from one end of the world to the other.[25] Then, Rabbi Menahem Nahum of Chernobyl (1730–1797) adds that the place where the light is hidden for the righteous is in the Torah itself.[26]

If we think about what that means, we begin to see why people would want to study Torah and be so involved with it. Learning

---

23. It is a widespread custom for Jewish worshippers to kiss the Torah scroll when it is removed from the ark and carried around the synagogue before and after it is read publicly. It is also common to kiss other sacred objects (ark cover, *atarah* and *tzitzit*, holy books, *mezuzah*, etc.). See Ronald Eisenberg, *The JPS Guide to Jewish Traditions* (Philadelphia: Jewish Publication Society, 2004) 618–19.

24. The acronym for Rabbi Shlomo (Solomon) son of Isaac (RaSHI), the most widely read medieval commentator on the Bible and Talmud.

25. The explanation in the Talmudic passage is that God foresees the sinfulness of the generations of the flood and the Tower of Babel and hides the light away to avoid its misuse and corruption.

26. See, for example, *Me'or Einayim*, *Shemot* (Jerusalem: *Makhon Ma'or ha-Torah*, 5758 [1997–1998]), 155–56. Interestingly, the author states that the Ba'al Shem Tov would gaze into the Torah until he saw the "hidden light," accessing both theoretical and practical insight. See Reb Zalman and Rabbi Daniel Siegel's translation of the beginning of this text in *Credo of a Modern Kabbalist*, 127–28. See also Arthur Green's translation of the entire *Me'or Einayim* (Stanford, CA: Stanford University Press, 2020).

Torah becomes a way to rediscover that light which illumines all of existence from one end of the world to the other, that light of the first day which reappeared for that timeless moment at Mt. Sinai.[27] And I'm hearing something else that feels very much like a Zen insight in this idea of the light of the first day. The first light . . . [allows a person] to see the world like one has never seen it before . . . When one sees the world with such eyes, one can see from the beginning of the world to the end, because those eyes are not yet blinded by subsequent stories, doubts, and experiences . . .

This distortion and constriction exist in the way we often approach Torah itself, giving the appearance that we are identifying the Torah with God. There are those who have thought, looking at the way we relate to the Torah, the Jews are Torah worshippers. What God says, is saying, is less important than what the Torah says, and Torah here includes the many subsequent legal decisions and codes. We say that people shouldn't worship objects (Exodus 20:4–6), and then we carry the Torah around and we kiss it. People have this notion that Jews are "Torahlaters" [as in idolaters].

What it is that we are really seeing in the Torah is that light of the first day. And that light of the first day actually exists in tension with the whole notion of tradition. To observe tradition means to accept the way my parents saw the world. My father and mother were good children to their parents by seeing the world as they did and continuing to live as they did. And so, to continue tradition and be a good child myself, I need to do the

---

27. In Hasidic and Kabbalistic literature, creation and revelation are often linked as two moments of great divine disclosure. See, for example, the opening teaching in *The Language of Truth: The Torah Commentary of the Sefat Emet, Rabbi Yehudah Leib Alter of Ger*, translated and interpreted by Arthur Green (Philadelphia: Jewish Publication Society, 1998), 3–5. Further, there are several classical teachings that describe Sinai as a radically inclusive experience, containing all future Jewish generations and insights. See, for example, Exodus Rabbah 28:6, https://www.sefaria.org/Shemot_Rabbah.28.6?lang=bi.

same. This is the sense of what tradition or being traditional means. However, imagine that our argument really is that we Jews have been transmitting a vision of how our ancestors saw the world and experienced God. And we've been transmitting that and making it current generation after generation in an unbroken chain since Moses stood on Mount Sinai to receive the Torah for the first time.[28]

Now we can see what an amazing tunnel tradition is, reaching back and connecting us to that flash our ancestors experienced 3,000 years ago! This is what really makes us rise and kiss the Torah, the scroll which makes it possible to bridge the gap between that moment so long ago and this present moment, that allows us to recognize that the moment of the flash of insight is not very far away at all. It is right here, so palpable that you can hold it, touch it, make a blessing, and read it. There is still inspiration to gain from it, something we actually expect to find when we read the Torah on *Shabbat* morning.

—*Credo of a Modern Kabbalist*, 106–8

IS IT REALLY KOSHER?

Sometimes I think we Jews exist so that in every age we will be able to ask our eternal question: is it kosher? Kosher means clean, pure, and, by extension, good for the natural processes of the universe. The opposite of kosher is *treif*, which means unclean, impure, polluted, and hence polluting. Kosher is energy-efficient and productive; *treif* is wasteful and eventually destructive.

---

28. The tension between the continuity of transmission and the need to *make it current* is boldly illustrated in a teaching ascribed to the Ba'al Shem Tov: "We say: 'God *of* Abraham, God *of* Isaac, and God *of* Jacob,' and not: 'God of Abraham, Isaac, and Jacob' [in the opening of the *Amidah* prayer], for Isaac and Jacob did not base their work on the searching and service of Abraham; they themselves searched for the unity of the Maker and his service." Authentic personal experience of the Divine—represented here by the phrasing "God of" each patriarch—enabled all three figures to act as faithful links in the chain of transmission. Martin Buber, "Themselves," *Tales of the Hasidim* (New York: Schocken Books, 1947), 48.

Taken in its eternal sense, keeping kosher is seen as a matter of obedience and submission to the law. In this view, the law is approached as statutes decreed by human beings. But the laws of religion, like the laws of nature, are integral elements of the cosmos. The law of gravity, for example, was not legislated; it was discovered. It was discovered because it exists, because it is natural. And so, too, the laws of religion—which are God's message to us on how to live in harmony with the rest of creation—were revealed/discovered to be embedded in existence.

In the past, many people were attracted to religion by burning bushes, supernatural occurrences introduced into their routine lives. Extraordinary miracles proclaimed religions and legitimized them. Today, when I talk about religion, I stress the miracle of the obvious. God reveals and creates constantly in the ordinary. There we find the real expression of God's "Minding."

In an age of increasingly rapid technological change, the issue of what's kosher has widened its focus to an inclusive concern for the well-being of all our fellow human beings, our planet, and the entire universe. As soon as we orient ourselves to the path of planetary survival, we must ask about a whole range of things: are they kosher?

We want to know if nuclear power is kosher, and the electricity produced by it. (And what about nuclear waste, and all the other toxins with which we pollute the air, the earth, the seas, and eventually ourselves—are they clean or unclean, kosher or *treif?*)

Eggs are generally considered kosher, but what about eggs from chickens who spend their entire lives imprisoned in a cage one cubic foot in size? Food pellets are brought to them on one conveyor belt; their droppings and eggs are taken away on another. The Bible forbids us to torment animals or cause them any unnecessary grief.[29] Raising chickens who can go out

---

29. See the discussion in the Babylonian Talmud, Bava Metzia 32a–33a.

sometimes and see the sky or eat a worm or blade of grass is one thing but manufacturing them in the concentration camp conditions of contemporary "poultry ranches" is quite another.

According to Jewish dietary laws all fruits and vegetables are kosher. But what about green beans or tomatoes harvested by ill-treated, underpaid, and exploited migrant workers—are they kosher? What about bananas from countries ruled by despots where the workers have few rights, and the bananas are heavily sprayed with DDT, picked green, and then artificially ripened in the holds of ships by being gassed—are they kosher?

Are chemical food additives kosher? They give food a longer shelf-life, but what do they do to our lives? Who really knows what all those chemicals do to our livers, kidneys, stomachs, or intestines? And artificial coloring dyes which make food look "pretty" but may cause cancer—are they kosher? And cigarettes, which we already know cause cancer, heart disease, and other health problems—are they kosher and pure?[30]

—*First Steps to a New Jewish Spirit*, 49–50

BODY AWARENESS

Awareness of your actual body experience is one of the most important keys to spiritual work. Windows to this awareness are built into the tradition. For example, after you go to the toilet and relieve yourself, there is a blessing for the successful completion of this most elementary and necessary act: "I worship you God. You are a cosmic God. You made me with passage and duct, vein and orifice. You made me wisely. If one of those were

30. Reb Zalman's pioneering work on *eco-kashrut*—a blend of traditional and contemporary ethical and legal considerations—helped lead to heightened awareness and concrete action across the Jewish spectrum. His student and colleague, Rabbi Arthur Waskow, has also been a crucial voice in this effort. See, for example, Waskow's book *Down-to-Earth Judaism: Food, Money, Sex, and the Rest of Life* (New York: William Morrow, 1995).

clogged, or if it seeped and leaked, I could not live and breathe, eat, or eliminate. In less than an hour I would be dead. So when it all works right, I am amazed at your goodness and your wisdom. And I worship you, Healer of my body, amazing us with daily wonders."[31]

From this blessing, you get a sense of the body's involvement in spiritual work and its role in the natural processes of the universe . . .

The recognition that it is a *mitzvah* to take care of the vehicle which is the body[32] should be one of your first recognitions. For this reason, we must stress again that any work done in the area of your spiritual consciousness *must* be preceded by care of the body. If not, your path becomes dangerous, because you are ignoring and overriding body signals. It's like driving your car when the oil pressure signal flashes red: the car *seems* all right, but you are burning out the engine. If your way of doing things allows you to override your body signals, you are very likely going to override the signals of the heart and of the mind. It is best to break this pattern as early as possible at the level of the body.

So tune in to your body. Listen to it. It comes from God and is one of the ways that lead back to the Divine.

—*First Steps to a New Jewish Spirit*, 42–44

A BODY ATTUNEMENT EXERCISE

Try this exercise: sit in a comfortable chair. Get the feel of how the chair is supporting you. Now, starting with your head, check out each part of your body for tensions, aches, or other forms the body's messages may take. Turn your head slowly from side

---

31. This blessing, known as *Asher Yatzar* (Who Fashioned), is also included in the traditional, daily Blessings Upon Rising (*Birkhot Ha-Shahar*).

32. See, for example, Maimonides, Mishneh Torah, Book of Knowledge, Laws of Personal Conduct, ch. 4. See also *Jewish Voices, Jewish Choices: Body*, edited by Elliott N. Dorff and Lewis E. Newman (Philadelphia: Jewish Publication Society, 2008).

to side, looking back over your shoulders. After turning it a few times, rest your head on your neck and shoulders in such a way that you don't have to carry it consciously.

When your head is balanced, take a deep breath and let it out. Now check your shoulders. Are they just hanging freely? Are your neck and shoulder muscles loose, resting easily on the frame of your body as it rests on the frame of your chair? (If you can't find a chair that is truly comfortable and suitable for this purpose, it is better to stand.)

Now ask yourself, "Are my shoulders resting on my spine? Is my spine resting on my pelvis?" And if you are sitting, "Is my pelvis resting on my buttocks, and is the chair carrying the whole thing, so I don't have to do anything?" Work at this until the answer to all the questions is yes.

Exhale deeply and ask yourself, "What stands between me and total physical well-being? Is my body humming with ecstasy, or is it informing me that there are still things to be taken care of?" It's important to remember that you are not looking for *ideas*. Remind yourself, "I am scanning that me which is my body for a signal—its most current message on my state of being."

Few of us reach an ecstatic sense of well-being on our first try, so don't worry if you're feeling something less than ecstasy at this moment. Just take a deep breath and repeat the process. Ask yourself, "What stands in the way between where I am now and the place where I'd feel that sense of well-being?"

Probably several answers will quickly come to you (eat better; get more exercise; lose weight). Don't seize on them, because in all likelihood they come from a preprogrammed and inappropriate place that will lead you away from the present moment. Go back to your *body* and let the answer well up from it: "What stands between me and well-being at this very moment?"

The answer has nothing to do with what you *ought to do* or what you *need to do* (responsibilities and obligations). It has only to do with what *your body is feeling right now*.

The message from your body will consist of a feeling which may or may not be translatable into words. If words do form, there will be only one or two. They are important words; try to remember them.

Next, ask yourself how to acknowledge the body's message. What has to be done about the words or feeling, so that your body will know you've gotten the message and that you intend to do something about it? What step is necessary to move from the place and condition in which you now are, past the obstacles indicated by your own body, to a place of well-being?

Wait for the answer. When it comes, it too will be a body sense, but it will concern something that can be done now (like, relax the muscles in your forehead; take off your shoes; release the tension in your calves).

When you have done this, check with your body once again. Has the action you've just performed taken care of the immediate problem? Is your body at ease, is it sighing ("A sigh is a break for one's body," said Reb Moshe Leib of Sassov [1745–1807])? Or is there still something else in the way?

If there is, repeat the procedure. Repeat it until your body is content, until every fiber and cell begin to hum. Repeat the process until your body is clarified and lucid, so transparent it seems to have disappeared.

When you have reached this state, you've given your body to God and your soul is sure to follow.

—*First Steps to a New Jewish Spirit*, 45–46

BREATHING THE DIVINE NAME

In the Kabbalah, the phases of breath also correspond to the letters in the Divine Name *(Y-H-V-H)*.[33] Visualizing the letters stacked one on top of the other, in a human form, try the following breathing meditation practice:

---

33. See Mark Verman, *The History and Varieties of Jewish Meditation* (Northvale, NJ: Jason Aronson, 1996), 111–30.

1. After an exhalation, when there is no breath left in your lungs, imagine the letter *Yod* of the Divine Name in the place of your head;
2. When you inhale and expand the lungs, imagine the upper *Heh* of the Divine Name in your shoulders and arms;
3. Now hold the breath in your lungs for a moment and imagine the letter *Vav* of the Divine Name in your spine;
4. Then when you exhale and deflate the lungs, imagine the lower *Heh* of the Divine Name in your pelvis and legs;
5. With the last exhalation complete, your lungs are empty, and you imagine the letter *Yod* of the Divine Name in the place of your head again, and you continue this breathing pattern through several cycles.

This powerful practice gives us a rhythmic awareness of *Y-H-V-H* in our very body and breath. To do this breathing meditation, and to become aware of one's own inner Divinity, is a great blessing.   —*Gate to the Heart*, 36

SACRED LOVE-MAKING

Making love in a sacred and committed relationship is the paradigm of the God-Israel relationship. Loving, intentional, and conscious relating is a *mitzvah*, a double *mitzvah* when hoping to beget children.[34] Kabbalists suggest that in making love

---

34. Having children is traditionally considered a *mitzvah* derived from the Torah—in fact, it is the very first *mitzvah* (and simultaneously blessing) given to the first human beings in Genesis 1:28: "Be fruitful and multiply." The Mishnah initiates the discussion of regular sexual relations as a

we visualize the *Yod* and *Heh* of the Holy Name in constant embrace, while the letters *Vav* and *Heh* are oneself and one's partner—the *Vav* generally being regarded as the male partner, and the *Heh*, the female. Reb Tzvi Elimelekh of Dynov [1783–1841] asks the question, "Why don't we make a blessing over the enjoyment of making love?" Since you cannot experience it without enjoying it, and to enjoy anything of this world without thanking God is not good. Therefore, he suggests that one should say in one's own language, "Thank you God for giving me a *mitzvah* which a person cannot complete without feeling pleasure."[35]

Allow that pleasure to connect you with God in your heart, taking your time with the anthem of embraces and kisses. The holy Ba'al Shem Tov taught us that, "It was revealed to me from Above that the reason for the delay of the coming of the Messiah is that people don't enter enough into the mystery of kisses before the great loving."[36] Connect the consciousness of kissing to the kisses given to *tzitzit, mezzuzah, Torah, tefillin*[37] and holy books.

When intending to bring a holy soul down into this world, pray that the Holy Blessed One and the *Shekhinah*, the Divine Presence [i.e., the transcendent and immanent or male and female dimensions of God], join you in the love-making. Visualize yourself in that heavenly sanctuary where Elijah the prophet connects parents and children [Malachi 3:23–24], and commit

---

mitzvah (called *mitzvat onah*) in its own right in Ketubot 5:6, https://www.sefaria.org/Mishnah_Ketubot.5?lang=bi. See also *Jewish Voices, Jewish Choices: Sex and Intimacy.*

35. This teaching is cited in the name of another contemporaneous Hasidic master, R. Tzvi Hirsch of Ziditchov (1763–1831), in Rabbi Simkhah Rabinowitz, *Piskei Teshuvot le-Shulkhan Arukh ve-Mishneh Berurah*, #240 (Jerusalem, Israel: 5762 [2001–2002] edition), 998 and n.18.

36. Cited by Rabbi Ya'akov Yosef of Polonoye (1710–83) in *Toledot Ya'akov Yosef*, Va-era (Jerusalem, Israel: *Agudat Beit Vaylifeli*, 5733 [1972–1973]), 143.

37. See the glossary for translations of these Hebrew terms.

yourselves to serving as hosts and educators to this new soul, to helping it in growing toward God.

After the descent from the holy union, give thanks in a fitting way and share with your partner some holy insight gained. When alone, offer your longing and yearning to God as a form of compassion with the *Shekhinah* and Her longing for union with the Holy Blessed One.[38]   —*Gate to the Heart*, 88–90

38. The notion that the female and male aspects of the Divine are separated and longing for reunion is a core teaching of the *Zohar* and many subsequent mystical texts. See, for example, Daniel C. Matt's translation and explanation of the text entitled "Secret of Sabbath" (*Zohar* 2:135a-b), in *The Essential Kabbalah: The Heart of Jewish Mysticism*, 80, and the explanatory notes on 189–90.

5

Jewish Renewal and Paradigm Shift

INTRODUCTION

Judaism is like an ancient tree. At the heart of any mature
tree is old wood. The old wood is crucial to maintaining
the tree's structure, its ability to withstand the changing winds, but no growth is going on there. The living
processes that are the *growth* of the tree, its message
to the future, take place only in the tree's newest and
outermost ring.   —*Jewish with Feeling*, 149

*Reb Zalman was fond of using the image of a tree's grow-
ing edge—which he adapted from his mentor, Howard Thurman—to describe the evolution of Judaism (and all other
traditions). While he loved many inherited ideas and forms—the
inner rings of the tree—he felt an urgent need to think creatively
about how to renew Judaism in conversation with the past and
the present. As he wrote, "The better we learn to listen to the
voices of the past, the more we can learn of ancient wisdom
that, with a little imagination, is still precious and applicable
today." But, as he adds, there are some things "the past cannot
teach us."[1]*

---

1. *Jewish with Feeling*, 149–50.

Reb Zalman *also made regular use of the term* paradigm shift, *a term popularized by the philosopher of science, Thomas Kuhn (1922–96).[2] In Reb Zalman's adaptation of this term, he sought to communicate the need to adapt Jewish thought and practice in light of such recent devastating events as World War II and the Holocaust as well as a series of constructive developments, including the Hippie, Feminist, and Environmental Movements.*

Beginning in the mid-1960s, he grew steadily from acting, in his own words, as an Orthodox restorationist to a heterodox renewalist. Renewal, he stated, requires one to carefully reflect on the worldviews and experiences of past Jewish actors—legalists, philosophers, mystics, and liturgists—asking why they did what they did, and if their religious responses remained compelling in the current age or paradigm. *Reb Zalman readily admitted that this was necessarily a disruptive and iterative process, requiring thoughtful experimentation—some of which would not stand the test of time. This is why he often referred to those engaged most intensely in the project of renewal as members of the Jewish avant-garde, whose explorations would, sooner or later, impact the community as a whole.*

One can hear in this description echoes of Hasidism and prior Jewish mystics but also the influence of Mordecai Kaplan and prior religious and philosophical pragmatists. While the early Hasidim challenged certain ideational and social conventions, they generally remained thoroughly committed to traditional halakhah *(Jewish law and practice), despite the claims of some of their opponents. Kaplan, on the other hand, was much more radical when it came to law and practice, advocating for informed democratic processes.[3] Reb Zalman largely agreed with Kaplan albeit from a mystical theological perspective rather than Kaplan's naturalistic (or transnaturalistic) vantage point.*

---

2. See Thomas Kuhn, *The Structure of Scientific Revolutions* (Chicago: University of Chicago Press, 1962).

3. To learn more about Kaplan, see Mel Scult, *The Radical American Judaism of Mordecai M. Kaplan* (Bloomington: Indiana University Press, 2013).

Reb Zalman referred to his own approach to Jewish praxis as psycho-halakhah (some of his students later called it integral halakhah). As his first musmakh (ordainee) and longtime colleague, Rabbi Daniel Siegel, writes, "It means a [halakhah] which incorporates and accepts the validity of personal experiential data in determining what changes from past practice have value." As Rabbi Siegel adds, this approach to Jewish practice also recognizes that "we are all now Jews by choice [a term usually used for converts to Judaism] and our communities are voluntary ones."[4] Finally, as Reb Zalman insisted, the introduction of the category of psycho-halakhah does not replace all previous Jewish legal proceedings but is meant to simultaneously include and transcend these discussions and rulings.[5] Reb Zalman understood the complexity of this project, and the delicate balance between continuity and innovation that it called for. Not surprisingly, his attention to the need for balance between the two became more acute in his later years, as the Jewish Renewal Movement he seeded grew and began to have a more significant impact on the Jewish community as a whole. He called on his students (and their students) to be bold in their convictions and cognizant of the fact that they are an organic part of k'lal Yisrael (greater Israel), just as Jews are a part of the larger human community.[6]

ANCESTRAL WISDOM

Many of us are looking for roots today, feeling disconnected from our traditions by the fragmentation of contemporary life. We've lost our sense of being legitimate members of the universe; we feel like strangers passing through someone else's territory.

---

4. Reb Zalman spoke of the need to develop a "consensus of the committed" among renewal practitioners to establish shared norms and to consult on contemporary dilemmas and future possibilities. See, for example, *Integral Halachah: Transcending and Including*, 36–38.

5. Ibid., iv.

6. Ibid., 66–68.

But this disorientation is not a necessary feature of modern life. There are ways to anchor ourselves, ways to regain a sense of belonging. One . . . [vital way to do so] is to reacquaint ourselves with our ancestral legacies.

It is important to know where we're coming from in order to understand where we are, and perhaps even where we are going. This requires a look backward into the past of our ancestors. The exploration is not without risk—there is always the danger of being trapped and tyrannized by the past. People sometimes slip into the assumption that whatever was done back then was the real thing; if it was good enough for them, it's good enough for us; give me that old time religion! These are the sentiments of the fundamentalists, but they are not the sentiments we are talking about here.

When we look back at our ancestors, our aim is not to be locked into the past. We want to use the past as a reference point, a source of tradition, and a living history so that we will be able to see ourselves as links in a long chain of continuity.

If we open ourselves to the potential impact of our ancestors and allow ourselves to be influenced by the accumulated experience of the Jewish past, we begin to tap a great source of energy. This energy, in one form or another, is readily available, but many people ignore it or pretend it doesn't exist.

To get in touch with it, we must project ourselves into the experience or frame of mind of our ancestors. This is easier than it sounds, for in practice what we have to do is follow certain procedures or perform certain acts in the style our ancestors have used for thousands of years. When we do this (and let's say we go back around 3,000 years to the time of Moses), we contact and, in some way, resurrect at least one hundred generations of ancestors behind us and within us.

A hundred generations represent an immense mountain of human experience; the encounter creates a very real impact. If you view your ancestors as a pyramid—two parents, four grandparents, eight great-grandparents, sixteen great-great-grandparents, 2,048 great-great-great-great-great-great-great-great-great grandparents (eleven generations)—and if you tap the energy concentrated at the tip of the pyramid, which is your location, you can begin to make use of your birthright.

It's the anniversary of your grandfather's death, his *yahrzeit*, when tradition requires the lighting of a twenty-four-hour candle and the recitation of the mourner's prayer for the dead. Sometimes you have a strong sense of your grandfather's presence, but usually this feeling occurs spontaneously, or is evoked by an accidental, unplanned chain of associations. This day, however, when you feel a special need to be in touch with your grandfather, he is not very present. So you make a conscious effort.

You think about him, try to remember what his voice sounded like, or the aroma of his body when he hugged you, or some other intensely personal feature. Then you look around for a memento, an object your grandfather used—a wine cup, penknife, prayer book, watch fob. You pick up the object, handle it, and in some way which you cannot entirely understand, a connection is made. Perhaps the physical object jogs your memories. Perhaps something of your grandfather has been absorbed by the object.

But whatever the cause, the experience remains. Once again, you feel close to him, and perhaps you also feel some sadness that he is no longer alive. But beyond your grandfather, in fact *by way of him*, you also feel connected to the pyramid of all your ancestors in a very conscious way. You feel rooted and grounded, and full of an energy and strength that comes from a sense of continuity and belonging. Your grandfather was the source of one quarter of your *you*, your *being*, so the grandfather within you always has the power to energize you.

The search for roots is a perfect metaphor for what people want. Roots connect us with our environment and absorb nourishment from it. In their quest to reconnect with their roots and find their legitimate places in the universe, many people open themselves to experiences and rituals from which their ancestors derived meaning and ecstasy. For Jews, one of the strongest of these stimuli is the sound of the *shofar*, the hollow ram's horn that is blown on certain holy occasions. When a Jew hears the call of the *shofar*, it is a rich, many-layered experience encompassing a wide range of feelings. When we are in earshot, this ancient sound pierces our thoughts, our feelings, the very core of our being. It raises goosebumps on our souls. This is because we hear it with our own ears and also with the ears of our great-grandparents and great-great-grandparents.

At times like this, when we touch a live wire of tradition, something mysterious takes place, something we cannot name or rationally assess. These experiences are the kinds of phenomena that [Carl] Jung (1875–1961) and many anthropologists have talked about, though they too have had no explanation. The moments remain mysterious, but their authenticity is undiminished.   —*First Steps to a New Jewish Spirit*, 51–53

JEWISH RENEWAL

As a HaBaD-Lubavitcher Hasid in the 1950s and '60s, I was breathing the same Existentialist air as Martin Buber and others, but with a difference: I still belonged to the traditional Orthodox world of the Hasidim. So I was one part religious Existentialist and one part Orthodox Restorationist. As a HaBaD-Lubavitcher Hasid, my writings in academic journals were mostly apologetics, and in my talks, I preached the restoration of the vitality of the Orthodox Jewish tradition.

Over time, I graduated that position and evolved what I call a "renewal" perspective. You see, Hasidism was once on the growing edge of the Jewish tradition, a radical movement[7] attempting to vitalize its relationship with God. Conservatives always want to be in the center, where things are safe; but as with a tree,

---

7. Scholars continue to debate just how *radical* the founders of Hasidism were (or in what ways they were radical), and when and why they upheld, challenged, and revised earlier and contemporaneous ideas and practices. See, for example, the opening section (chapters 1–9) of *Hasidism: A New History*, edited by David Biale et al. (Princeton, NJ: Princeton University Press, 2018).

the center is dead matter; the *livingness* is on the growing edge. Clearly, Hasidism used to be on this vital edge; but over time, as movements often do, it opted for the centrist position of safety and preservation.

Restoration is basically a centrist position and seeks to hold onto a dying paradigm, to pound the square block of the past into the round hole of the present. In contrast, renewal embraces new paradigms without abandoning our sacred and cherished traditions. Renewal realizes that it is not necessary to toss tradition out with its outworn cosmologies.

Today, we are privy to information that floods us with wonder at a rich and evolving cosmos, and we do not want to pawn our intellect and what we know from science for the price of staying wedded to the traditions of the past. We look to fulfill our spiritual needs, as experienced in the present, with a maximum of tradition; but in order to make this happen, we have to retro-fit our spiritual technology to the demands of our era, being sensitive to feminism, expanded notions of human potential, and ecological thinking.

Nor is there anything particularly new about renewal. It has been going on from the beginning. Anything that is alive renews itself continually. But there is also the teaching in Judaism that says that nothing has changed since Sinai.[8] That is the architectural point of view. Many of the Orthodox Hasidim insist that nothing has changed in Hasidism, and thus have put a lot of their energy into rebuilding and transplanting the old *shtetl*

---

8. One example of this type of thinking is the interpretation of Exodus 24:12 attributed to Rabbi Shimon ben Lakish in the Babylonian Talmud, Berakhot 5a (https://www.sefaria.org/Berakhot.5a?lang=bi) in which he claims that at Mount Sinai, Moses was not only given the Ten Commandments but the Five Books of the Torah, the entire TaNaKh (Hebrew Bible), as well as the Mishnah and the Talmud. See Abraham Joshua Heschel's discussion of this and other rabbinic visions of the revelation at Sinai in his classic work, *Heavenly Torah: As Refracted through the Generations*, edited and translated by Gordon Tucker with Leonard Levin (New York: Continuum International Publishing, 2006), 563–68.

(village) of Eastern Europe in a modern Jerusalem and New York. But what is interesting is that they did not exactly rebuild it—*they improved it*—like in a movie where all the cars from the 1950s are shiny and clean. If you have ever seen pictures from the *shtetl*, some of the *shtreimel*s [fur hats] were pretty ratty. But just look at the *shtreimels* today; they are all beautiful and nicely shaped. In the *shtetl*, the buildings were often ramshackle; but today, they are pristine. Clearly, they did not have it as good in old Zolkiew[9] as they have it now in Brooklyn! So even restoration is a minor renewal.

Jewish Renewal as a movement is basically the *avant-garde* of a more inclusive and far-reaching paradigm shift. When Reconstructionist Judaism first arrived on the scene, many people were saying, "We don't want to hear about it; it's new; we don't want to have anything to do with it." But today, even in Orthodox settings, they are having bat mitzvahs [which Mordecai Kaplan first inaugurated for his own daughters]. And it is similar with Jewish Renewal. Go to the Holy Wall *(Kotel)* in Jerusalem and you will see people wearing the "rainbow *tallit*" I designed, people who have no idea where it came from, and if they had an idea, they might not wear it! Or they will be singing Reb Shlomo Carlebach's melodies without knowing anything about the unconventional spiritual figure who wrote them. That is simply how it is.

Hasidism, though rooted in a past paradigm, is an eminently usable model for Jewish Renewal. In many ways, Hasidism was also well ahead of its time, taking a *sui generis* approach to Judaism without throwing anything out.

—*Wrapped in a Holy Flame*, Introduction

RENEWAL IS PARADIGM SHIFT

As consciousness evolves over time and the world changes, traditions must reclaim their primary teleological impulse in order to adapt to the needs of the evolving consciousness. This process

---

9. The Ukrainian (then Polish) town in which Reb Zalman was born in 1924.

of unfolding within and adapting without, we call "renewal." Renewal itself is characterized by the struggle to marry the *magisterium* of a religious tradition, i.e., its inherited body of knowledge and wisdom, to a new reality map or paradigmatic understanding of the universe. On a small scale, renewal is happening continuously; but it is also a process that we witness on a larger scale in certain epochs or axial moments in history,[10] like ours, when religions and religious forms are breaking down and slowly re-organizing and re-forming over time.

An awareness of this process can help to keep our current religions and spiritual traditions healthy. For as we engage and become aware of the process of renewal, we must re-evaluate our traditional spiritual teachings and practices, considering their "deep structures,"[11] analyzing their function in different historical periods to better understand how they might apply, or be adapted for use in our own time. This new understanding and adaptation allows us to utilize the maximum of our historical traditions, without at the same time turning a blind eye to the true needs of the present.[12]

—*Foundations of the Fourth Turning of Hasidism*, 17–18

THE STRUGGLE BETWEEN PARADIGMS

Now what happens between paradigms? For instance, what happens when polytheism is making the transition to monotheism . . .? When this is happening, the old paradigm starts to break down, and often a "battle" ensues between the old and new paradigms. Can you imagine the argument? "No, no . . .

---

10. The German philosopher Karl Jaspers (1883–1969) famously described the middle of the first millennium B.C.E. as an "Axial Age," a period of profound cultural change reflected in transformed spiritual consciousness throughout the world. See his book, *The Origin and Goal of History* (New Haven, CT: Yale University Press, 1953).

11. Noam Chomsky popularized this term in the 1960s. See his book *Aspects of the Theory of Syntax* (Cambridge, MA: The MIT Press, 1965).

12. This passage was authored by Netanel Miles-Yépez, but approved by Reb Zalman, whose thought it also represented accurately.

We're not going to have this god who looks like a human being. God is a bull!" This is why the Hebrew tribes made the golden calf after Moses disappeared on Mount Sinai [Exodus 32]; it was the comfortable "old-time religion" of that period.

Whenever we decide to let go of an older paradigm, there is always a struggle between those who say, "We have to do it just like our parents did it!" And those who protest, "We can no longer afford to do it the way our parents did it!" Both will insist that they are right, and the situation will get pretty tense. It is a battle between two competing paradigms. Those who are holding onto the old paradigm are tenacious and ask, "How do you know that you are right? We have time-tested material here; what do you have to support something new?" It is a good question.

There is always a point at which it becomes apparent to a new generation that the growth-cycle of the old point-of-view has reached its limit, and the greater organism needs to shed the old skin in favor of a new one. And during this process of "shedding," especially in religion, there is a moment between paradigms when people feel the need to go back to the primary experience that first gave birth to the religion. Because the question of the "old paradigmers" was right—"How do we know what is real and right if we can no longer trust the words that come from the past?" And the answer of those who are calling for a new paradigm is often, "Let us experience what our forebears experienced, and we will know for ourselves!" These people are gnostics, or "knowers," people who look for direct experience. The gnostic is wont to say, "Unless you experience it yourself, you don't know what you are talking about; because words are inadequate to describe it." The Sufis were gnostics, as were the Hasidim . . .

Now, in talking about paradigm shift, I am talking about a history of spirit, a history of mind that helps me take every writer of religious or spiritual material and acknowledge their accomplishment by going into that paradigm in which that individual appeared and taught. But then comes the question, "What good is such teaching today if it is obsolete?" The answer is that it is not obsolete. There is still a primitive part of us that acts as if polytheism, for instance, is the truth. Look at the stock market . . . is it a "bull" or a "bear" today? We see those energies in zoomorphic forms! Sometimes we act in the service of one or the other, and not necessarily in the service of the One.

When we touch a *sefer Torah*, a Torah scroll, and kiss it—I hesitate to say—there is something akin to idolatry in that act.[13] Of course, idolatry is not what we intend, but nevertheless, there is a tangible presence that we can hug, that we can kiss, with which we can interact! It is a powerful experience, and that pattern still lives in us.

There is also a dualism of spirit and matter that still lives in us. We have a sense that there is a difference between animal behavior and acting like a *mensch*, a spiritual being. We say, "Stop it! You're acting like an animal!" We aspire to "spirituality." Here again, we see that separation between spirit and matter living inside of us.

Today, we understand these paradigmatic holdovers in terms of "processes" and "functions," and ask ourselves, "What function is that holdover fulfilling?" Imagine you are feeling guilty about something you should not have done. If the Temple were still standing, you would bring a sacrifice. Imagine it in terms of the children's rhyme, "Mary had a little lamb." Wherever Mary went that "little lamb was sure to go." But when the Mary of that period did something bad, something that culture considered wrong, she had to take her beloved lamb to the Temple and say, "Dear God, I should have died for what I've done wrong, but I am offering this animal that I've nurtured in my stead."[14] Can you imagine what would be going on inside of Mary, seeing this animal sacrificed for what she had done, and then having to

---

13. See, "Why Do We Kiss the Torah?" in Chapter 5 of this volume.

14. See Nahmanides (1194–1270) on Leviticus 1:9, https://www.sefaria.org/Ramban_on_Leviticus.1.6?lang=bi.

eat a portion of it? It's unpleasant to consider; but that was how this act was understood then.

Now, if I were to ask myself, "What is it that I need to do to expiate my guilt today?" I can learn something from the process of sacrifice in that paradigm, as I just did. That is, reconstructing the function of the act in the past. That is what Mordecai Kaplan and the Reconstructionists originally intended, to see what the function of a particular behavior was in the past and try to re-create that same function in the present.

This is my thinking-tool, my mind operating system, for dealing with many religious issues. Each successive paradigm shift was considered heresy by the people who came before, and they judged their successors as wrong because they did things differently than was done in the past. That is why I say from that many people today are "driving by the rearview mirror." They are superimposing the past onto the present and heading for an accident.

—*Wrapped in a Holy Flame*, Introduction

THE ESSENTIALIZING OF JEWISH RENEWAL

Because of the paradigm shift that has occurred in religion today, most of the world's spiritual traditions will no longer be able to do "business as usual." All of us have to adapt. The hard and fast changes that have occurred in recent history, science, and society, have made it necessary for us to alter our traditions. But this also requires a keen understanding of what is essential to them, and what is superfluous.

The conscious changes we make to our religions today cannot be made without sophistication. It is simply foolish to do so; for, unless the deep structures and functions of a religion are understood, and truly appreciated, a mere cutting away of the bulk is not going do the job. A tradition which does not admit of both conservation and change will be dead and gone.

Some have tried to do this in Judaism in recent history, and being rationalists, ended up cutting the heart out of Judaism. While others, favoring the heart over the head, have tried to remove reason and the intellect. Neither camp respected the holistic "organicity" of the tradition in their process. There are others out there who would like to see a return to the "yesteryear" of Judaism; but we cannot afford to deny how our situation has changed and evolved. And yet, neither can we deny that Judaism has deep historical roots and a remarkably diverse *magisterium*.

The 20th century Indian philosopher, Sarvepalli Radhakrishnan (1888–1975), sums up the situation perfectly when he writes:

> The only revolutions that endure are those that are rooted in the past. We can make our own history, but we cannot do so at will, in conditions of our own choosing. Culture is tradition and tradition is memory. The duration of this memory depends on the continuous appearance of creative personalities.[15]

Those "creative personalities" are the ones who will adapt the tradition to new circumstances, endowing it with a new meaning . . . For it is only by taking-over and re-interpreting elements of our own *magisterium* that our tradition will survive in this new atmosphere. How can we make a Judaism for the future? We need to understand more of the function of what we do in Judaism and be less concerned with the details of how we do it. We also need to find better uses for our current social units.

What is the function of *tzimtzum* (Hebrew for "contraction" or "concentration")? . . . How many oranges would you have to eat in order to get the amount of vitamin C contained in one tablet of vitamin C? Probably many more than you could eat in one sitting. That is a *tzimtzum*. It does away with the bulk and ephemeralizes the essence.[16]

---

15. Sarvepalli Radhakrishnan, *Religion and Society* (London: George Allen & Unwin, 1969), 113.

16. *Ephemeralization* is a term coined by R. Buckminster Fuller (1895–1983) to describe the human ability to progressively accomplish more with less through developing technology, which he saw as a progression from

Imagine a fertilized ovum. In it is the *tzimtzum* of a human being. Likewise, an acorn is a *tzimtzum* of an oak tree. *Tzimtzum* contains the seed of growth, as well as the seed of further seeding. For Jews, the Passover *seder* is also a *tzimtzum*, an attempt to teach the seed-light of Judaism in just one night, in one incredibly dense transmission! We take the most abstract notions of freedom and divine providence and reduce them to sociemes we can repeat each year in a new setting. Then we see how much is carried over to the next year, and the next generation. If you look at why most Jews are Jews today, it is likely that you will find a Passover *seder* somewhere in their past that, even in the most anemic form, contained in itself much of the larger message of Judaism.

Now, in the same way, if we would make Jewish Renewal more effective, we need to be able to make a *tzimtzum* of it. We have to become more and more effective in making transmissions of Jewish Renewal.

In the distant past, if you wanted to write a book, it would take a great deal of time, and a lot of costly materials. Think of all the people that had to be involved in producing the materials and the content of a holy book in the past. There was a whole social pyramid of people involved in one way or another. It took a village! And these kinds of pyramids produced much inspiring and wonderful material. But it is not going to work in the same way for us.

We need to create smaller, less time and space-consuming systems and tools, while ever increasing our effectiveness. We need to be able to pack more information and God-consciousness into smaller ergs of expended energy.

Yet each change we make in this direction must also be considered with an eye to its consequences. For instance, we can afford to have a Passover *seder* once a year, but we can't afford to have one every week. It wouldn't be Passover any more if we

---

the material to the increasingly abstract. See Fuller's *Nine Chains to the Moon* (Garden City, NY: Anchor Books, 1971), 252–59.

had it every week; part of its power comes from having it only once a year.

However, the functions of our everyday spiritual life have to be made more and more effective in order to work for us today. Every aspect of life—our use of time and energy—has to become more effective than it has been up to now. We have to take the 613 *mitzvot*, our inherited God-connections,[17] and bring about a *tzimtzum* with them also. This is hard to say, but there are just too many details in them. But when we ask—how are we going to make a Judaism for the future? Then it is clear that we have to ephemeralize the container. And who is going to handle that? Are we going to wait for a new revelation from above? . . .

The challenge is to take our tradition into our own hands now, and to make a *tzimtzum* of it for ourselves and future generations.

—*God Hidden, Whereabouts Unknown,* 49–53

TEFILLIN IN THE NEW PARADIGM

Here, we offer a concrete example of Reb Zalman's psycho-ha-lakhic or integral thinking. Given his love for prayer, we have chosen a reflection on tefillin, *the prayer boxes traditionally worn on head and arm during weekday morning prayer services (and minor festivals). This text also illustrates Reb Zalman's do-it-yourself spirit, which is reflected in his design of the rainbow* tallit *and others of his creative projects. The selections in the previous section on* eco-kashrut *and Shabbat practice in*

---

17. The Hasidic masters are fond of the teaching that the Hebrew word for commandment, *mitzvah*, is related to the Aramaic *tzavta* (based on common roots and sound) meaning "bind" or "be together." Through the intentional fulfillment of a sacred deed, the devotee can come closer to God (the Commanding One, *Metzuveh*). See, for example, Rabbi Menahem Mendel of Vitebsk, "Fear and the Divine Will" (*Peri ha-Aretz, Noah*), in *The Religious Thought of Hasidism: Text and Commentary,* translated and edited by Norman Lamm (Hoboken, NJ: Yeshiva University Press/KTAV Publishing House, 1999), 107–8.

contemporary life are also good examples of his approach to Jewish ritual exploration and innovation.

When I look at the rulings and practices that have to do with *tefillin*, my sense is that this is a place where the consensus may soon shift. We now find that there are good kids about to become bar or bat mitzvah, who don't want to have *tefillin* made from leather that costs an animal its life. Adults as well, who want to take on the practice of wearing *tefillin*, often share this difficulty. But, according to tradition, you can't do it any other way[18] . . . So my sense is that we need to be prepared for this . . . consensus to shift.

I do not think that this shift will begin from the head, meaning from formally constructed arguments made by knowledgeable leaders, which will then spread to the people. Rather, I think it will start from grassroots experiences and experiments as people look to deepen the meaning of their practice.[19] For example, people who like to work with wood will find suitable precious hard woods from which they will make their own *tefillin* boxes. This is no less a renewable resource than animal skin, and by choosing the forest from which the wood comes, these *tefillin* boxes can serve as a special connection to the ecology of that particular place. In so doing, the boxes themselves will reinforce the message of the second paragraph of the *Shema* (Deuteronomy

---

18. Rabbinic tradition understood the Torah as requiring *tefillin* to be made from the skin of kosher animals. See Babylonian Talmud, Shabbat 108a, https://www.sefaria.org/Shabbat.108a?lang=bi. See also Louis Isaac Rabinowitz, "Tefillin," *Encyclopedia Judaica*, 2nd ed., vol. 19, edited by Fred Skolnick and Michael Berenbaum (New York: Thomson Gale, 2007), 577–79.

19. This comment brings to mind the ancient sage Hillel's instruction to his colleagues that it is important to observe how common people enact a particular *mitzvah* when the sages do not have a precedent in hand (Babylonian Talmud, Pesahim 66a, https://www.sefaria.org/Pesachim.66a?lang=bi). Reb Zalman clearly goes further here, suggesting that even when knowledgeable leaders have a firm grasp of a law or norm, grassroots practice can create change and shift consensus.

11:13–21), which so many of us now see as a call to ecological responsibility.[20] And, while I can't at this moment see how to do this, it would be interesting to think of making ceramic *batim* (houses or boxes for *tefillin*). What is easier to imagine is boxes and straps made from natural fiber cloths.

There are other possibilities that are closer to the classical approach and may be acceptable to many people. One is to use the skins of animals which died of natural causes, rather than being slaughtered.[21] I also realize that old *tefillin* were made from rawhide, from which one can do many things not possible with tanned leather. We now have the technology to make leather from used *tefillin*, chop it up finely, and take these leather particles and put them together again using the same hydraulic press that produces the regular *batim* for *tefillin*. I would love to see all these possibilities explored.

For a period of time, I think the most important thing is to encourage people to experiment without needing to commit to any particular approach. For example, what would it be like for someone to write out the *parshiot* (portions of the Torah that go into the *tefillin* boxes) by herself? Perhaps she would choose to write them on recycled paper, rather than parchment, or even on paper that she made herself. Can you imagine the power of first contact with *tefillin* if a bar mitzvah *bokher* ("boy" in Yiddish)

20. This biblical text speaks of a direct, causal relationship between obedience to God's statutes and divine reward and punishment through rain patterns and crop growth. Reb Zalman and others have called on contemporary practitioners to think in more organic or *karmic* terms about human behavior and ecological consequences. See Reb Zalman's translation of this portion of the *Shema* in his siddur, *Sh'ma': A Concise Weekday Siddur for Praying in English,* edited by Netanel Miles-Yepéz (Boulder, CO: Albion-Andalus, 2012), 27–30.

21. As Reb Zalman implies, such skins (as long as they are derived from kosher animals) are acceptable for *tefillin* according to classical legal sources. See, for example, Babylonian Talmud, Shabbat 28b and 108a (https://www.sefaria.org/Shabbat.28b?lang=bi, https://www.sefaria.org/Shabbat.108a?lang=bi). See also Aryeh Kaplan, *Tefillin* (New York: Orthodox Union/National Conference of Synagogue Youth, 1993).

were required to learn how to make paper from fibers of cloth and then to inscribe the words of the *parshiot* of the *tefillin* on that paper, and finally sealing them inside the boxes himself?

While these experiments would result in finished products that are departures from classical *halakhah*, they would restore the traditional personal connection to this practice. If, in the end, this experimentation allows a new consensus of the pious to emerge, which expands the range of acceptable *tefillin*, then so much the better. If it doesn't, it will at least raise awareness of this powerful practice. For all the above, what I am saying is that it's not an issue of waiting for someone else to give you permission to try something. Once people have actually experimented with other ways and have reported on their experiences then the practice will begin to shift. I myself would like to put on such a pair of *tefillin* to see what happens when I *davven* with them.

—*Integral Halachah*, 70–72

DENOMINATIONALISM AND RENEWAL

Nowadays, we generally understand "denominations" through a range of liturgical form, theological orientation, and social status, dividing the polity of congregations and their affiliations according to a spectrum, or a continuum extending from the most secular and humanistic elements of the Jewish populace to the most religiously observant elements, those who are often called, Ultra-Orthodox.

In an article I wrote over twenty years ago,[22] I already claimed that this continuum is *not* the continuum on which Hasidism and Kabbalah operate. Hasidism and Kabbalah are perpendicular to the continuum that goes from Humanism to Ultra-Orthodoxy. There is a dimension of seriousness, a piety in which the reality of God is taken into deep consideration, that applies

---

22. Zalman Schachter-Shalomi, "Neo-Hasidism and Reconstructionism: A Not-Only Imaginary Dialogue," reprinted in *Paradigm Shift: From the Jewish Renewal Teachings of Reb Zalman Schachter-Shalomi*, edited by Ellen Singer (Northvale, NJ: Jason Aronson, 1993), 63–73. 127–33.

equally, whether one is praying from the Reform *Union Prayer Book* or *davvenen* out of traditional *siddur* with an Ultra-Orthodox *minyan* in Me'ah She'arim . . .

So where does Jewish Renewal fit into the current continuum, including secular Jews, humanistic Jews, Reform Jews, Reconstructionists, Conservative Jews, and the entire palette of Orthodox Jews? Do we need to understand renewal as a new denomination? It is true that you will find congregations and *havurot* (informal prayer groups) that label themselves "Renewal," that there is an organization called, ALEPH: Alliance for Jewish Renewal (and congregations affiliated with it and its biannual *Kallah* (national "Gathering"), and that there is even an association of Renewal rabbis called, Ohalah. Nevertheless, my sense is that Jewish Renewal is a *process*.[23]

Of course, there are and will continue to be fellowships of like-minded people who wish to identify with that process and renewal values who will wind up naming themselves "Jewish Renewal," but I want to stress that aspect of Jewish Renewal which is, as I said, perpendicular to the continuum of denominations. After all, there are some Conservative congregations, and even some Reform and Orthodox ones, that will want to offer their members occasional Renewal-type services, or rabbis who will use various innovations born of the Renewal process [even if they do not know where they came from] . . . Far from being dismayed by this, I take it as an indication of how much the process of Renewal has penetrated into the continuum of Judaism and has reached the stage of common usage . . .

The more important issue behind the question of denominationalism is to be able to see everything as part of *K'lal Yisrael*, the entire community of Israel as an organic body. From that perspective, using the organismic model as a means of understanding an entire people, then it is clear that the diversity in the range of form and content within Judaism is necessary for the health of its body. And it is not only in relation to Judaism that

---

23. To learn more about this association of rabbis, cantors, and rabbinic pastors, visit https://www.ohalah.net/.

we need to see things *organismically*; one must also see Judaism as part of the planetary totality, with all religions, all people, and all life on this planet. In this way, I have been teaching that every religion is a vital organ of the planet. It would be absurd to expect that the entire body be made up of liver or heart. Rather, each organ of the planet needs to do its part for the healthy functioning of the other organs, and most of all for the health of the entire body. So every religion, in order to be healthy, is *interdependent* with all others. And within this vital organ of Judaism, the same necessities prevail.

—"Denominationalism and Jewish Renewal," 26–33

RENEWAL FOR ALL

Based on his extensive experience working in interreligious spaces and with seekers moving between spiritual communities, Reb Zalman developed a keen interest in questions of borders and bridges. One manifestation of this thinking was his suggestion that the Jewish Renewal community make creative use of the ancient concept of the ger toshav, *the resident alien. Using various biblical and rabbinic precedents, he sought to create a place for non-Jews (including the growing number of gentiles married to Jewish spouses and/or raising Jewish children) to participate in aspects of Jewish religious life without undergoing full conversion. Like other contemporary rabbinic figures, Reb Zalman was concerned both about welcoming non-Jews into the community with respect and care and preserving the integrity of this age-old tradition. This is reflective of his broader organismic religious vision, in which he speaks of the world's religions as distinct but interconnected parts of a global body. This requires each religion to maintain its distinctiveness, while also sharing vital nutrients.*

Rabbi Elijah Benamozegh (1822–1900), Livorno, Italy, was visited by Aimé Pallière (1875–1949), a man who grew up as a Roman Catholic and went on to embrace the way of the Salvation Army until later feeling an attraction to Judaism. Rabbi Benamozegh, who was an eminent Kabbalist as well as a legalist, counseled Pallière not to take on the full Jewish *halakhic* [legal] observance but to become an affiliate under the category of *Ger Toshav* [*"Resident alien," e.g., Deuteronomy 1:16*]. This is what he did and described in his book that was published in translation as *The Unknown Sanctuary* (1928).

I have encountered many people who would fit under the category of *Ger Toshav*. Dr. Jean Houston speaks of such people as "psycho-Semitic" souls. There are as many of them today as there were in the time when the apostle Paul traveled to invite them to join the nascent new branch arising out of Judaism.

When I wrote my book, *Jewish with Feeling*, I had a different working title: *If You're So Universal, Why Be Jewish?* If I were to check on the basic reality map shared by progressives, I'm sure I would find that many of them are in harmony with those who adhere to Jewish Renewal. We share the concern for the planet. We are no longer in the place where we see ourselves in a triumphalist vision. We recognize the impact of the spirit that rises from the earth and shapes the rituals and celebrations of different ethnic groups. We welcome them all as expressions of the Divine on the earth. The feminine mind holds for us the hope for some answers to the problems the masculine mind has created. Ecology is, for us, the major motivator for ethics and morality . . .[24]

---

24. Reb Zalman does not actually answer his own question about "Why Be Jewish" in this reflection. In the latter part of *Jewish with Feeling* and elsewhere, however, he argues that while there is much that is *generic* about religion, each tradition also possesses teachings, practices, institutions, organizing principles, and histories that make them substantively different. He believes that Judaism is a beautiful life path (one among many others) that should be practiced, studied, and renewed with care and creativity. This, of course, requires a committed and passionate collectivity working on this grand cultural project. At the same time, he feels strongly that Judaism does not only exist for those who identify exclusively as Jews but that it possesses resources that can be of great assistance to others seeking to live good and upright lives.

In this spirit, we want to issue an open invitation to those who would like to be affiliated with us in the generic religious[25] quest that seeks to heal the planet. We would like to share some of our spiritual and social tools for generating value experiences in the family.[26] We want to make the rabbis and congregations of Jewish Renewal open to the participation of affiliates in such ways as will not disturb our own social "community-immunity" response.[27]

In Jewish Renewal we have fostered social settings that create a safe and sacred space and allow for lively rhythmic chanting and speaking as well as for shared contemplative silence.[28] We have also updated the liturgy. All of this makes for engaged participation and creates a context for development of conscience, which makes for better moral and ethical decisions . . . This then is an invitation to people who feel an affinity for the distinctive

---

25. In using the term *generic religion* he means that many traditions share a range of common concerns, ideals, and aspirations, and have crafted their cultures using similar forms and structures. Of course, these traditions have also influenced one another (directly and indirectly) over the centuries.

26. Reb Zalman believed that among Judaism's most compelling teachings were family- and home-based ritual practices, including Sabbath and Passover rites.

27. Again, he is raising the question of how a Jewish community can be both open to outsiders while maintaining its distinctiveness. Rabbi Daniel Siegel and other leaders in the Renewal Movement continue to explore the category of *Ger Toshav*, accepting and challenging Reb Zalman's proposals. See, for example, Rabbi Daniel Siegel et al., "Renewing Ger Toshav: Opening the Gates that More May Enter to Praise God," Integral Halachah Institute of Aleph Canada, https://www.alephcanada.ca/catalogue#!/ RENEWING-GER-TOSHAV/p/80234570/category=5386144.

28. It is noteworthy that in describing some of the hallmarks of a Jewish Renewal prayer service, Reb Zalman mentions several practices that he and his students adapted eclectically from Jewish and non-Jewish sources. He was blessed to see various of his experiments grow into established traditions within and beyond the renewal community.

flavor of Jewish generic religion to affiliate with those congregations that will welcome them.   —*Unpublished*[29]

ISRAEL AT FIFTY

Reb Zalman wrote relatively little about the State of Israel, focusing much of his attention on developing a Jewish spiritual agenda for the North American life. As previous scholars have noted, Jewish Renewal is largely a diasporic phenomenon, (with some recent growth in Israel) with its unusual blend of Eastern European piety, American pluralism, and more.[30] Still, as a refugee from Nazi-occupied Europe and lover of Jewish religion and culture, Reb Zalman felt that the modern Jewish state offered the Jewish people both a safe haven and an unprecedented, and potentially sacred, opportunity to develop a Jewish and democratic society.[31] In keeping with his organismic model of human relations (and building creatively on previous Zionist thinkers such as Ahad Ha-Am (1856–1927) and Mordecai Kaplan), he believed that Jews in Israel and the diaspora should view themselves as one body, each playing distinct roles while sharing religious and cultural resources. In this piece (1998), he articulates his deep concern for the spiritual–ethical direction of contemporary Israeli society, both with regard to intra-Jewish affairs (i.e., Orthodox hegemony) and the Israeli–Palestinian conflict. While critical in his tone, he ends the article on a hopeful note (as he so often does in his teaching).

---

29. Unpublished text edited by Netanel Miles-Yépez for this volume.

30. See Shaul Magid, "Jewish Renewal Movement," in *Encyclopedia of Religion*, https://www.encyclopedia.com/environment/encyclopedias-almanacs-transcripts-and-maps/jewish-renewal-movement. See also Magid's "Jewish Renewal: Toward a New American Judaism," in *Tikkun* 21, no. 1 (January/February 2006): 57–60.

31. See Reb Zalman's comments in *Credo of a Modern Kabbalist*, including his affirmation of the Law of Return, providing Jews from around the world the right to Israeli citizenship. See ibid., 164–65.

Let me share with you some reflections as *Medinat Israel* [the State of Israel], on the threshold of the new century-millennium, is entering her fiftieth year, her first Jubilee or *Yovel*.

When our prophets spoke of the future, they gave us a vision of Zion and Jerusalem that is yet to be fulfilled, saying: "My house shall be a house of prayer for all people" [Isaiah 56:7]; "Even from them [the non-Jews] shall I [God] take priests and Levites" [Isaiah 66:21]; and, "Out of Zion shall come forth Torah, and the word of God from Jerusalem" [Micah 4:2]. This served as a wonderful vision of Israel as a flowing fountain, from which would come forth inspiration and a light that would proceed to the whole world . . .

Now that the Zionist ideal has found its realization in the State, what can we look forward to? Any move from an ideal to reality entails a certain amount of degradation; more shadow energy, what we call *kelipah* [shell or husk] in Jewish mysticism, begins to adhere. As long as a Jewish state was a dream, a myth, a hope, we saw the good and it looked to us that it could be sustained out of justice. But now that we meet it in palpable reality—Oy, does it need mercy.[32]

The myth that sustained us throughout our diaspora was that of the return. Now that we have returned and have a sovereign country, we have little to propel us into the future. We are scared mythless. It will take poets, dreamers, and mystics to reach into a yet unrealized future to dream the next story of our people.

---

32. This is a reference to the rabbinic and mystical notion that all of life requires a balance between justice (*din*) and mercy (*rahamim*). See, for example, Genesis Rabbah 12:15 (in reference to creation as a whole, https://www.sefaria.org/Bereishit_Rabbah.12.15?lang=bi) and 21:8 (in reference to the individual person, https://www.sefaria.org/Bereishit_Rabbah.21?lang=bi). See also the diagram of the ten *sefirot* in Daniel C. Matt's *The Essential Kabbalah: The Heart of Jewish Mysticism* (San Francisco: HarperCollins, 1995) (found between the Foreword and the Introduction), and his explanation of these attributes or potencies; ibid., 7–11. Reb Zalman returns to this theme later in this piece.

Without an active myth, a dynamic transpersonal story, Israel will be bereft of the invisible means of sustenance and support.

Herzl was more a futurist than many others. He wrote a novel, *Altneuland* ["The Old New Land" in German],[33] which was his stab at science fiction. In it he explored a European capitalist democracy and made room for non-Jewish Zionists. He still lacked, however, a forward-looking vision of what an Israel seated in the heart of the bridge between Asia and Africa could become in the global village.

The hopeful believer in me is not willing to give up. Seeing the hand of God in history, I trust that we will be led through these transitions: the dreams and visions will come, yet the labor and contractions are painful.

Without having an attractive vision of what is yet to come, we have created an Israel which now must face a daunting situation. Jerusalem is becoming more and more dominated by the ultra-Orthodox, to the point that some secular Jews are fleeing to other parts of the country. People in one enclave feel less connected with those of others, and even more at odds with each other in the same milieu. The *haredim* ["tremblers," as in Isaiah 66:2, ultra-Orthodox Jews] believe in an ultimate future in which they will triumph and prevail as a result of their *mesirat nefesh*, their tenacious sacrificial devotion.

Our Palestinian cousins have their own triumphalists as tenaciously contending that *Allah* has promised them that they will prevail. Both the *haredim* and these Palestinians have little understanding of the compromises necessary for a negotiated peace. So, we have two kinds of triumphalists confronting each other, unable to recognize that Israel is an experiment that cannot be called off. Providence has seen to it that the most difficult

---

33. Herzl published this utopian novel in 1902. It expands on ideas he articulated in his political pamphlet, *Der Judenstaat* (The Jewish State), six years earlier. Both are considered foundational Zionist texts. For a sampling of Herzl's writings, see *The Zionist Ideas: Visions for the Jewish Homeland—Then, Now, Tomorrow,* edited by Gil Troy (Philadelphia: Jewish Publication Society, 2018), 11–17.

partners that could be involved in this struggle had to wrestle with each another. When we have learned how to collaborate in peace at least as well as we collaborate in creating strife, we will have a model for others. The people in Rwanda and Bosnia and others all over the globe are waiting for the results of our experiment. The messiah we are waiting for is us: Israelis and Palestinians . . .

So all this is the dark side.

But if we could take Isaiah's future vision into the present, we could begin to think in very different terms: about a United States of the Middle East.[34] I draw a certain kind of hope from the collaboration that is already taking place between some groups in Jordan and Israel on the level of commerce. In hope, I extend that vision to other domains.

We have to move away from nationalism to an organ-based understanding—what I call an organismic understanding—of our place on the planet. We need some of each of the organs of the whole body of the Jewish people in Israel. It makes sense that we need the B'nai Yisrael from India and the Falashas from Ethiopia[35] in Israel along with the Edot Ha-Mizrah [those from North African and Arab lands] and the Ashkenazim [Eastern and Central Europeans]. We must be prepared to give up the idea that the Northern Hemisphere is the only decent place from which to learn, as if the Ashkenazim have the corner on wisdom.

---

34. Earlier in his career, Reb Zalman wrote about his dream of a federated Middle East (as part of a larger global governmental system), with independent states functioning with unprecedented economic, political, and cultural interdependence. In this vision, Jerusalem would become an internationalized city and the world capital of the United Nations. See his brief essays, "The Condition of Jewish Belief" (1966) and "Jerusalem and the Complete Redemption," written the following year "in response to the gathering clouds of the 1967 war"—both are available in *Paradigm Shift*, 117–25 and 75–78. See also Scott Kommel Meyers, "Religion of Reason in the New Age: Zalman Schachter-Shalomi, Hermann Cohen, and Messianic Politics" (master's thesis, University of Colorado at Boulder, 2017).

35. While this was a common designation for Ethiopian Jews at the time, they prefer the term *Beta Israel* (House of Israel).

At the same time, I don't think it's useful to think of Israel as our homeland as if we all were ever to live there. If we, who are in the diaspora, form a good part of the body of the Jewish people, then Israel is our heart . . . If you have an organismic understanding, you can see that we in the diaspora bring nourishment to the heart and we get nourishment from the heart. We are vitally important and necessary. The flow of vigor from us to Israel and from Israel to us can be seen like a circulation system.[36]

The Palestinians in the diaspora could also bring the wisdom of their experience to their community in the Holy Land. Among the Palestinians there are *yordim*,[37] émigrés, all over the globe. They too visit their home from time to time and need a way to keep their identity in their diaspora. So it is not an issue of *Lebensraum*[38] for either of us. Both sides need to recognize that we

---

36. As mentioned above, here, Reb Zalman builds on the views of previous Zionist thinkers who viewed the relationship between Israel and the diaspora Jewish community as symbiotic. This is different from classical or contemporary thinkers who view living in Israel as an elevated form of Jewish existence. One current outspoken proponent of this position is the (secular) writer A. B. Yeshoshua. See Troy's *The Zionist Ideas* for a detailed categorization of different forms of Zionist thought (political, cultural, diaspora, etc.).

37. *Yordim*, those who descend, is usually used to refer to Jews who have left Israel to live elsewhere. Related to the previous note, the term carries with it the theological legacy of undertaking a spiritual descent when leaving the Land of Israel. It is for this reason that those who emigrate to Israel are said to go on *aliyah*, ascent. Reb Zalman is purposely using this term inclusively here, to indicate that Palestinians, like Jews, view their relationship to the Holy Land as sacred or otherwise deeply consequential. One ongoing issue with Reb Zalman's vision is that international travelers cannot get directly to and from the West Bank and Gaza; they must go through Israel, Jordan, or Egypt, often having to navigate complicated political and security issues.

38. Living space (German). This term was used in the early twentieth-century to justify colonization. It is most strongly associated with the Nazis, who used it as the basis of their invasion of Poland and the desire to occupy Russia, removing *undesirable* populations from these territories. It

are not talking about land, but about cultural centers to which we and they could come, and then it would not make so much of a difference exactly where the territorial line is being drawn . . .

However, we cannot totally deny the reptilian brain, even if we wanted to. Every human being needs that part, even though we need the higher brain functions as well.[39] The reptilian brain connects us to the soil, and so we need *Eretz Yisrael* [The Land of Israel]. The chthonic [subterranean] power issuing from the dark places in our being that connect us to the voice of the earth cannot be denied, as the Jungians well understood.[40] There is some way in which the land itself nourishes our being, and we cannot abandon that connection. We cannot remain Jews for many generations without a connection to that particular piece of land.

Mythically we, as Jews, are tied into this land, and our very understanding of how we should live and be as Jews in the universe is organically tied into our connection to the Land of Israel. The calendar of Judaism is the most organismic one I know: it connects us both to the moon and the sun, it honors time and it honors the seasons . . .

The diaspora consciousness helped us to think in universal terms . . . We made a theology to fit our diaspora situation. But we always retained the prayer in which we call for God to return

---

became a cornerstone of their brutal nationalist–racist agenda. See https://encyclopedia.ushmm.org/content/en/article/lebensraum.

39. This is a reference to the triune brain model proposed by the American physician and neuroscientist Paul D. MacLean. The model, designed to describe the evolution of the brain, includes the reptilian complex, the paleomammalian complex (limbic system), and the neomammalian complex (neocortex). While the theory has been challenged over the years, it was used widely in lay contexts while Reb Zalman was active.

40. He is referring to the work of Carl Jung and his school in which there is extensive discussion about the relationship between mythology and identity, including the power of earth-based spiritual traditions. See, for example, C. G. Jung, *Jung on Mythology*, selected and introduced by Robert A. Segal (Princeton, NJ: Princeton University Press, 1998).

the *Shekhinah*, God's Presence, to dwell in the Holy Land.[41] We prayed for the transcendent God to become immanent in the Holy Land in Her feminine aspect (as the *Shekhinah*). In this vision, God would honor all of Her children (not just Jews), and thus "the Mother of many children is made happy" (Psalm 113:9) . . .

According to the Kabbalistic roadmap, the first fifty years is governed by God's attribute of forgiving loving-kindness (*hesed*), while the second *Yovel* is governed by limit-setting severity (*gevurah*).[42]

The next *Yovel* is the *Yovel* of *gevurah*, demanding a certain amount of self-control and a certain amount of *teshuvah* ("return," repentance). The mistakes that we made in Israel over all these past fifty years came into being in the context of a very forgiving matrix—that is part of what I mean by saying that the first *Yovel* was *hesed*. We didn't get slapped by instant karma when we did something wrong—we were in a forgiving environment. I don't think that is going to remain the case in the next fifty years. I think we are going to get some very quick karmic response, and that is *gevurah*. I think that we are going to face some harsh realities in the next fifty years that will massage us into being a better people (and that's the hopefulness in *gevurah*).

To envision this future, we will need nurturing womb-men and women. The way to overcome the difficulties of *gevurah* is through *rahamim*, compassion (from *rehem*, "womb"). We need to nurture the place of compassion in our dealings with the problems of the State of Israel. The key is to really validate the pain of whoever is on the other side. For Israel, that may be a nobler way to relate to the Palestinians. (Wouldn't it be wonderful if Jews could prepare food for Muslims during Ramadan, when they fast to honor their traditions, wouldn't it be wonderful if

---

41. This blessing is traditionally recited three times daily during the *Amidah* prayer. Similar sentiments can be found throughout Jewish liturgy.

42. To learn more about Kabbalistic cycles of cosmic rebirth, see Gershom Scholem, "Earlier Worlds, Lower Worlds, and Cosmic Cycles," in *Kabbalah* (New York: Quadrangle/New York Times, 1974), 116–22.

we could go to each other's circumcision ceremonies, sharing the legacy of Abraham as we do?) Any negotiation process must begin by recognizing the other and validating them for who they are. We must honor the other person first before anything that is to happen at the negotiating table is to work.

As Herzl said a century ago, "If you will it, it is not just a legend." May we see it in our day. Blessings to you in hope for the world's *tikkun* [healing].　　　　　—"Entering Israel's Second *Yovel*."

6

Hasidism and Neo-Hasidism

INTRODUCTION

While Reb Zalman traveled great distances from his early years as a HaBaD devotee, he remained a passionate student and teacher of Hasidism throughout his adult life. Broadly speaking, he sought to carry forth the devotional spirit of Hasidism into the New Age. Like the Eastern European mystical masters he so admired, Reb Zalman believed that prayer and meditation were foundational to the spiritual life, and that the goal of the seeker is to carry the insights and intentions of these sacred experiences into the rest of life. As the Ba'al Shem Tov and so many other Hasidic teachers taught, "There is no place devoid of God's presence" (citing the medieval work Tikkunei Zohar*); the challenge is to uncover the* holy sparks *in our midst, to discover the sacred in the mundane.*

Reb Zalman was also drawn to the pioneering spirit of the founders of Hasidism and their willingness to challenge certain established norms in an attempt to renew Jewish life, even in the face of harsh criticism and opposition. These mystical leaders served as models of spiritual integrity and communal responsibility for him. In fashioning his vision of Jewish Renewal, he gleaned creatively from these pioneering spirits, as well as from his masters and fellow Hasidim in HaBaD. His explorations of other Hasidic communities—Bratzlav and Bobov were particularly important—also informed his evolving religious vision. Neo-Hasidic figures such as Hillel Zeitlin, Martin Buber, and Abraham Joshua Heschel served as models of Jewish intellectuals who thoughtfully translated the beauty and depth of Hasidism for modern seekers.

Below, the reader will find a selection of Reb Zalman's teachings on Hasidism and Neo-Hasidism, including recollections of his Hasidic travels, interpretations of homilies and tales, and reflections on the relationship between Hasidism and Neo-Hasidism. Characteristic of his approach to various historical phenomena, Reb Zalman was most interested in the insights of the rebbes *and how these might apply to contemporary life. While he read some scholarly studies on Hasidism, he also made liberal use of legend and hagiography in trying to convey the ideals, aspirations, and yearnings—the* spiritual juice, *as he sometimes called it—of the masters and their disciples. We offer several footnotes throughout this section to help clarify specific historical and textual matters. As you read, you may wish to consider the descriptions of the relationship between master and disciple (*rebbe *and* hasid*) throughout this section (both classical and Reb Zalman's revisions of it). Does this model speak to you at all? Are there elements of it that might be translatable today? How does it compare with teacher–student or mentor–mentee relationships you have experienced?*

THE BA'AL SHEM TOV AND THE QUALITY OF *MAMMASH*

Israel ben Eliezer, the Ba'al Shem Tov, was born in 1700, lived sixty years, and passed away on the first day of *Shavuot* [Feast of Weeks, Pentecost] in the year 1760. He left no books and little documentary evidence of his existence. Nevertheless, his influence on his environment and future generations was immediate and profound. Indeed, the change he brought about in the people around him was nothing short of miraculous, leading to an explosion of spirituality that was ultimately to dot the map of Eastern Europe with his influence . . .[1] Who would have even noticed towns like Bratzlav or Lubavitch had they not become identified with important leaders of the Hasidic Movement?

What was it that set the Ba'al Shem Tov's teachings apart from the others who had come before him? Perhaps, more than anything else, it was the *mammash* quality of his spirituality, the "palpable" immediacy of his relationship with God. He used to quote Isaiah 6:3, saying, "The whole Earth is filled with God's glory," suggesting that God is available to everyone, everywhere, equally![2] What good is a God who plays favorites, or who merely created this world a long time ago, and has since been deaf, dumb and blind to us? . . . For the Ba'al Shem Tov, there were no accidents. To him, a tinker asking if one had pots and pans in need of repair was also the voice of Providence asking a person if they needed to repent . . . Revelation was available to the learned and unlearned alike. He looked constantly for ways to reunite the people of Israel with their God, often acting as the people's advocate.

—*Wrapped in a Holy Flame*, Preface

---

1. As noted in the introduction, The Ba'al Shem Tov (Master of the Good Name), was a mystical healer, teacher, and prayer leader in the Ukrainian town of Mezibozh. His shamanic talents (including the use of divine names in incantations and amulets) attracted both common folk and members of the elite. Several of his associates and disciples formed the nascent Hasidic movement, crediting him as the inspiration for their activities. To this day, the BeShT (acronym for Ba'al Shem Tov) is viewed by Hasidim as the founding father of the Movement, and by Jews the world over as a major religious personality. See Moshe Rosman, "Ba'al Shem Tov," *YIVO Encyclopedia of Jews in Eastern Europe* (2010), https://www. yivoencyclopedia.org/article.aspx/Baal_Shem_Tov.

2. Indeed, this phrase became a watchword in Hasidism and is repeated countless times by various masters. This teaching also stands in tension with the notion that the Hasidic master is a uniquely gifted and advanced spiritual being, who serves as a bridge between heaven and earth. See the collection of primary sources in and the editorial introduction to the chapter "Zaddik," in *The Religious Thought of Hasidism: Text and Commentary*, edited by Norman Lamm (New York: Yeshiva University Press/KTAV Publishing, 1999), 251–322.

THE DIAMOND-CUTTER HASIDIM

In the following text, Reb Zalman reflects on his first substantive experience with HaBaD Hasidism as a fifteen-year-old boy in Belgium. As he and his family fled the Nazis, he underwent a painful period of theological questioning and searching. While he continued to ask some of the same existential questions for years to come (see Chapter 1), he regarded his Antwerp experience as a spiritual awakening and touchstone, and his small group of coworkers a model for the communities he sought to create as both a Hasid and Neo-Hasid. It was through his association with this group that he later met the sixth and seventh Lubavitcher rebbes.

The next few months in Antwerp were among the happiest of my youth. Nazi Vienna had receded into the background. Every morning except for *Shabbat*, of course, I would join a group of young men in a large work room filled with special lathes. Diamond cutting is noisy work, and we would sit around a large table and often sing Hasidic melodies at the tops of our voices. At other times, one fellow would sit with a microphone and teach the Talmud while we all wore earphones and cut diamonds together. If someone had a question, he would give a signal, and the speaker would shut off the machines temporarily. The question would be answered, and then we would all continue with our work.

Although resembling a high-spirited *yeshiva*, it was also an ecumenical group. We listened to inspiring secular books such as *Jean Christophe*, by Romain Roland (1866–1944), and those by Anker Larsen (1874–1957), a Danish playwright and novelist. It was a wonderful school and workplace for me, and I enjoyed both the physical and spiritual aspects . . .

One *Shabbat* afternoon, I went outdoors with the HaBaD group. I felt something stirring within me and strolled off to be alone. In recent weeks, one key question had challenged and perplexed me: why is God hiding in the world?[3] I was filled with the mood of exaltation. It was strange at the time, but since then, I experienced it as a preparation for spiritual disclosure. Everything around seemed connected. A luminous brightness surrounded me, and now the answer became totally clear: God bestowed free will to us so that we might grow spiritually, and therefore this is how human life had to be. I felt exhilarated and suffused with a wonderful sense of wholeness and unshakeable faith. At that moment, I prayed with all my soul that God should not let me lose this insight. In a real sense, that epiphany in Antwerp has stayed with me ever since.

—*My Life in Jewish Renewal*, 30–31

TRANSLATING HASIDISM FOR TODAY

Years ago, when I first read William James' *Varieties of Religious Experience* (1902) and Aldous Huxley's *Perennial Philosophy* (1945), I was both thrilled and disappointed—thrilled at the beautiful parallels and similarities between traditions I found there, but disappointed to find that neither had much in the way of analogous teachings from the Jewish mystical tradition. There was an ache in my heart that Hasidism was not well represented in these popular books. It troubled me that the internal world of a Hasid was not available in English in a way that people could easily access.

How wonderful it would have been to discover the many little Hasidic teachings and stories that parallel those of other traditions in James' and Huxley's classic works. For instance, the

---

3. The Hasidic masters often speak of God "hiding in the world," using the older Jewish mystical notion of *tzimtzum* (contraction, self-limitation) to describe this theological perspective. See, for example, Norman Lamm (editor), "Chapter 1: God and Providence (specifically texts #14, 15, 16)," in *The Religious Thought of Hasidism: Text and Commentary* (Hoboken, NJ: Yeshiva University Press and Ktav Publishing House, 2003), 40–49. See an example of Reb Zalman's application of this term to the process of Jewish spiritual renewal in the text "The Essentializing of Jewish Renewal" in the previous chapter.

story of the man who came to Reb Menahem Mendel of Kotzk intending to vilify the local *shohet* (ritual slaughterer) over some trifle, and was surprised when the Kotzker Rebbe reprimanded him, saying, "Why are you so worried about what goes *into* the mouth, and not about what comes *out* of it?"[4] Now, I don't suppose that the Kotzker Rebbe was quoting the famous saying of Jesus (Matthew 15:10), or that he had ever even read the New Testament; nevertheless, it is the same teaching.

Even today, there is still a vast landscape of Hasidic literature and wisdom that remains untranslated and largely hidden from the world.[5] It is waiting for someone to come along and make it accessible to a new audience. And this is becoming more and more imperative as we all begin to emphasize the "hearts" of our respective traditions. There have always been people who were satisfied with the exterior of religion, for instance, with the exterior of Hinduism or Islam, while others have felt the need to go deeper, into the interior terrain of Vedanta or the Sufi tradition. Today, this need is being addressed by a stream of accessible translations from representatives of those traditions; but the interior life that Hasidism could produce, and has produced for many generations, has not yet been well represented for the general reader . . .

---

4. See the story entitled "Not What Goes in at the Mouth" in Martin Buber's *Tales of the Hasidim: Later Masters*, translated by Olga Marx (New York: Schocken Books, 1991), 229. There, the protagonists are two older mentors of the Kotsker Rebbe, Rabbi Jacob Isaac (The Holy Jew, c.1766–1814) and Rabbi Simhah Bunem (1765–1827).

5. While Reb Zalman is correct about the many Hasidic materials that await translation and explication, it should also be noted that there has been significant growth in this area (including digital resources) over the last several decades. This includes the work of Hasidic and Neo-Hasidic teachers and scholars, published by such entities as Habad (Chabad) and Bratzlav (Breslov), Jewish Lights and the Jewish Publication Society, as well as Paulist Press, Shambhala, and Albion-Andalus. He and his colleagues and students have played a major role in this ongoing effort.

I have lived most of my life as a Hasid, the disciple of three great *rebbes*,[6] studying the teachings of Hasidim and visiting *rebbes* all over the world. And yet, my perspective has also grown to include the perspectives of other spiritual traditions—Sufism, contemplative Christianity, Vajrayana Buddhism, and Hindu Vedanta—and has been deeply influenced by emerging scientific theories. Thus, I am not the Hasid I was fifty years ago. When I approach a Hasidic text of insight and meditation today, a teaching or a Hasidic tale, I measure it mostly according to my emotional reaction: *Does it inspire me? Does it open me to something deeper? Does it make my soul bigger or smaller?* I have the feeling that there are already enough religious teachings in the English language that make your soul smaller, and I have no intention of adding to them by translating them. Thus, I present to you my own distillation of the Hasidic inner world, as a person who is aware of the inner worlds of other religious paths and who also believes in a generic spirituality that pervades all spiritual paths, from Shamanism to Judaism.

—*Wrapped in a Holy Flame*, Preface

THE ECUMENICS OF THE BA'AL SHEM TOV

"Straightforward are the ways of God; the righteous walk in them, the wicked stumble" (Hosea 14:10). There are numerous (godly) paths, and God wishes to be served in all ways; sometimes in this way, sometimes in another. When a person finds their path blocked, this may mean that God now wishes to be served in another

---

6. In addition to his experience studying under the sixth and seventh Lubavitcher *rebbes*, Reb Zalman also visited other Hasidic communities in North America and Israel. The third *rebbe* he is referring to here is Rabbi Shlomo Halberstam (1907–2000), the third *rebbe* of Bobov. Rabbi Shlomo and his son, Rabbi Naftali Halberstam (1931–2005), rebuilt this Galician dynasty in the United States and elsewhere after it was decimated in the Holocaust. See David Derovan, "Bobov," in *Encyclopedia Judaica*, 2nd ed. vol. 4, edited by Fred Skolnick and Michael Berenbaum (New York: Macmillan Reference USA, 2006), 23–24.

manner. Do not despise anyone for their kind of service,
for all ways lead to God. (*Tzava'at Ha-RYBaSh*)

The *Tzava'at Ha-RYBaSh*, "Testament of the Rabbi Yisra'el
Ba'al Shem," is a book of prescriptions.[7] All Hasidic masters
gave prescriptions, usually a short set of notes written for their
disciples, as if to say, "If you want to be one of my disciples, follow these prescriptions," or "These are the things most necessary
at this time and age to bring one to balance."

In the *Tzava'at Ha-RYBaSh*, the Ba'al Shem Tov quotes the
prophet Hosea (14:10)—"Straightforward are the ways of God;
the righteous walk in them, the wicked stumble." [It does not
state] the "way of God," but the "ways" in plural. For sometimes, says the Ba'al Shem Tov, you find one path blocked and
another path open to you, or one path blocked for you, which
may not be blocked for another person. There are many paths
that lead to God; do not exalt any path above God.

When you translate this teaching into the discussion of religions and spiritual paths, it makes a lot of sense. Sometimes
paths are blocked for us that are open for others. Once, Reb
Shlomo Carlebach, of blessed memory, quoting the Ishbitzer
Rebbe [Rabbi Mordecai Joseph Leiner, 1801–54], pointed out
that for many Jews after the Holocaust, the path via Judaism
was "blocked" by the weight of this tragedy. Many of them
could not get close to God until they first took a detour through
other religions. So the teaching of "numerous paths" is relevant
for us today.[8]

---

7. While the title of this anthology suggests that it was written by the
Ba'al Shem Tov (*RYBaSh* is an acronym for Rabbi Yisrael Ba'al Shem Tov),
it is actually a collection of prescriptions (*hanhagot*) and aphoristic teachings primarily drawn from the teachings of his disciple, Rabbi Dov Baer,
the Maggid of Mezritch. It was first published in 1793; several editions of
the book (with some textual differences) have been printed since that time.
See, for example, *Tzava'at Harivash: The Testament of Rabbi Israel Ba'al
Shem Tov*, translated and annotated by Rabbi Jacob Immanuel Schochet
(New York: Kehot, 1998).

8. For a fuller version of this story, see *My Life in Jewish Renewal*, 179.

But the sentence goes on, "the righteous walk in them, the wicked stumble." The point is that even the nicest teachings can be subverted by someone who has the wrong attitude, or by the wrong application of them.[9] For example, imagine someone in an argument about scripture screaming vociferously, "You should love your neighbor as yourself!" [Leviticus 19:18]. That is such an inappropriate application for that sentiment.

The medium and the message have to fit together; but sometimes you find that the medium in which the message is delivered is not at all what it ought to be. To speak of kindness in an unkind way is a contradiction. This is how the wicked stumble in "the ways of God."

"The righteous," however, "walk in them." People are capable of finding and following the ways that suit them best, provided they do not stand still. There is a great Yiddish work by Menahem Boraisha (1888–1949) called *Der Geyer* (literally, "The One Who Walks"), whose dedicatory sentence is "Seven times will the righteous fall and yet rise" (Proverbs 24:16). Boraisha then quotes from Reb Shneur Zalman of Liadi—"The *tzaddik* (righteous one) is called one who walks" (*Tanya, Hinukh Katan*).[10] In walking, one does not stand still, the head bobs up and down, up and down. Even *halakhah*, the word for Jewish law, means "the walking." Thus, to be open and fluid, "walking," is the way of the Hasid. When one is static and certain of life's

9. Rebbe Nahman of Bratzlav also read this verse to mean that Torah teachings, improperly received, can distance a person from God or even act as a kind of "poison," despite the Torah's potential to be life-giving. See Rebbe Nahman's *Likkutei Moharan*, Volume 2, Lesson 91, edited and translated by Moshe Mykoff, annotated by Chaim Kramer (Jerusalem, Israel: Breslov Research Institute, 1999), 15:318–45. See also Babylonian Talmud, Yoma 72b, https://www.sefaria.org/Yoma.72b?lang=bi.

10. See the introduction to the second part of [Schneur Zalman of Liadi, *Likkutei Amarim—Tanya: Bi-Lingual Edition* (New York: Kehot, 1984), 283–86, and n.39.

limits, when one stands still, one is closed to the joy of endless possibilities, even on the spiritual path.[11]

The Jewish philosopher, Franz Rosenzweig (1886–1929) said that the whole problem with becoming what we *can* become, and doing what we need to do, may be the lack of a moment of generosity on our part. That is to say, it may be a failure to look at what is really "do-able" for us in particular, to be open to our inner guidance and deep inclination. We have all had some experience with this. Think of those moments when you said to yourself, "I couldn't do that" or "What will people say?" We have to be generous with ourselves, and with our deep inclinations, in order to find those "straightforward ways of God."

—*Wrapped in a Holy Flame*, Chapter 1

THE TOTALITY OF SOULS

Someone asked Reb Pinhas of Koretz, "How can we pray for someone else to repent when that prayer, if granted, would curtail another person's freedom of choice? Do not the rabbis say, 'everything is in Heaven's hands, except the fear of Heaven (Babylonian Talmud, Berakhot 33b)?'"

The Koretzer answered, "What is God? The totality of souls. Whatever exists in the whole may also be found in the part. Therefore, in any one soul, all souls are contained. If I turn in *teshuvah* (in repentance), I already contain in me the friends whom I wish to help; and, likewise, they contain me in them. My *teshuvah* makes both the 'them-in-me' better, and the 'me-in-them' better. In

---

11. See Elliot Wolfson, "Walking as a Sacred Duty: Theological Transformation of Social Reality in Early Hasidism," in *Hasidism Reappraised*, edited by Ada Rapoport-Albert (London: Littman Library of Jewish Civilization, 1997), 180–207.

this way, it is easier for the 'them-in-them' to become better as well." (Rabbi Pinhas of Koretz, *Imrei Pinhas*[12])

In this wonderful teaching, a great insight of Hasidism can be married seamlessly to one of Sufism. For, in it, I find a parallel to the great "Toward the One" prayer of Hazrat Inayat Khan (1882–1927), who first introduced Sufism into the West . . .

> Toward the One,
> the Perfection of Love, Harmony, and Beauty,
> the Only Being, United with All the Illuminated Souls,
> Who Form the Embodiment of the Master, the Spirit of
>   Guidance.

When Reb Pinhas says that God is the "totality of souls," it is very close to Inayat Khan's "the Only Being," who is "United with All the Illuminated Souls," forming the "Embodiment of the Master, the Spirit of Guidance." From this we come to understand from whence the rebbes derive their remarkable insight; for whatever insight we may receive (whether through the outer *rebbe* or from the inner *rebbe)* can be understood to derive from "the Spirit of Guidance," or the "Great Rebbe," if you will, a collective superconscious of illuminated beings producing a greater awareness than any individual is able to contain in him- or herself alone.

This Great Rebbe then filters this awareness into the right moments through precisely the right people for that moment. Now, the local *rebbes*, who are able to make themselves especially transparent to the will of God, become willing conduits of this grace and, therefore, are often thought to *own* this territory because of their consistency in doing so. But the truth is, we are all a part of that collective, and thus we are all contributors to and conduits of that grace. As Murshid Samuel

---

12. Rabbi Pinhas of Koretz, *Imrei Pinhas ha-Shalem*, edited by Rabbi Elimelekh Elazar Fraenkel (B'nei B'rak, Israel: 5763 [2002–2003]), *Sha'ar ha-Tefilah*, #46), 295.

Lewis (1896–1971), a disciple of Inayat Khan, later wrote, "It is a mistake to assume there is any 'teacher.' The teacher is the positive pole of the cell, and as the pupil or pupils—the negative pole—show more aptitude, the electromagnetic field of the cell increases and knowledge comes through the teacher which would have otherwise been impossible."[13]

As great as this insight may be, we must not forget that it is meant to set up another point in the Koretzer's teaching, to explain why prayer is effective. For the Koretzer says that the best way to help someone else is to do our own spiritual work of *teshuvah*, turning ever back to God, thus creating a positive effect in the outer world for our friends but also healing the us-in-them in the inner world. *—A Heart Afire*, 141–42

TEIKU—ELIJAH LIVES!

Why do the Rabbis promise that all questions will be answered by Elijah the Prophet when he comes to announce the Messiah, and not by Moses, who will then be resurrected?

The answer is that Moses died, and we cannot hope to be helped with our current problems by Moses, peace be upon him, who completed his life.

Since that time, the Torah has been placed in our hands. If one's soul is from the side of grace (*hesed*), everything is pure, permitted, and kosher; and if it is from the side of rigor (*gevurah*), the opposite is true. Yet, each person, according to their own rung is a vehicle for the word of the living God. This is why the sages, realizing the need for grace in this world, set the *halakhah* (law) down according to the teachings of Hillel, for this is according to the world's need.

---

13. Samuel L. Lewis, *Sufi Vision and Initiation: Meetings with Remarkable Beings*, edited by Neil Douglas-Klotz (San Francisco: Sufi Islamia/ Prophecy Publications, 1986), 322.

Now, one who is alive and participating in this world is aware of the needs of the time and the attributes by which we need to live. But one who does not live on this plane does not know the attributes by which we need to live in this world. Since Elijah is yet alive, having never tasted the taste of death, remaining connected to this plane, he, and no other, is capable of resolving our questions. (Rabbi Levi Yitzhak of Berditchev, *Kedushat Levi, Likkutim*[14])

What is the meaning of the word *teiku?* In Aramaic it literally means "let it stand." There are times in the Talmud when the Rabbis delve deeply into an issue, question and debate, but come to a standstill, unable to reach a firm conclusion. In such cases, they proclaim, *"Teiku!"* Now, some say that in addition to its literal meaning, *teiku* is also an acronym for *Tishby Yitaretz Kushiyot V'Aba'yot* (the Hebrew letters *Taf, Yud, Kuf, Vav*), meaning "Elijah the Prophet will resolve difficulties and questions."

Picking up on this tradition, Rabbi Levi Yitzhak of Berditchev (1740–1809) asks the question, "Why don't we ask Moses?" After all, he is our most direct source of Torah; shouldn't we turn to him for help? Why go to Elijah?

The answer is that Moses lived and died while Elijah lives on. According to the Bible, Elijah was taken up to heaven in a whirlwind while still alive (2 Kings 2:11). It is also said that there will come a day when Elijah will return: "Behold, I will send unto you My messenger, Elijah. And he will reconcile the hearts of parents unto the children, and the hearts of the children unto the parents" (Malachi 3:23–24).

Over the centuries, many legends have been told about the prophet's surprise visits to people in need. In Jewish folklore Elijah is regarded as something like the figure of Hermes in Greek mythology. If you have a conundrum and seek a way out of it, he will manifest and reveal the answer. It is for this reason that

---

14. Rabbi Levi Yitzhak of Berditchev, *Kedushat Levi, Likkutim* (Warsaw, Poland: Yitzhak Goldman, 5636 [1876]), 218.

on occasions like the Passover *seder* or a circumcision, when we need intergenerational connection, we invite Elijah to join us. On Saturday night, as we bid farewell to the *Shabbat*, we sing the song "Elijah the Prophet" as we attempt to connect *Shabbat* to the rest of the week. Elijah is uniquely suited to see us through moments of change or transition—both in the here and now and in the future—drawing on the wisdom of the ages, providing us with insight appropriate for this particular moment in time.

A brief Hasidic story illustrates the difference between Moses and Elijah: A man comes to Reb Elimelekh of Lizhensk (1717–1786) and asks if he should go forward with a certain business deal. The Rebbe says yes: "It's going to be good; God will help." The man then goes to the Rebbe's disciple, Reb Ya'akov Yitzhak of Lublin (1745–1815), and asks him the same question. And Reb Ya'akov Yitzhak says, "You're going to get wiped out." So the man says to himself, "I asked the teacher and he said I'm going to do well, and then I asked the disciple, and he said I'm not going to make it. Which one should I listen to: the teacher or the disciple?" The man decides to go with the teacher and makes the deal. At first, it goes exceedingly well, but in the end, he loses his shirt. The man returns to Reb Ya'akov Yitzhak and asks him, "Why did things turn out this way?" Reb Ya'akov Yitzhak answers, "Because my master, my teacher, Reb Elimelekh, saw only until his dying day. And to his dying day, you were successful. But he didn't see any further. I can't see past my dying day either, but I saw further because your failure was within my lifetime."

Moses, as great as he was, could only see until the end of his lifetime, while Elijah can see far beyond.

Reb Levi Yitzhak continues his teaching by saying that every soul comes into the world with a kind of imprint from a particular branch of the Tree of Life (the *sefirot*, source of all souls).[15]

---

15. See the text entitled "The Cosmic Tree" (from *Sefer Ha-Bahir*) in Daniel C. Matt, *The Essential Kabbalah: The Heart of Jewish Mysticism* (New York: Castle Books, 1997), 77, 188 (explanatory notes).

Some people come from the branch of grace (*hesed*), while others come from the branch of rigor (*gevurah*). Sometimes, when two souls like this meet they feel as if they are banging their heads against a wall. "Why don't you see things the way I do?" Hillel and Shammai are perhaps our most famous examples of two such souls. Hillel saw everything through the lens of *hesed*, and Shammai through the lens of *gevurah*.[16] Both are necessary, and each is a vehicle for the word of the living God. However, realizing the need for more grace than rigor in this world, the Rabbis tipped the scales of *halakhah* (Jewish law and practice) in Hillel's direction.[17]

It is said that when God created the world, it was created with the attribute of justice; but seeing that the world would not be able to exist that way, God added the attribute of mercy.[18] This is what allows us a "second chance," the opportunity to learn and grow without being beaten down by our mistakes. Therefore, in pre-messianic times the world needs *more* Hillel than Shammai, because we haven't yet reached the kind of righteousness that Shammai demanded. God willing, we will one day reach that level of consciousness and then be able to go with Shammai's

---

16. Rabbi Hayyim Vital, one of the great exponents of Lurianic Kabbalah, explores this subject in *Sha'ar ha-Gilgulim*, edited by Rabbi Shmuel Vital (Jerusalem, Israel: *MoHaRaR Yisrael*, 5623 [1862–63]), *hakdamah* 34, 37a.

17. These early rabbinic figures and their disciples are remembered for their intense and ongoing debates about various Jewish ritual and ethical matters. See, for example, Babylonian Talmud, Yevamot 14a, https://www.sefaria.org/Yevamot.14a?lang=bi. While Hillel and his students are deemed the winners of vast majority of these debates, the opinions of both academies are recorded in the Talmud and described as "words of the living God" (Babylonian Talmud, Eruvin 13b, https://www.sefaria.org/Eruvin.13b?lang=bi).

18. See Rashi's comment on Genesis 1:1 (https://www.sefaria.org/Rashi_on_Genesis.1.1?lang=bi), which draws on Genesis Rabbah 12:15, 15:1 and Exodus Rabbah 30:13.

rulings.[19] But now it is the grace and mercy of Hillel that are necessary. And it is only the person who is alive and present to the needs of the world who understands the attributes we need to live by.

Very often people will refer you to this authority or that holy text saying, "You have got it all wrong; that is not the way to do it." But you must ask from what time period did this text come or out of what paradigm did it emerge? Yes, it may have been true in that time, but is it true in our time? The answer may be yes, but it may be *no*. Since Elijah is ever alive, having never "tasted death," he is uniquely suited to resolve our questions. In his vital, living presence, he can assess the needs of the hour and offer guidance for our time.

It is no surprise that this teaching comes to us from Rabbi Levi Yitzhak of Berditchev, for he is known as a *rebbe* of great kindness and compassion, whose loving spirit was felt throughout the Hasidic world.[20] He would often travel to surrounding communities to acquaint himself with the village Jews, to better understand their challenges and help support them. And like Abraham (Genesis 18:16–33), he was known for debating with God on behalf of other people. For no one knew better the aches and pains of the Jewish community and how hard his community tried to remain faithful to the Master of the Universe. Once, along with a group of others, Reb Levi Yitzhak watched as a wagon driver greased the wheels of his wagon while wearing his *tallit* and *tefillin*. The others laughed and scolded the filthy man, but Reb Levi Yitzhak was amazed. "Look," he said to God,

---

19. See Rabbi Shalom Buzaglo, *Mikdash Melekh* (Amsterdam: Meldola, 5510 [1749–1750]) Volume 1, 71b.

20. See Zalman Schachter-Shalomi and Netanel Miles-Yépez, *A Merciful God: Stories and Teachings of the Holy Rebbe, Levi Yitzhak of Berditchev* (Boulder, CO: Albion-Andalus Inc., 2010).

"how your servant praises and honors you, even while greasing his wagon wheels!"[21]

Like Elijah the Prophet, the Berditchever (as the master is affectionately known) was keenly aware of the need to provide his community with a vision of Judaism that was in deep dialogue with the past and responsive to life in the present. And like Hillel, he was a brilliant sage who understood that in his generation the world needed a Torah of *hesed*. May the memory of Rabbi Levi Yitzhak continue to serve as a blessing.

—*Jewish Mysticism and the Spiritual Life*, 217–20

THE REBBE AND THE HASID

One element of Hasidism that Reb Zalman found both profound and complex was the relationship between the rebbe *and the* Hasid. *In particular, he was fascinated by the phenomenon known as* yehidut, *in which the disciple would come to the* rebbe *for guidance and support—spiritual and material. Reb Zalman's interest in this mystical/magical/therapeutic convention was, of course, shaped in part by his own experiences with his* rebbes, *and by his desire to weave together insights from Hasidism with other forms of psychological and pastoral counseling. This led him to devote his doctoral dissertation to the subject of Hasidic counseling, which he used as the basis for two books:* Sparks of Light *and* Spiritual Intimacy.

In the following text, Reb Zalman recounts a story he heard from the seventh Lubavitcher Rebbe, Rabbi Menahem Mendel, about the power of yehidut, *as reflected through the eyes of the children of a previous HaBaD leader. Reb Zalman then adds a brief word of commentary.*

Once, the two eldest sons of Reb Shmuel of Lubavitch (the fourth leader of the dynasty, 1834–1882) were playing the game

---

21. Martin Buber's version of this story is entitled "The Drayman" and can be found in his *Tales of the Hasidim*, translated by Olga Marx (New York: Schocken Books, 1991), 222.

of *rebbe* and Hasid. Zalman Aharon (1858–1908), then seven years old, was playing *rebbe*, while his younger brother, Shalom Dov Ber (who became the fifth rebbe), then five years old, played Hasid. The younger brother girded his waist with a *gartel*, a prayer sash, knocked softly at the door, and when invited to enter, approached his older brother cautiously, saying, "*Rebbe*, please give me a *tikkun* (healing prescription) for my soul."

"What have you done?" asked the elder brother and *rebbe*.

"I took a pickle when *Imma* (Mama) wasn't looking."

Zalman Aharon laughed, whereupon Shalom Dov Baer, frustrated, turned to his older brother and said, "You are not a *rebbe*—a *rebbe* never laughs at the Hasid's distress!"

Another time, the two brothers were playing the same game. The younger Shalom Dov Baer asked for a *tikkun* [remedy] for not having recited the blessing after eating an apple, and the elder Zalman Aharon replied, "For the next forty days you are to recite the blessing out of the prayer book after eating anything [for added focus]."

"You didn't do it right," his younger brother reproached him.

"What do you mean? I watched *Abba* (Papa) through the keyhole myself when a Hasid asked him the same question, and this is what he said," argued Zalman Aharon.

"I watched him, too," Shalom Dov Baer replied, "but you don't do it right; *Abba* always sighs before he answers."

To the Hasid—and this is still the practice today—all matters fall properly under the guidance of the *rebbe*. The Hasid, considering an apparently minor matter, shrugs and says, "Who is to know what is *major* and what is *minor*?" Matter, spirit, soul, Torah—in all of these one must unify the Blessed Name. The consequences of this seemingly unimportant step may actually involve one's entire life (or lives). Thus, the Hasid looks to the *rebbe*.

Many seekers have found their way to *rebbes* of our own day in Lubavitch, Satmar, and Bobov in Brooklyn, Belz and Ger in Israel, modern *ba'alei teshuvah*, "returnees" to Judaism and Hasidism, have found their place there.

Others, having found their consciousness expanded in a new paradigm of spirituality, see in Hasidism a way to discover "guidance" within, and also through interpersonal sharing. They consult with the *rebbe* as a channel of the greater guidance available in the universe, understanding that the *rebbe* performs a "function" in doing this, but is not identical to role that is played in the game of Hasid and *rebbe*.[22]

—*Fragments of a Future Scroll*, Part I

IMAGINING *YEHIDUT*

Following on the previous selection, here we include Reb Zalman's narration of an imaginal journey into the yehidut *experience between* rebbe *and Hasid. We assume that this loving and vivid depiction includes elements from his own experiences in HaBaD and other Hasidic courts.*

Let us imagine ourselves with the Hasid and *rebbe*. Close your eyes for a moment and in your visualization, you too are now in the *rebbe*'s chamber.

With a kindly and thoughtful look, the *rebbe* takes the items [*pidyon* (payment) and *kvittel* (note with request for help)] from the Hasid's outstretched hand. Placing the *pidyon* into an open drawer, the *rebbe* slowly surveys the Hasid, who stands nearby, refusing to sit down even when invited to do so. The Hasid's clothes, stance, appearance, and facial expression—all of these the *rebbe* examines with care.

As he turns to the *kvittel*, he gazes at the name and uses a mnemonic device to remember it. Having stilled his mind prior to the meeting, the *rebbe* now feels a surge of impressions flowing through him, taking him to the root of the Hasid's soul. Before reading further, the *rebbe* begins to sense the real needs

---

22. See the "The Geologist of the Soul" and "*Rebbe*-Talk: A Conversation with Reb Zalman" below in this chapter for further elucidation of this final point.

of the Hasid—not those necessarily listed on the *kvittel*—as well as how those needs can best be fulfilled.

The *rebbe* perceives the soul in front of him as it stood in the fullness of the original, divine plan—and the blocks and hindrances that are keeping the soul from advancement.

Looking deeply into the *kvittel*, the *rebbe* examines its manifest content and compares it with his estimate of what could have been written. He also notices whether the *gabbai* [attendent] or the Hasid wrote it. Shifting the focus of his eyes, the *rebbe* gazes at the entire *kvittel*, turns away, then looks again.

The Hebrew letters seem to dance and sway, forming new patterns of hidden meaning. The *rebbe* begins to sense further revelations about the other's soul; he feels the presence of the departed ancestors who have spiritually accompanied the Hasid to the sacred encounter. For a timeless instant, the *rebbe* integrates all of this within; he becomes the Hasid, and standing in his place, sees how far the Hasid is from being able to accept the right counsel for himself. Flooded with immense compassion, the *rebbe* sighs. Simultaneously, he meditates on his own life and seeks a corresponding experience for the Hasid's predicament.

Blushing with embarrassment at the *rebbe's* sigh, the Hasid is sorry for the grief and concern for his soul he has caused. He's about to apologize, but the *rebbe* has begun his questioning. He inquiries about the Hasid's family and background, livelihood, and progress in study and prayer. Some questions seem remote from the matter of the *kvittel*, but the Hasid diligently offers his replies.

The *rebbe* takes one of the Hasid's answers and repeats it to him, either in the same manner, or with a different inflection. Thus, the *rebbe* begins to elevate the communication to a higher plane, from which he can give the *eitzah* or prescription for action. As the Hasid appears ready, having already experienced the shock of insight through the *rebbe's* repetitive remarks, the next stage of the session is reached. First, though, the *rebbe* quotes a few relevant words from the Torah.

The Hasid thereupon sees that the *rebbe* is about to offer his counsel, as he has shifted in his seat. His face takes on more authoritative lines as his voice becomes commanding and yet remains compassionate. The Hasid is "all ears" to absorb the *eitzah*.

Having finished his council lasting several minutes, the *rebbe* allows the Hasid to ask questions clarifying his mentor's comments. Some of these seem strange and unrelated to the Hasid's problem, but he trusts in the *rebbe*'s guidance. In an act of faith, he now stands near and inclines his head for the blessing. Again, the *rebbe* alters his expression and manner; alert to this shift, the Hasid strains to catch every syllable of the blessing.

When the *rebbe* has concluded his blessing, the Hasid utters a fervent "Amen," and starts to move backward. Without turning his back to his master, and without averting his gaze, the Hasid backs toward the door. The *yehidut* is over.

The *rebbe* makes a few notations on the *kvittel*, placing it where he can later use it to intercede for the Hasid. Stepping out of the *rebbe*'s chamber, the Hasid is suddenly accosted by others. As they eagerly question him with, "*Nu*? What did the *rebbe* tell you?" He fixes the details in his mind, still aroused from the power of the *rebbe*'s assistance.

—*Sparks of Light: Counseling in the Hasidic Tradition*, 95–97

THE GEOLOGIST OF THE SOUL

Once, when I was still a Hillel director at the University of Manitoba in Winnipeg, I took a group of my students to meet my *rebbe*, Rabbi Menahem Mendel Schneerson, the seventh Lubavitcher Rebbe . . . I served as the translator for them, translating into English from the Rebbe's Yiddish. When the students got the opportunity to ask questions, one of them boldly asked the Rebbe, "What's a *rebbe* good for?" I could have sunk through the floor in embarrassment; but the Rebbe wasn't offended at all and gave this wonderful answer: "I can't speak about myself; but I can tell you about my own *rebbe*. For me, my *rebbe* was the geologist of the soul. You see, there are so many treasures in the earth. There is gold, there is silver, and there are diamonds. But if you don't know where to dig, you'll only find dirt, rocks, and mud. The *rebbe* can tell you where to dig, and what to dig for, but the digging you must do yourself." More than any other spiritual analogy I know, this *mashal* (analogy) from my *rebbe* best puts the role of the *rebbe* into its proper context, emphasizing the *rebbe's* function over identity, and not taking responsibility for doing the spiritual work for the disciple.

—*The Geologist of the Soul*, xi

REBBE-TALK: A CONVERSATION WITH REB ZALMAN

Or Rose: As a young man, you spent a decade studying and living in the Lubavitch community of Brooklyn, New York. What do you remember most vividly about your *rebbe* (master), Rabbi Yosef Yitzhak Schneersohn, the sixth leader of this storied dynasty?

Reb Zalman: To this day, I still feel that Reb Yosef Yitzhak was more my *rebbe* than anyone else. When he spoke or *davvened* (prayed), I felt a sense of attunement with him. When I was with him, I felt all of the fibers in my being drawn to him; it was not just what he said, but his facial expressions and body language. When Reb Yosef Yitzhak told a story, he would tell it with such rich detail, even though he had a speech impediment. But he did not want to deny us any part of the description because he wanted to take us into an imaginative space. And when he *davvened*, he opened my heart; I sensed that he was talking directly to God and inviting us to join him in this sacred landscape. The same was true at the *rebbe's tish* (table). While it wasn't a beautifully ritualized experience like that of Bobov Hasidim,[23] there was a palpable sense that, *Zeh ha'shulhan asher*

---

23. As noted above, Reb Zalman visited the Bobov court many times and had great respect and admiration for Rabbi Shlomo Halberstam. He was drawn to the Rebbe's warmth, grace, and attention to religious aesthetics (including his famous iridescent blue caftan). Reb Zalman's close

lifnei Ha'Shem—"This table is set before God" (Ezekiel 41:22). At the *Pesah* (Passover) *seder* there was an understanding that when you raised the first piece of *matzah* (unleavened bread) to your mouth, your *kavvanah* was not simply to feed your body, but to feed your *emunah*, your "faith," as well.

Or Rose: And what about Rabbi Menachem Mendel Schneerson, the seventh Lubavitcher Rebbe?

Reb Zalman: I actually met Reb Menachem Mendel before I met his father-in-law. I first encountered him in Marseille, France.[24] I was immediately impressed by his intelligence and erudition, and I was very excited by the potential I saw in him to help people integrate religious and secular ideas. He was remarkable in his ability to communicate with all different types of people; his world spanned from the Sorbonne[25] to Lubavitch. I must say that my connection to him was much more of the head than the heart.[26]

Or Rose: While you were very close with both of these towering figures, you ultimately left the Lubavitch community. Can you say something about that decision?

Reb Zalman: Let me tell you a story. When Reb Noah of Lakovitch (1774–1832) took over from his father and became the *rebbe* of his community, the followers saw that he wasn't

---

students, Rabbi Phillip (1939–2016) and Malka Goodman, were a part of the Bobov community in the 1960s and helped their teacher and others of their Neo-Hasidic colleagues access this court in Brooklyn, NY.

24. Reb Zalman and his family were held in an internment camp outside of Marseille while they were fleeing from the Nazis. See "Revelations at Marseille," in *My Life in Jewish Renewal*, 43–48.

25. It appears that Rabbi Schneerson did not study formally at the Sorbonne. He did, however, earn a degree in engineering from École Spéciale des Travaux Publics du Bâtiment et de l'Industrie in 1938. See Samuel C. Heilman and Menachem M. Friedman, *The Rebbe: The Life and Afterlife of Menachem Mendel Schneerson* (Princeton, NJ: Princeton University Press, 2010), 121–25.

26. The relationship between Reb Zalman and Rabbi Menachem Mendel is worthy of scholarly study given the significance of their contributions to modern American Jewish life.

doing things as his father had done. So, they said, "Why don't you do it as your father did?" And he said, "I'm doing exactly what my father did: my father didn't copy anyone, and I don't copy anyone."[27]

A second relevant story: when the Ishbitzer Rebbe (Rabbi Mordecai Yosef Leiner) decided that he had to leave Kotzk, he went to say goodbye to his *haverim* (friends and colleagues). As he said goodbye to Reb Dovid (Morgenstern, 1809–1893), the son of the Kotzker Rebbe (Rabbi Menahem Mendel Morgenstern, 1787–1859), the Kotzker's son asked him for some money as a parting gift [a common practice among Hasidim]. When the Ishbitzer reached into his pocket for some money, a *kvittel* (written request for spiritual or material need) fell out of his pocket. "Ah," Reb Dovid said, "so you are already acting as a *rebbe* [by praying for or otherwise intervening on behalf of a community member, while still in the court of his master]." So the Ishbitzer answered, "Reb Dovid, what do you think, I came to learn from your father to be a shoemaker?"

There is a time when you have to leave the nest. Many things contributed to my departure from Lubavitch. This included my inability to maintain a certain set of Orthodox theological views and practices. There are times when you must say, "*Ad kan*, I can go with you this far, but from here on I have to be my own person." But I didn't leave only because I needed more individual fulfillment, but because I wanted to be a good shepherd to the people who were coming to me for spiritual support. I simply couldn't lead most of them in the direction of a traditional Lubavitch lifestyle.[28]

Or Rose: Do you consider yourself a *rebbe*?

---

27. See Martin Buber, "In His Father's Footsteps," *Tales of the Hasidim: The Later Masters* (New York: Schocken, 1961), 157.

28. See the biographical introduction to this volume to learn more about Reb Zalman's break from Lubavitch. See, also, his comments in "Chapter 24: Leaving Chabad: The Fallout from My Washington, D.C. Lecture," in *My Life in Jewish Renewal*, 175–76.

Reb Zalman: I *function* as a *rebbe*, but it is not constant. When I'm finished serving in that role, I'm done. I can go out, even take in a movie and get a pizza. This is very different from *rebbes* of the past. They were expected to maintain that role all the time. In the hierarchical world of traditional Hasidism, the roles of *rebbe* and Hasid (master and disciple) are clear; each needs the other, but they interact in specific ways. I believe that in our day, living as we do in a democratic context, we need different people—men and women—in a community to function as *rebbes* at different times, helping people grow in their relationships with God. Like the earlier Hasidic masters, Neo-Hasidic *rebbes* will bring different strengths and experiences to this work.

Or Rose: What do you do when you function as a *rebbe*?

Reb Zalman: Mostly, I try to listen to what people say, how they say it, and when they say it, and then I ask what lies behind these presentations. What does this person's *neshamah* (soul) need in order to live more harmoniously with God and creation? Unlike many *rebbes* of the past, I claim no supernatural abilities, but I have tried to cultivate my own inner life and my skills as a teacher, *shaliah tzibbur* (prayer leader), and counselor so that I can be of service to those who seek me out as a *rebbe*. It is important to add that as in traditional Hasidism, not every *rebbe* can serve every Hasid. If I don't feel a soul connection with a person, if we are not a good fit, I advise him or her to seek help from someone else. We must be honest with ourselves and others about our abilities and limits, knowing that we do not serve ourselves but a greater purpose.

— "Rebbe-Talk: A Conversation with Reb Zalman Schachter-Shalomi,"
Sh'ma, 10–11

HASIDISM AND NEO-HASIDISM

For many people, Hasidism is identified almost exclusively with the ultra-Orthodoxy of Jews in Brooklyn and Me'ah She'arim (in Jerusalem). But we believe that Hasidism is actually something larger, something perpendicular to a continuum that stretches from the furthest reaches of liberal spirituality to the most strictly defined orthodoxy. That is to say, there is a dimension of holy sincerity and piety associated with living in the authentic presence of God, *nokhah p'nai Ha'Shem* [Lamentations 2:19], that applies equally to all, whether one is a Reform, Conservative, Reconstructionist, or Orthodox Jew (or even, as we have discovered over the years, an evangelical Christian or Universalist Sufi!) . . .

Some have called this "Neo-Hasidism." That is to say, it belongs to the spirit and values of a loosely organized movement of people inspired to create their own unique spiritual practice based on the model of the Ba'al Shem Tov. The term "Neo-Hasidism," or new Hasidism, was first used in earnest [in North America] in the 1950s and '60s to describe the Hasidic-inspired work of people like Martin Buber (1878–1965) and Abraham Joshua Heschel (1907–72). Often it was applied pejoratively, marking that work as inauthentic, as if it were an artificial invention. But this was not the case. Many of the personalities involved in this movement were themselves Hasidim, came from Hasidic families, or were from families that had moved away from Hasidism and who now wished to return in some way.[29]

Moreover, those who looked on Neo-Hasidism as an artificial invention had forgotten the historical context in which the prior Hasidic Movement had arisen. For Neo-Hasidism was not the first "new" Hasidism to arrive on the scene. In the time of the Ba'al Shem Tov and the Maggid of Mezeritch [1704–72], people spoke of that movement in the same way, likewise calling it "the new Hasidism."

---

29. While Reb Zalman mentions only Buber and Heschel in this context, as noted in the introduction, another important, but lesser-known, figure was the journalist and writer Hillel Zeitlin (1872–1942). See the introduction for more on this figure. In addition to these three religiously oriented individuals, there were also cultural figures from roughly the same period who drew inspiration from Hasidism, including Y. L. Peretz (1852–1915), Micha Josef Berdyczewski (1865–1921), and Shmuel Yosef Agnon (1888–1970).

You see, Hasidism had been known before. This is why we like to speak of it as something perennial, arising again and again over the centuries in various group-oriented, contemplative movements in Judaism. Sometimes it even bore the name "Hasidism" in one form or another—the Early Hasidim of the 1st and 2nd centuries BCE;[30] the Hasidim of Ashkenaz in 12th and 13th century Germany; and the Hasidism of the Ba'al Shem Tov. These are what we tend to think of as the "Three Turnings of Hasidism."[31] And now, it seems, we are on the cusp of a Fourth Turning, the very beginnings of which can be traced to the first years of the 20th century.

It was for the purpose of connecting these two Turnings that I made my pilgrimage in 2005 to the grave of the holy Ba'al Shem Tov in Mezhibuzh (Ukraine). I prayed there for continuity between the Third Turning and the Fourth; I wanted the holy Ba'al Shem Tov to understand our reasons, as Neo-Hasidim, for moving in a new direction. For we too felt that the divine flow was being blocked, often by people who wanted to make sure others would behave according to traditionally defined religious norms before receiving divine blessing and inspiration. Thus, the channel of the great flow that had opened in the time of the Ba'al Shem Tov had become so progressively narrowed that barely a trickle of the original flow remained by the middle of the 20th century.[32] Then came the overwhelming release of the 1960s and

---

30. See Mishnah Berakhot 5:1, https://www.sefaria.org/Mishnah_Berakhot.5.1?lang=bi, and Babylonian Talmud, Berakhot 32b, https://www.sefaria.org/Berakhot.32b?lang=bi, which speak of the contemplative prayer practices of this legendary group.

31. This term is adopted from the Buddhist notion of the three turnings of the dharmic "wheel," that is, the transformation of the teachings of the Buddha into later forms of Mahayana Buddhism. See His Holiness the Dalai Lama, *The End of Suffering and The Discovery of Happiness: The Path of Tibetan Buddhism* (Calabasas, CA: Hay House, 2012), 11–71.

32. In Hasidic thought, the biblical scene of Isaac and his servants (Genesis 26:18–19) reopening the wells his father Abraham once dug is often understood as a metaphor for the need to open blocked channels of spiritual vitality. See, for example, the teaching from the *Me'or Eynayim*,

'70s. In this period, not one person but many began to dig under the sluice gate to release the flow. This allowed those who could not immediately comprehend and integrate *halakhah*, the laws of Judaism, to taste divine love, compassion, and grace directly. As a result, these previously deprived people began to find new ways of bringing tradition and *mitzvot* into their lives, ways that were in accord with feminist, ecumenical, and ecological values.

—*A Heart Afire*, xviii–xx

GRAFTING TO THE BA'AL SHEM TOV'S TREE

In 2005, I made a pilgrimage with my youngest son to the graves of the great Hasidic rebbes of the 18th century—the Ba'al Shem Tov, the Maggid of Mezeritch, Reb Pinhas of Koretz, and many others. My intention was to bring the spirituality of Jewish Renewal and Neo-Hasidism back to the land of my birth and the source of its inspiration in these holy men. My sense was that if what is called Neo-Hasidism today is not firmly rooted in the Hasidism of the Ba'al Shem Tov and these masters then it will lack spiritual depth and the strength to endure for many years to come. This is why I went to the Ukraine.

When I arrived in Mezhibozh—the most important stop on my pilgrimage—I went to the *mikveh* (ritual bath) and then proceeded to the grave of the Ba'al Shem Tov. I began to pray that those of us who are now being called Neo-Hasidim should be allowed to connect directly to him. There was no doubt that we were part of the same tree, but it seemed to me that a branch of a branch can begin to feel disconnected in its great distance from the trunk. So my intention was to take this branch of Neo-Hasidism and graft it directly onto the trunk of the tree of *Hasidut*, tapping into the very spirit of the Ba'al Shem Tov himself.[33]

---

in *Speaking Torah: Spiritual Teachings from Around the Maggid's Table*, edited by Arthur Green, with Ebn D. Leader, Ariel Evan Mayse, and Or N. Rose (Woodstock, VT: Jewish Lights Publishing, 2013), 118–19.

33. In speaking about this "grafting" process, one image Reb Zalman had in mind is an artistic work known as "The Family Tree of the Ba'al Shem Tov" (1926), which depicts several generations of the BeShT's

"So what happened?" you might ask.

I don't know how to express it exactly. If I were to convey it in the language of *midrash* (myth and legend), I would say, "The Ba'al Shem Tov spoke to me"; but we live in different times, and I want to be clear about what I am saying. There were no voices, no appearances, and yet . . . a consciousness arose in me at that moment and I felt I received a "message" from the Ba'al Shem Tov.

There is a divine *shefa*, a "flow" that comes from God that descends into our world and creates a holy response in us. That response then returns to the source of the flow . . . like an alternating current between us and God. This is what energizes everything we do in the world in relation to the Divine. But, inevitably, someone comes along and says, "We need to control the flow," someone who appoints him or herself as the guardian of the tradition, limiting access to who may benefit and how. This person wants to say, "Only after you have done all of these preliminaries will we give you a taste of the waters of Eden." These limitations become a kind of dam or sluice gate on the flow, which the guardians lift and close at will. This was the situation in the Ba'al Shem Tov's time, which he attempted to correct by digging underneath that sluice gate to release the flow once more,[34] so that the self-appointed guardians could no longer control it.

---

offspring, including many prominent Hasidic leaders. See a copy of this document in the Israel Museum's online version of the exhibit, "A World Apart Next Door: Glimpses into the Life of Hasidic Jews," https://museum. imj.org.il/exhibitions/2012/Hasidim/index-e.html. Reb Zalman actually experimented from time to time with the creation of his own tree, connecting various Neo-Hasidic teachers (himself included) to traditional Hasidic figures.

34. The imagery is taken from a letter believed to have been written by the Ba'al Shem Tov (c.1752) to his brother-in-law, Rabbi Gershon of Kuty (c.1701–61). In the correspondence, the BeShT describes a "soul ascent" in which he encountered the Messiah. According to the Ba'al Shem Tov, the Messiah implored him to actively spread his teachings, to allow his "wellsprings" to "burst forth to the farthest reaches" (Proverbs 5:16). For

I now felt as if the Ba'al Shem Tov were saying that the flow had once again become dammed up—over the past 300 years—and was only now being rereleased in our time.

In that moment, I was deeply certain the holy Ba'al Shem Tov had given us his *heksher*, his seal of approval, and the right to connect to him directly.　　　　　*—A Heart Afire*, xvii–xviii

---

a translation of the letter, as printed in the work of his student, Rabbi Ya'akov Yosef of Polnoye, see "The Mystical Epistle of the Ba'al Shem Tov," in *The Schocken Book of Jewish Mystical Testimonies*, edited by Louis Jacobs (New York: Schocken Books, 1996), 182–91. See also Emanuel Etkes' discussion of this document (and different versions of it) in *The Besht: Magician, Mystic, and Leader* (Waltham, MA: Brandeis University Press, 2005), 272–88.

7

Deep Ecumenism and the Interreligious Encounter

INTRODUCTION

While Reb Zalman earned a certain acclaim as an interreligious leader and international spiritual elder in the last two decades of his life,[1] he began his exploration of other religious traditions more quietly much earlier in life. One important marker in his ecumenical journey took place in the fall of 1946. After being dispatched by his rebbe to New Haven, Connecticut, to help establish a yeshiva, he stumbled upon a book about Catholic contemplative prayer and an anthology of teachings from the world's religions in a local public library.[2] As he said on numerous occasions, reading these materials "changed his life" in ways he could not foresee at the time, leading him to redraw his "reality map."

After years of study in the more insular world of HaBaD-Lubavitch in Brooklyn, he (re)discovered the wisdom and power of other religions.[3] An inherently curious person, this led the

---

1. As noted in the introduction, the success of Rodger Kamenetz's *The Jew in the Lotus* (1994), in which Reb Zalman is presented as a wise, daring, and playful spiritual master, helped introduce this unusual Neo-Hasidic figure to many Jewish and non-Jewish readers, and to *reintroduce* him to others (particularly those in the "mainstream") who may have not appreciated his gifts and growth as a teacher and leader.

2. Eugene Boylan, *Difficulties in Mental Prayer* (Princeton, NJ: Scepter Publishers, 1997); and Robert O. Ballou, ed., *The Portable World Bible* (New York: Penguin Books, 1977).

3. We say "(re)discovered" because Reb Zalman reported on several experiences earlier in life that served as precursors to his explorations of

young rabbi to explore various Christian houses of worship in the area and other religious phenomena in his travels as a HaBaD emissary. This included attending a Voodoo ceremony in Haiti in the summer of 1949, while in the region fundraising for HaBaD and assisting underserved Jewish residents. Soon after, he also had an unexpected, powerful experience with a medium in a small house church in New England.[4]

In 1955, Reb Zalman began to study formally with non-Jewish religious teachers and mentors for the first time as a graduate student in the psychology of religion at Boston University (BU). His experience at BU was deeply moving, including his time learning with the Reverend Howard Thurman. Thurman was, by that point in his life, a nationally regarded public intellectual, preacher, and community builder. Thurman served as the Dean of Marsh Chapel at BU and taught in its school of theology. His unapologetic mystical worldview, pioneering ecumenical and interracial efforts, and creative teaching style greatly impressed his new Jewish student.

After graduating from BU and moving to Winnipeg, Manitoba, Canada, in 1956, Reb Zalman began an intensive exploration of Catholic monasticism, which led to a formative friendship with the renowned Trappist monk and writer, Thomas Merton. Through an exchange of letters and visits to Merton's monastery in rural Kentucky, the two men carried out intense theological and praxis-oriented discussions. Among Reb Zalman's many fond memories of his time with Merton was sitting on the porch of the monk's makeshift hermitage on the monastery grounds, chanting the psalms in Hebrew and Latin.[5]

---

the world's religions as an adult. See the opening chapters of *My Life in Jewish Renewal* about his childhood and adolescence in Europe (including the piece in the previous section entitled "The Diamond-Cutter Hasidim").

4. See *My Life in Jewish Renewal*, 79–81.

5. See Rabbi David Zaslow, "Staunch Friendship for the Love of God," *What I am Living For: Lessons from the Life and Writings of Thomas Merton* (Notre Dame, IN: Ave Maria Press, 2018), 177–82.

Reb Zalman's exploration with hallucinogenic drugs with Timothy Leary (Summer 1963) and others also served to broaden his spiritual worldview. These trips *helped concretize his study of Jewish mystical teachings on* soul ascents *and other such voyages, demonstrating that one could engage in such mind-altering quests with Jews and non-Jews alike. Having opened these* doors of perception,[6] *Reb Zalman continued to explore other religious and spiritual phenomena, including Islam and Eastern traditions. This included striking up meaningful relationships with Pir Vilayat Inayat Khan, a leading voice of universal Sufism, and the American guru and best-selling author, Ram Dass (formerly Richard Alpert).*

As the texts in this chapter attest, Reb Zalman's attraction to the interreligious realm involved a blend of interest in people, practices, and ideas. As he grew as an independent, Neo-Hasidic seeker and teacher, he sought out the company of other fellow travelers, whose own journeys took them into uncharted waters. It was a dive into what Reb Zalman later called, Deep Ecumenism, *a term he adapted from his friend and colleague Matthew Fox.[7] In his dialogues with these individuals, he was most interested in sharing* spiritual technologies, *learning and teaching about the* upaya *or techniques for human development. What are the practices, he would ask, that help you move from your* is *to your* ought? *How do your prayers, meditations, dances, or incantations bring you closer to the Divine and motivate you to engage other people with greater compassion?*

---

6. See Aldous Huxley, *The Doors of Perception* (New York: Harper & Brothers Publishing, 1954). In addition to reading Huxley's work avidly, Reb Zalman also developed a close relationship with the author's long-time friend and mentor, Gerald Heard (1889–1971). See "Gerald Heard, My Irish Rebbe," in *My Life in Jewish Renewal*, 189–91.

7. See Matthew Fox, *One River, Many Wells: Wisdom Springing from Global Faiths* (New York: Tarcher/Penguin, 2004). While this term is often to describe intra-Christian (Catholics, Protestants, etc.) activity, Fox and Reb Zalman also use it to describe interfaith or interreligious engagement.

Among the ways in which Reb Zalman identified himself over the years was as a Gaian *Jew. Inspired by the nascent environmental movement and other related influences, he became outspoken about the need for people across religious and other lines of difference to adopt a new holistic understanding of their interconnection and interdependence. As he stated on many occasions, the great religious icon of the second half of the 20th century was the vision of the earth from outer space. Seeing pictures of our shared planet moving through space and time is a call—a Divine call—to move beyond the traditional us vs. them thinking of past ages. The old and destructive patterns of triumphalist thought and behavior needed to be replaced with an organismic model in which different communities see themselves as part of the greater body of the planet. For Reb Zalman, this meant that religious and secular communities would view themselves as semipermeable membranes, proudly practicing the best of their traditions, while exchanging vital nutrients with others. This requires ongoing attention to issues of particularism and universalism, learning to honor both our commonality and difference.*

TRUSTING THE HOLY SPIRIT

In 1955, after years of intensive study in the seminary and service in various Orthodox Jewish congregations in New England, I began to feel the need for a broader education and a wider range of experience. Up to this point, my entire religious education had taken place within the Jewish world, and it was beginning to feel somewhat narrow. I also had a sense that I could be doing more with my life, and so, with the permission of my *rebbe*, I enrolled in Boston University to study Pastoral Psychology and the Psychology of Religion. But of greater importance for my later life was my meeting with the Reverend Howard Thurman [1899–1981], who was then Dean of Marsh Chapel at the university.

At the time, I was living in New Bedford, Massachusetts, which was then a two-hour drive from Boston. And since it was winter, I had to be on my way under a dark sky, too early to say the morning prayers. So I would leave at five o'clock in the morning in order to arrive there at seven, leaving me an hour to pray and have a bit of breakfast before my first class at eight. Once I was there, the problem was to find a suitable place for a Jew to pray. The Hillel student organization building was still closed at that hour and the only building open that early was the chapel, but this also presented a dilemma. The main chapel upstairs was full of statues of Jesus and the Evangelists. As an Orthodox Jew, I simply wasn't comfortable praying there. Downstairs was a smaller, more intimate chapel for meditation, but there I was likewise inhibited by a big brass cross on the altar. Having no other option, I chose a public room called the Daniel Marsh Memorabilia Room in the same building. There I found myself a corner facing east, toward Jerusalem, and began to pray.

One morning, after I had been doing this for a while, and just after completing my prayers, a middle-aged black man came into the room and said in a casual way: "I've seen you here several times. Wouldn't you like to say your prayers in the small chapel?" I shrugged my shoulders, not knowing what to say. The man was so unpretentious that I thought he might have been the janitor. And his offer was so forthcoming that I did not want to hurt his feelings, but how could I explain that I couldn't pray in the chapel because of the cross on the altar? After a moment of looking at me earnestly, he said: "Why don't you stop by the chapel tomorrow morning and take a look? Maybe you'd be comfortable saying your prayers there."

The next morning, I was curious and went to look into the little chapel. There I found two candles burning in brass candleholders, and no sign of the big brass cross! The large, ornate Bible was open to the Book of Psalms, Psalm 139, "Whither shall I flee from Thy presence." From then on, I understood that I was at liberty to move the cross and say my morning prayers in the chapel. Afterward, I would always put the cross back and turn the pages to Psalm 100, the "Thank you" psalm.

Sometime after this, I read an announcement about a new course in Spiritual Disciplines and Resources, which would include "labs" for spiritual exercises to be taught by the Dean of the Chapel. The course intrigued me, but I was apprehensive about taking it. The Dean of the Chapel was also a minister, and I worried that he might feel obliged to try and convert me. So, after giving it some thought, I made an appointment to speak with him about my concerns.

When I walked into the office, the friendly black man from the chapel was sitting behind the desk, none other than Dean Thurman himself. He smiled and offered me a chair and mug of coffee. I felt a little ashamed of my initial assumption; I should have understood from our first encounter that this was a man to be trusted, but still I was hesitant.

"Dean Thurman," I said, "I would like to take your course, but I don't know if my 'anchor chains' are long enough." He put his coffee mug down on his desk and began to examine his hands. Slowly, he turned them over and over. I noticed that the backsides were very dark, while his palms were very light. He looked at them slowly as if considering the light and dark sides of an argument. This lasted only a few minutes, I'm certain, but it felt like hours to me. He did this with such a calm certainty that he seemed to possess great power. Moreover, he had this prominent bump on his forehead (above and between his eyes) and I could swear that it was about to open and reveal the "third eye."

Finally, he spoke: "Don't you trust the *Ru'ah Ha'Kodesh*?" I was stunned. He had used the Hebrew for the "Holy Spirit," something I had not expected from a Gentile. And in so doing, he brought that question home to me in a powerful way. I began to tremble and rushed out of his office without answering him.

For the next three weeks I was tormented by that question: did I indeed trust the *Ru'ah Ha'Kodesh*, trust It enough to have faith in my identity as a Jew? Or was I holding back, fearful of testing my belief in an encounter with another religion, unnerved by the prospect of trusting my soul to a non-Jew? If I was fearful, did it mean that I didn't truly believe? Finally, I realized that his question could have only one answer. "Don't you trust the *Ru'ah Ha'Kodesh*?" Dean Thurman had said. I had to answer, "Yes, I do," and so I signed up for his course.

It was marvelous and tremendously impactful, especially his use of "labs." In the labs, we experimented with various spiritual exercises, which frequently took the form of guided meditations. In one exercise, we were instructed to translate an experience from one sense to another. We would read a psalm several times then listen to a piece by Bach to "hear the meaning of the psalm in the sounds of the music." Another exercise was to "see music as an abstract design moving through space." In these ways, our senses were released from their usual, narrow constraints and freed to tune into the Cosmos, to touch God.

People seldom have those primary experiences in religion referred to by William James [1842–1910], Aldous Huxley [1894–1963], and others. But without this first-hand knowledge, the study of religion is impoverished. Such primary experiences allow the student to understand what is being taught, and the use of experiential labs is now part of my method. In fact, I have often found that they turn out to be extremely important in the spiritual growth of many individuals.

In the exchanges with Dean Thurman and the other members of the class, I learned an important lesson that is still at the center of my thinking: Judaism and all the other Western religions are suffering from having become over-verbalized and under-experienced. Someone else's description of ecstasy or spiritual *at-oneness*, given second or third hand is simply not enough for us. We want to have these experiences for ourselves, and I wanted to make it possible for other people to have them, too. That is part of what a living, breathing, religion is about, and I learned this from Dean Thurman.   —*My Neighbor's Faith*, 217–20

TRADE SECRETS FROM THE MONASTERY

While teaching Pastoral Psychology and Psychology of Religion at the University of Manitoba, I would often talk to various people about the Reverend Howard Thurman, a great African American contemplative and my mentor at Boston University. As The Canada Council sometimes made grants available to invite a speaker, I eventually arranged to invite Dr. Thurman to speak at the university. He came by train (as he said that flying affected his sense of time), gave some wonderful talks in different places, and even led a chapel service for us.

During his talk and sermons, he had a wonderful way of pausing that was simply amazing. It was as if he was looking for just the right word, looking and looking, until everyone wanted to help him with the word, but didn't dare. But in that pausing, people also tended to fall into the space and silence he had created, until finally he would speak again and cover you with the word. He would say something like "that luminous . . . *darkness*" and catch you on the insight of the paradox.

Between talks, I asked him if there was anything that he would like to do in Winnipeg. I told him about all the various sights to see, but he was not interested in the real estate.

So I asked him, "Would you like to go out to St. Norbert's monastery [Our Lady of the Prairies]?"

He said, "Yes, that I'd really like to do."

"Good, I'll call up and arrange it. Who would you like to talk to while you're there? Would you like to speak with the abbot?"

"No, the abbot is a manager."

So I called the abbot and said, "I think my guest would like to talk with the Master of the Novices, Brother Franciscus."

The abbot said, "That's fine; we'll arrange it."

After we arrived, we sat down in a room with the novice master and they began to talk over tea and cookies.

Dr. Thurman asked the Master of the Novices, "What are the complaints that your novices have?" Brother Franciscus replied, "The hardest thing has to do with the ones who come and say, 'Why do we have to have these long hours of discipline in prayer when it's so easy to get into raptures out in the field doing our work?'" (St. Norbert's is a Trappist monastery where they do *ora et labora*, "prayer and work," and the work is often agricultural.)

So Dr. Thurman asked, "So what is it that you do when they say this?"

Brother Franciscus answered, "I forbid them to come to chapel, except on holidays and for Masses of obligation. After a while, they come and complain again, 'We didn't come here to be merely farmhands.' But it is in this way that they eventually realize that it is the time that they spend on their knees in prayer that prepares them for those raptures that they experience in the field. It is as it is said, 'Those who sow in tears, will reap in joy' (Psalm 126:5)."

Well, Dr. Thurman was very happy with this answer. You know, people sometimes want to talk theology and fight with each other. It's ridiculous. But when two clerics can sit down to talk with each other, saying, "Listen, you're working at the same trade that I'm working at; what do you do when people experience recalcitrance to the message?" Then things just fall into a softer place and we can do work across the borders of denomination, and even religious traditions.[8]

—"Trade Secrets from the Monastery"

MY FRIEND THOMAS MERTON

Among the most remarkable persons I've been blessed to know was Thomas Merton. The first time we met at Our Lady of Gethsemani monastery in Kentucky, until his life was tragically cut short by a freak accident in Thailand six years later, we were staunch colleagues and friends.[9] I continue to be inspired by his

8. Thurman has a moving reflection on his visit to the Canadian Midwest and his interactions with Reb Zalman in *The Papers of Howard Washington Thurman: Volume 5: The Wider Ministry, January 1963–April 1981*, edited by Walter Earl Fluker et al. (Columbia: University of South Carolina Press, 2019), 14–34.

9. Merton died (December 10, 1968) of a heart attack caused by accidental electrocution while meeting with a group of Asian Benedictines and

hopeful vision of ecumenical harmony and cherishing of humanity's diverse spiritual traditions. In some ways, his outlook is even more important today than when he advanced it during the Cold War and its nuclear tensions . . .

I well remember that August day [in 1962 when we first met face to face] . . .

It was already evening [when I arrived at the monastery], and the gate was officially closed. Having made reservations to stay at the guest house, I arrived with my baggage at the front gate. To my dismay the entrance bell announcing visitors was attached to a rope with a cross at its end. As a Hasidic rabbi, I really didn't want to grasp the rope, but it was necessary to pull the rope in order to ring the bell. After a moment's thought, I grabbed the rope *above the cross* and yanked. The bell instantly rang!

Suddenly, a Trappist monk emerged from the shadows, who had obviously been standing silently all along. Striding over, he opened the gate for me and said, smiling, "An interesting solution to a problem of conscience."

He led me to the guest house, and the next morning, after eating breakfast, I was to meet Thomas Merton. Having never seen a picture of him, I had no idea what he looked like. In those days, Pope Pious XII had appeared quite ascetic, and I unthinkingly assumed that Merton, as a fellow clergyman of the Catholic church, was the same type of person. Suddenly, I felt a tap on my shoulder. I turned around and there was Thomas Merton—who resembled a football coach! He was husky with broad shoulders and a big grin. He took me to Shangri-La, his hermitage, which the Gethsemani administrators had given him permission to have.

We were hardly strangers, having written to each other regularly for over a year and a half. So, what did we talk about? Everything. The first topic I wanted to discuss concerned the

---

Cistercians near Bangkok, Thailand. See Morgan Atkinson, ed., with Jonathan Montaldo, *Soul Searching: The Journey of Thomas Merton* (Collegeville, MN: Liturgical Press, 2008), 174–180.

real differences between meditation and contemplation. Nowadays, thanks to the New Age movement of the 1980s, everything involving the mind is simplistically dubbed "meditation" by practitioners of yoga, Buddhism, Kabbalah, and a host of other popularized spiritual paths. But in those days, especially among Catholics, the language was precise and clear. Meditation was discursive reflection, and contemplation was something that moved away from words and got to that place where—when grace overcame the individual—he or she would experience infused contemplation, meaning that the *shefa* (divine overflow) descends from the transcendent and fills the mind.

Then we talked about the obstacles to reaching a deep state of consciousness. We gave our views about Saint John of the Cross (1542–1592), and why one has to pass through a "dark night of the senses" and a "dark night of the soul."[10] After all, one does not achieve the experience of infused contemplation by opening a box of Cracker Jacks![11]   —*My Life in Jewish Renewal,* 155–57

THE SHAMAN BLOWS THE SHOFAR

The Hasidic approach to the religious experience aims at empirical realization. I use empirical in its classic meaning—basing my knowledge of the religious experience on direct observation

---

10. John of the Cross wrote about progressive stages of purification and spiritual development—body and spirit—in the aspirant's journey to intimacy with the Divine. These involve deeply painful experiences of "darkness," of physical and existential disorientation, loneliness, and a sense of meaninglessness along the winding road to unity with God. See St. John of the Cross, *Dark Night of the Soul,* translation and introduction by Miribai Starr (New York: Riverhead Books, 2002).

11. Mary Helene P. Rosenbaum has gathered and published letters from Reb Zalman to Merton in *Merton and Judaism: Holiness in Words,* edited by Beatrice Bruteau (Louisville, KY: Fons Vitae, 2003), 198–207. She also includes a list of letters from Merton to Reb Zalman published in Thomas Merton, *The Hidden Ground of Love: On Religious Experience and Social Concerns,* selected and edited by William H. Shannon (New York: Farrar, Straus, and Giroux, 1985).

and experiment. As an empiricist, I recognize the validity of non-Jewish religious experience, so over the years I've explored other religions, as well as other methods for enhancing spiritual growth. These forays have provided me with validation for my own religion.

A few years ago, in Calgary, Canada, I participated in a symposium on mysticism, with spokesmen for several other traditions. Among us was Brother Rufus Goodstriker, a medicine man from the Blood Indian Reservation. We were all put up at a modern plastic motel, a place that didn't seem to hold much promise for a group of mystics. But the setting was glorious—to the east, the Canadian prairies stretched for miles; and to the west, the Canadian Rockies soared into the sky.

When I woke up the first morning and began preparing to say my prayers, I remembered where I was and decided to go up to the roof. So I took my *tallit, tefillin,* and a *shofar* (hollowed ram's horn) and rode the elevator up to the top floor. I found the door to the roof and pushed against it slowly in case it made a lot of noise or touched off an alarm. But it made just a slight noise; I closed it softly behind me.

The sky was still dark in the west, but in the east there were streaks of light. The roof was a forest of air conditioners, vent pipes, and chimneys, but I found myself a corner facing the east and began to get into my prayers.

After a few minutes, I heard the door open again and Brother Rufus stepped out onto the roof. He, too, had a small bundle under his arm. We acknowledged each other's presence with wordless nods. He also took up a position facing east and began to perform his morning ritual.

First, he took out a prayer blanket, which reminded me of my *tallit.* Then he lit a small charcoal fire, offered some incense, and made a burnt offering of a pinch of meal or flour. Facing the east with his arms raised in the air, he swayed back and forth, chanting in a language I did not understand. But I did not have to understand the language to know that he was calling to God.

At the moment of sunrise, he placed a small whistle to his lips and blew a sharp note in every direction.

I continued my own prayers and concluded by blowing my *shofar*. Then I wrapped up my things and saw that Brother Rufus was doing the same. He approached me and asked in a gentle, direct way, "May I please see your instruments? If I were at home I would have had a sweat lodge this morning to be ritually clean before I touch them. Here at this place all I could have was a shower. Is that all right?"

I told him it was and unwrapped my things. He looked at the *tefillin*. "Ah, rawhide," he said. Then he handled them and noticed they were sewn together with natural gut, not with machine-made thread. He nodded to let me know he understood the significance of using gut, a natural material with an animal's power, instead of cotton or nylon.

Then he carefully examined the knots in the *tefillin*, ran his fingertips over them, and said with respect, "Noble knots." Next, he shook the *tefillin* and heard something move. "What is inside the black box?" he asked. I told him there was a piece of parchment on which was written God's name and other holy words. He nodded, and I saw respect on his face. I knew that he understood my prayer instruments and my prayers.

Then he looked at my brightly striped *tallit* and thought it was beautiful—he loved the colors, which bore some resemblance to the colors of his own prayer blanket. He examined the *tzitzit* (the knotted fringes at the corners of the *tallit)* and saw the five double knots and the windings of blue thread that create a very specific design.[12] "What's the message?" he asked, revealing to me that he also understood that such designs are not random, but deliberate.

After a few moments, he picked up the *shofar* and looked it over. "Ram's horn," he commented. "We use a whistle made

----

12. See "Tzitzit: The Fringes on the Prayer Shawl (text and video)," *My Jewish Learning*, https://www.myjewishlearning.com/article/tzitzit/. See also "*zizit*," in the *Encyclopedia Judaica,* 2nd ed., vol. 21 (New York: Macmillan Reference USA, 2006), 642–43.

from an eagle bone. May I blow it?" He blew a few loud notes through the ram's horn, handed it back, and simply said, "Of course, it's much better than cow." For a moment I thought, "Better for what?" But Brother Rufus was a medicine man. He knew that you blow animal bones to blow the demons away, to clear the air, to connect with God, to bring about change, to say to the sleeping soul, "Hey, there, wake up! Pay attention!"

At every step of his examination of my sacred prayer tools, Brother Rufus asked the right questions. He was in tune with the technology of religious artifacts and he understood them. He, coming from a very different world, approached my religious instruments as if they were not so different from his own, and he affirmed each one.

His response reminded me of the common element of all religion, the inner experience which transcends external variations and differences.[13]   —*First Steps to a New Jewish Spirit*, xviii–xx

SAYING *ZIKR* WITH SUFIS

Some years ago, I was traveling around Israel looking for Sufis; but everywhere I looked, all I could find were rock hard fundamentalists. Eventually, however, I came to the *Makhpelah* (the Tomb of the Ancestors in Hebron) and asked some children on the street, "Can you help me to find the *sheikhs*?" They figured that they were going to get some coins out of it, so they took me through back alleys—through labyrinthine paths, past butcher shops and hanging meat covered in flies—and finally brought me to a little green gate,[14] which was itself a Sufi clue.

---

13. Reb Zalman's final words raise important questions about the relationship between the outer and inner dimensions of religion generally, and how similar or different the experiences of practitioners are within or across traditions. See Catherine Cornille's discussion of these and related issues in *The Im-possibility of Interreligious Dialogue* (New York: Crossroad Publishing, 2008). See, in particular, 110–135.

14. See Seyyed Hossein Nasr, ed., *The Study Quran* (New York: HarperCollins, 2015), 750–56, including the note to verse 65 on 751–52.

I gave the children their money and went through the gate and down some steps and there I found an old *sheikh*. He was blind and wore a green embroidered cap and was sitting there "telling" his beads.[15] There were two other men next to him, and not wanting to interrupt, I sat down in front of him. After a moment, he lifted his head to me and asked whether I knew an American Sufi called "Noor."

I responded, "*Aiwa*," yes. Noor was Nooruddeen Durkee, one of the founders of the Lama Foundation in New Mexico. Then he asked if I knew another American Sufi called "Maryam."

Again, I responded, "*Aiwa*," yes. Maryam was Maryam Kabeer, who was in charge of the Bawa Muhaiyaddeen center in Philadelphia.

"What do you want?" asked the old *sheikh*.

"I want to say *zikr* with you," I responded. I wanted to do the Sufi practice of "remembrance" with him.

"Thursday at 4 o'clock—come back."

So, I came back with a group of Jews on Thursday at 4 o'clock to the little *zawiyya* or *shtiebele* (prayer house) of Sheikh Abdul Latif. The old *sheikh* was sitting off to the side. Next to him was a man wearing a red fez hat with a white band around it. This was the *qadi* or judge from the local mosque. He wanted to know how it was "kosher" for a group of Jews to say *zikr* with them. We tried to talk to one another, but we needed a translator. The younger Arabs present wouldn't admit that they knew Hebrew, so they finally brought over the public health official, a doctor, to translate for us.

The doctor came in and began to say his afternoon prayers . . .

Standing at his side, I said the prayers along with him. When he had finished, "the trial" began.

---

15. On the use of beads for prayer and meditation in different spiritual traditions, see Gray Henry and Susannah Marriott, *Beads of Faith: Pathways to Meditation and Spirituality Using Rosaries, Prayer Beads, and Sacred Words* (Louisville, KY: Fons Vitae, 2008).

The *qadi* asked again through the translator, "What do you want?"

I said, "I'm here to say *zikr* with you."

"Why don't you pray with your own people?"

I said, "I *davvened* this morning with my own people."

"So why do you want to say *zikr* with *us?*"

I said, "Because, wherever I travel, I always search out my Sufi *ikhwan* (siblings) to say *zikr* with them; and to be in the Holy Land, and not to have the chance to say *zikr* with you would be sad . . . I'd like to be able to say *zikr* with you."

"Are you a Muslim?"

"No," I said, "I'm a believer, not a Muslim."

"What do you believe in?" he asked.

I said, "*Ash hadu,* I bear witness that 'there is no god but God, and God is One.'"

Okay. Not too bad.

"So, do you observe the *Shari'a* (Islamic law)?" . . .

I responded, "*Aiwa,* Yes, I do."

"What level of *Shari'a* do you observe?"

"I observe the *Shari'a* of the *bani Ishaq* and *bani Yaqub* (the children of Isaac and of Jacob).

So the *qadi* asked me, "Then why not follow the *Shari'a* of Islam?"

I responded, "Because it is not fitting for a child to depart from the path of their parents. I come from the *bani Ishaq* and *bani Yaqub,* and not from the *bani Isma'il* (Ishmael)—so I follow the *Shari'a* of my parents."

"And what about *tariqat?*" asked the *qadi.* He was now asking if I followed the path of a Sufi.

"In that path, I'm at one with you."

Then someone says, "Ask him! Ask him! What about the *Rasul* (Messenger)? What has he got to say about Prophet Muhammad, peace be upon him?"

Ah! They've got me now!

But I respond, "*Ash hadu,* I bear witness that there is no god but *Allah,* and Muhammad is God's Messenger."

So they said to me, excitedly, "Then you're a Muslim!"

"No, I'm a Jew."

"Then how can you affirm the mission of the *Rasul*, the Apostle of *Allah*?"

So I said, "Allow me to go back with you in your history. There was Isma'il, the son of Ibrahim *khalil Allah*, 'the friend of God,' and he and his children still had the *tawhid*, 'the knowledge of the Oneness of God.' But his descendants fell into darkness, into the *Jahiliyya*, 'Ignorance,' and lost their way to the Oneness of God. Then *Ya Rahman*, *Ya Rahim*, 'the Merciful One, the Compassionate One,' sent a Messenger to the children of Isma'il to bring them back to the *tawhid*—to the Oneness. And I believe that he was a true messenger."

Finally, the old blind *sheikh*, Abdul Latif, interrupted the proceedings and said definitively, "I don't want to talk anymore; I want to say *zikr* with this man!"

Then they brought in the drums and we began the *zikr*.

—"Saying *Zikr* with the Sufis: A Trial"

TORAH AND DHARMA

When I first encountered Buddhism, I was at a loss about what do I do with the fact that there is no God in Buddhism. But, in the sixties, when people were exploring psychedelics, I explored them also. And I got to a place at one point where I felt a merging with the divine mind, and there I realized that God was an atheist—*God did not have a God!* When your mind gets out of "two-ness" and into that "one-ness," there is no God; there is only "I Am That I Am" [Exodus 3:14]. Then you come to a pivot that flips very fast between *full* and *empty*, "emptiness" and "fullness," and the questions fall away.

In 1975, I was in Boulder, Colorado, teaching at the Naropa Institute (then in its second year) when I got the news that my father, of blessed memory, had died. They had taken the body to Israel, so there was no point in me "sitting" *shiva*, doing my mourning, anywhere but Boulder. Before long, the news got around, and all the Buddhists of Jewish families from Naropa came out of the woodwork and helped me to make a *minyan*, so that I could say *Kaddish*[16] for my father. Allen Ginsberg and Jack Kornfield were among them. And before I said the first *Kaddish*, remembering Allen's poem of the same name—a poignant work for me—I asked him to read Psalm 49. He then read what you read in the house of a mourner, "What can you do about death? A brother cannot save you; how could a stranger save you? Everyone, in the end, 'drops the body' and goes into the grave; recognize that what you share with animals is this life and death" [a paraphrase of the psalm]. It is a stark psalm, and he read it as if he had written it himself. It was very powerful.

Then, I said my first *Kaddish* and got into the *Aleinu* prayer.[17] In the usual translation, a part of this prayer reads,

> It is our task to give thanks to the Creator of all, to ascribe greatness to the Lord of creation, who has not made us like the other nations of the earth, and has not set us up like the families of humankind. God has not put our portion with them, nor our lot with all their masses—for *they* bow down to *emptiness and void*,

---

16. Traditionally, the *Kaddish* is recited only with a prayer quorum or *minyan* (ten Jewish adults, ten men in Orthodox settings). On the centrality of communal prayer in Judaism, see Rabbi Hayim Halevy Donin, *To Pray as a Jew: A Guide to the Prayer Book and the Synagogue Service* (New York: Basic Books, 1980), 14–16. See also Arthur Green, "Kaddish" and "Minyan," in *These Are the Words: A Vocabulary of Jewish Spiritual Life* (Woodstock, VT: Jewish Lights Publishing, 2000), 87–88, 162.

17. Originally composed as a prayer for Rosh Ha-Shanah, since medieval times it has been a core part of the three daily services and other rituals. This prayer opens with the worshipper "bowing and bending" before the "King of all Kings" and thanking God for the unique mission and destiny of the Jewish people. It ends with a more universal vision of the future when all peoples will recognize the Divine as the universal Sovereign. To learn more about this prayer, see *My People's Prayer Book, Volume 6—Tachanun and Concluding Prayers*, edited by Lawrence A. Hoffman (Woodstock, VT: Jewish Lights Publishing, 2002).

and *we* bow down to the *Sovereign of Sovereigns*, the *Blessed Holy One.*

But, just then, as I was saying this prayer after the *Kaddish*, I saw two tunnels before me. With one eye, I saw a tunnel going out into the universe where "they bow down to *emptiness* and *void*," in a Buddhist context, with the Buddhist definition of emptiness, *shunyata*. The prayer was no longer saying that they bow down to "vain foolishness," *narishkeit*, to "stupid things," but to *emptiness* in the Buddhist sense. "And we bow down to the Sovereign of Sovereigns, the Blessed Holy One." Then, for a moment, these two became one vision for me, and once again took me back to the center of knowing—*It is there. It is not there. It is there. It is not there.* I was "knocked out" and could not go on with the prayers for a while. When I recovered, I finished the prayers with a new understanding, "On that day, our Sustainer will be one, and God's name will be one."

—"Torah and Dharma: Torah *Hyphen* Dharma"

ALEINU—IT IS OUR DUTY

We rise to praise You,
Source of All,
Your generous work as
Creator of All;
You made us One
With all of Life
And help us to share
With all of Humanity;
You linked our fate
With all that lives,
And made our portion
With all in the world.
Some of us—
Like to worship You
As *Emptiness and Void*;
Some of us—

Want to worship You
As *Sovereign of Sovereigns*;
We all consider You
Sacred and blessed.

We stand amazed
At the vault of the sky,
At the firmness of earth,
And deem You enthroned
In the Highest realms,
But also dwelling
Within us.

You are our God;
There is nothing else;
Your Truth
Is supreme;
Existence is
Nothing but You;
So Your Torah
Guides us—
And you shall
Know today,
And take it to heart,
That Yah is God—
In Heaven above
And Earth below—
There is nothing else.[18]
Yah's sovereignty extends
Throughout the Cosmos;
Yah will indeed govern
Over all there is;

---

18. Deuteronomy 4:39. This is a key text in HaBaD thought as it is read as an expression of God's all-encompassing nature—"There is *nothing* else"—rather than simply an affirmation that there are no other gods. See Rabbi Schneur Zalman of Liadi's *Likkutei Amarim—Tanya: Bi-Lingual Edition* (New York: Kehot, 1984), 2:1, 287.

On that Day,
Yah will be One
And Her Name
Will be *ONE* [Zachariah 14:9].
—*Sh'ma': A Concise Weekday Siddur for Praying in English*, 49

UNIVERSALISM AND PARTICULARISM: THE DALAI LAMA

In 1989, the Dalai Lama, leader of the Tibetan people in exile, appealed to the Jews for help . . . The Dalai Lama's question to the Jews was simple. "Tell me your secret," he said, "the secret of Jewish spiritual survival in exile."

It was also unprecedented. Here was the head of a world religion turning to the teachers of another faith and saying, in effect, "We find ourselves in a situation about which we have no knowledge. We need to learn how to transform our faith so that it might grow again from the ashes of our destruction. We need to reshape our faith to survive without a homeland. You, the Jews, are experts in this. Please help us. Please teach us." And so a delegation of us went to Dharamsala, India, the Dalai Lama's home in exile, to consult with His Holiness on how he might keep his people's spiritual heritage alive in a diaspora that still has no end in sight. The full story cannot be told here: [Rodger] Kamenetz devoted his book *The Jew in the Lotus* to our dialogue, and the conversation between our people is still ongoing. I emphasized the importance of parent-to-child transmission through tools like the Jewish *seder*. Jews and Tibetans went on to celebrate seders together—one of our most potent teaching tools—with the Tibetans saying "Next year in Lhasa!"—their own Jerusalem, the capital of Tibet.

The Dalai Lama's plea to the Jews reversed the usual position that world faiths—including our own—take toward each other. Most Jews in Orthodox communities, for example, still hold on to a triumphalist vision of Judaism . . . [I]t's hard to draw boundaries around a triumphalist attitude: it infects our thinking at every level. I grew up in the Hasidic community, among the Lubavitchers. In the early days of Hasidism, the disciples of the Ba'al Shem Tov would reach a certain level of spiritual attainment with one *rebbe*, then continue their study with another . . . In my day, though, the Belzer Hasidim would say, "None are truly for God except Belz," and the Lubavitch thought the same of themselves. Each Hasid seemed to march to the slogan of "One God, one *rebbe*, one wife." Each sect adopted a uniform: to this day, you can tell which *rebbe* a person follows by the width of his hat brim or the color of his socks . . .

If we think of the world as an organism, then *triumphalism is a cancerous attitude*. The cells of triumphalist organs want to go wild; they want to spread themselves so much that they will consume all the other cells in order to glorify that which is *them*. This is clearly not the way to go.

We who do not share this hardline thinking sometimes go to *the other extreme* in coexisting with other faiths: "We are living in the modern world. We are all one global community now. We no longer want to see the world in terms of *us* and *them*. Of course, we need a little spice to life, so we'll keep our Hanukkah candles and they can keep their Christmas trees. But please, let's get rid of all the archaic stuff that has kept us fighting for so many centuries in the name of religion." This is clearly a more peaceful and benign way than the triumphalist attitude. Sometimes it's not even a belief we stand up and declare, but something we express by inaction, by staying away, by allowing our celebrations and rituals to slip away from our grasp.

But this, too, would homogenize the organism. To give up our own special way of being misses the mark. Certainly, we can make utopian statements that look forward to a future where religious and ethnic differences have been eradicated. But right now, I believe there is still a lot of mileage left in the contributions that we Jews—and other religions as well—have to offer to the world.

The Dalai Lama's vision was neither triumphalist nor what we might call "homogenist," but organismic. What happens in a living being? The skin and the bones, the heart, brain, lungs,

liver, spleen all have different functions. Yet they are all connected. No life can survive if one of the vital organs were gone.
Each organ needs to maintain its integrity in order to function. A
person can live only because the liver is "livering" and the heart
is "hearting." We understand that instinctively. Our stubborn
assertion of our individuality as a people, even here in America,
is like a gland saying, "Don't you assimilate me. I need to do my
work!"

When we look at our planet itself as an organism, we realize that every expression of diversity on this planet is part and
parcel of Earth. At the highest level we are all one. But nowhere
in nature do we find pure universalism: the universal always
expresses itself in the particular. The nations and faiths of the
world are the organs of this planet. And we as the Children of
Israel have functions to carry out in this world for the benefit
of the organism as a whole. That is why, having survived the
persecution of two thousand years, we need to survive also the
danger of dissolving into mere secularism or into a vaguely spiritual New Age soup in which the distinctive contributions of the
various religions would be wiped out. That is why our instinc-
tive reluctance to be the last link in the chain is a healthy one . . .

The Dalai Lama's extraordinary question shed new light on
what it means to be Jewish—or to be Christian, Muslim, Hindu,
or Buddhist. Why be Jewish? Because as Jews, we are stewards
of certain types of knowledge and experience that the world
needs. Of course, we are being Jewish for ourselves and our children, and for the Jewish faith, nation, and community as well,
but there's more to it than that. "Because of my love for *all* of
humankind, I want to be Jewish"—this is really the only answer
that can justify our stubborn refusal to cave in to the brutal pres-
sures of history and the subtler ones of the modern world. This
realization allows us to feel called not only by our past, but by
our present and future as well.[19]   —*Jewish with Feeling*, 182–88

---

19. See "The Shaman Blows the Shofar," above, in which he places
greater value on the similarities across traditions.

THE PROBLEMS WE FACE TODAY

The problems we face today are not yielding to the solutions provided by our hallowed traditions and lineages in the past. Each of them had, built-in, almost from the beginning, a high degree of surface tension to separate them from other traditions. Even their most universal and inclusive statements were based on hegemonic and hierarchical notions of togetherness, suggesting to the others, "If you come under our umbrella, as a lesser adjunct, or a minor satellite, we will legitimate you."

The attitude was basically triumphalist, which is to say, "When the Messiah comes, *we* will be proven right, and you will know that *you* were wrong." Almost every tradition has a myth of a messianic figure to come, whether it is the *Mashiah* in Judaism; the second coming of the *Christos* in Christianity; the *Mahdi* in Islam; *Kalki*, the last *avatar* in Hinduism; or *Maitreya* in Buddhism. So triumphalism has largely defined how we have dealt with one another in the past.

Then came the Holocaust and Hiroshima, the moon-walk and the view of Earth from outer space, the Hippie revolution and the Internet; and it became clear that we could no longer afford to think of ourselves as separate, or to have reality maps that do not base themselves on an organismic view of life on this planet.

Our theologians, teachers and preachers, in order to defend themselves against existential terror and the high anxiety of the spiritual vacuum in which they have to operate now, have by and large been co-opted by those who have pockets deep enough to build walls around the status quo, and by the "have-nots" who want only a return to implausible security of the "old time religion."

More and more, deeper thinking eco-theologians are coming to the conclusion that each religion is like a vital organ of the planet, and that for the planet's sake, each religion needs to stay healthy, and to function well in concert with the others for the health of the greater body of the planet. Thus, for all my universalism, I still need to be the best and healthiest Jew I can be, and to urge my co-religionists to do the same, as their contribution to the healing of the planet.

While I have gained much from my tradition, which has provided me with many sacred tools and the means of achieving various elevated states of consciousness, many of these tools do not seem to be immediately applicable to our current situation. However, there is clearly a revelation coming down to us from helpers above our ken, as well as a chthonic push up from below,[20] from our mother the Earth. Thus, I am less inclined to offer answers than to raise questions at this point.

Every generation needs new answers for the problems that the old answers have created. For example, nuclear fuel, pesticides and herbicides were all answers to questions posed by previous generations. And now they are the problems of this generation. Soon we will also have to deal with questions raised by the genetic engineering of plants and livestock. And who knows how soon? Even with human genetic stock.

The urge we experience to grow in awareness is often blocked and opposed by forces that want to cut us off from that creative, life-affirming urge, flooding us with mind-deadening distractions and addictions to things we don't really need.

Yet, at gatherings like this one, we want to amplify that urge. We recognize that it is communicating with the push from the Earth, telling us of her need for healing, and with the teleological pull of the vision of organismic wholeness that wants to birth and grow itself in us. Here, in this place, at this time, we want to wake ourselves and others up to an even greater awakening.

—*The Emerging Cosmology*

SOURCE OF TIME AND SPACE

Source of
Time and Space,
Avinu Malkeinu,
Our Sovereign

---

20. From the Greek word for *earth*; often used in mythological contexts to describe subterranean forces.

Father and Mother,
Draw down to us
The great Renewal,
A stream from
The Infinite,
Attuning us to
Your timely intent.

Let Wisdom flow
Into our awareness,
Awakening us to foresight,
Guiding us to help
Instead of harm.

May every
Tool and device
Of human use
Be sparing and protecting
Of Your Creation.

Help us to set right
All that we have debased,
To heal what we
Have made ill,
To care for and restore
What we have injured.

Bless the Earth,
Our home;
Guide us in how
To care for her
So we might live
According to
Your promise,
Days of Heaven
Here on Earth [Deuteronomy 11:21].

May all the beings
You have fashioned

Become aware of You
And the gift of being
You grant them
In every moment.

May we realize
The Shaping
Of our lives,
And may everything
That breathes
Share breath
And knowing,
Delighting in the
One Great Breath.

Guide us in
The understanding
Of the art of partnering
With family, with friends,
And with neighbors,
New and old.

Aid us in dissolving
Old enmities;
May we come to honor,
Even in those
Whom we fear,
Your image and form,
Your-Light-Dwelling
In their hearts.

May our star soon
Rise on the day
When Your House
Will indeed be
A House of Prayer
For All Peoples [Isaiah 56:7],
Named and celebrated

In every tongue;
On that day
You will be known
As One with all
Cosmic Life [Zachariah 14:9].

—*The Emerging Cosmology*

8

Spiritual Eldering

INTRODUCTION

*As advances in medicine allow people to live longer lives, we
need to continue to develop the spiritual tools to grow in wisdom. This effort is challenged by contemporary Western culture
in which there is an obsession with staying young—and, above
all else, looking young. Can we shift our collective consciousness
and develop a more nuanced understanding of the rhythms of an
organic life cycle? Can we learn from the earth itself that there
are different seasons that bring with them distinct gifts, challenges, and opportunities?*

*Reb Zalman began to contemplate these questions as he
approached his sixtieth birthday, feeling that his body and spirit
were out of sorts as he tried to plow forward with business as
usual. Tired and frustrated, he decided to take a much-needed
extended retreat, during which he began to formulate his vision
of spiritual aging. Using the skills and insight he had developed
within Jewish, interreligious, and humanistic contexts, he set out
to reframe the discourse about aging, inviting people to openly
address issues of mortality, to engage in a process of deliberate
life review, and to consider their legacies. Reb Zalman also advo-
cated for elders—and society as a whole—to think about how
they could serve their families and communities distinctively. He
invited older people to take pride in their hard-earned wisdom*

and apply it intentionally and tactically in the winter *of their lives.*

With characteristic linguistic flair, Reb Zalman described this transformative way of thinking and acting as a movement from age-ing *to* sage-ing. *He explains his choice of phrasing as follows:*

> *According to the traditional model of life span development, we ascend the ladder of our careers, reach the zenith of our success and influence in midlife, then give way to inevitable decline that culminates in a weak, often impoverished old age. This is aging pure and simple . . . As an alternative to the inevitable senescence, this book proposes a new model of late-life development called sage-ing, a process that enables older people to become spiritually radiant, physically vital, and socially responsible "elders of the tribe."*[1]

As students of Reb Zalman, who had the opportunity to interact with him in his November *and* December *years, we can attest to the seriousness with which he undertook his own eldering process. We witnessed him reflect both privately and publicly about his failures, regrets, and unfinished work, as well as his successes, accomplishments, and joys. As an experimental person by nature and a pioneering public figure, he also regularly instructed his students to think carefully about issues of personal expression and integrity, and interpersonal and societal responsibility. Most importantly, perhaps, Reb Zalman modeled for us the need to* apologize *and to offer* forgiveness—*seeking to heal broken relationships whenever possible. Just as the world as a whole is in urgent need of* tikkun *(mending) so are individual lives. This includes our relationships with God, the other, and ourselves.*

---

1. *From Age-ing to Sage-ing, 5.*

FROM AGE-ING TO SAGE-ING

I was approaching my sixtieth birthday, and a feeling of futility had invaded my soul, plunging me into a state of depression that no amount of busyness or diversion could dispel. On the surface, I had much to be thankful for. During the preceding decade, I had worked tirelessly and joyously in a pioneering movement to renew Jewish spirituality in the contemporary world. As a rabbi schooled in Kabbalah, the mystical wisdom of Judaism, I had broadened my base of operations by studying with Sufi and Buddhist teachers, Native American elders, Catholic monks, as well as humanistic and transpersonal psychologists. Besides serving as a professor of religion at Temple University in Philadelphia, I was speaking at national conferences and giving retreats at leading growth centers on the need for an ecumenical approach in renewing Western religion.

Yet while my public life was bustling with activity, beneath the surface, away from my teaching and pastoral work, something unknown was stirring in my depths that left me feeling anxious and out of sorts whenever I was alone. To avoid these upsetting feelings, I threw myself back into my work with a renewed resolve not to yield to the depression. But despite my best efforts, I could not keep up the hectic pace that had marked my previous decades of work. At night, looking at myself in the mirror in unguarded moments, I realized that I was growing old. Feeling alone and vulnerable, I feared becoming a geriatric case who follows the predictable pattern of retirement, painful physical diminishment, a rocking-chair existence in a nursing home, and the eventual dark and inevitable end to my life.

New questions began assailing me at these times. With an extended life span guaranteed by medical advances and our health-conscious lifestyles, could I convert my extra years into a blessing rather than a curse? What does one do with one's extra years? Were there exemplary long-lived people, patron saints of the elder years as it were, who could serve as inspired role models whom I could emulate? For all the earlier phases of my life, I had models to inspire and guide me, but when it came to growing old, there were no good models, codes of behavior, scripts, or social expectations to shape and give meaning to my life. As a rabbi and spiritual leader, I was supposed to provide answers to other people, but as I confronted my own aging process, I didn't know how to answer the new questions that life so insistently was bringing to my attention.

To deal with my unanswered questions, in 1984 I took a forty-day retreat at the Lama Foundation, an ecumenical retreat center located near Taos, New Mexico. I lived in a rustic cabin overlooking the Rio Grande where I spent most of my time in solitude, praying, meditating, writing, studying, and taking long walks. I was on a Vision Quest, an ancient shamanic rite of passage in which the seeker retreats from civilization, goes to a sacred place in nature, and cries for a vision of his life path and purpose.

After a few days, when the surface noise of my mind died down, I realized that I was sloughing off an old phase of life that I had outgrown. At the same time, to my great surprise and wonderment, I was being initiated as an elder, a sage who offers his experience, balanced judgment, and wisdom for the welfare of society. As I followed the intuitive promptings that came from within, I instinctively began harvesting my life, a process that involves bringing one's earthly journey to a successful completion, enjoying the contributions one has made, and passing on a legacy to the future. To initiate the process, I asked myself, "If I had to die now, what would I most regret not having done? What remains incomplete in my life?" As a first tentative step toward harvesting my life, I devoted an entire day meditating on my children and praying for their welfare. I wrote each one a heartfelt letter expressing much of the "mushy" stuff that frequently remains unexpressed between parents and children. I also set new priorities for my professional life and personal relationships.

When I returned from the retreat, I had a new spring in my step and a buoyancy in my heart. Having been to the mountaintop where I had glimpsed a vision of elderhood, I set about slowly at first, then with increased momentum, to bring my vision down to earth. Fueled by a sense of urgency and excitement, I did extensive reading in gerontology and life extension. I consulted with well-known consciousness researchers, such as Jean Houston and Gay Luce, who were doing remarkable work in developing the potentials of older adults. I applied the teachings of spirituality and transpersonal psychology to the issues of aging. Most of all, I studied my own eldering process, piecing together from my own quest the tools that lead to successful life completion. From this exploration, in 1987 I founded the Spiritual Eldering Institute, which sponsors nondenominational workshops that provide the emotional support, along with the psychological and spiritual tools, to help people become elders within our modern culture.

Giving these workshops across the country, I have witnessed firsthand how people are searching for a new approach to aging. Most of us have grown up with a deep-seated fear and loathing of old age. Our youth-oriented culture, while touting aerobically perfect bodies and lifestyles as life's *summum bonum*, focuses obsessively on the physical diminishments associated with old age. In the popular imagination, old age means wrinkled skin and chronic disease, rather than the wisdom, serenity, balanced judgment, and self-knowledge that represent the fruit of long life experience. Fortunately, our culture's limited, one-sided view of aging is undergoing a profound reconceptualization in our time. We are the first generation to apply the insights of humanistic and transpersonal psychology and contemplative techniques from our spiritual traditions to the aging process itself, giving birth to what some people call the conscious aging movement . . .

We don't normally associate old age with self-development and spiritual growth. According to the traditional model of life span development, we ascend the ladder of our careers, reach the zenith of our success and influence in midlife, then give way to an inevitable decline that culminates in a weak, often impoverished old age. This is *aging* pure and simple, a process of gradually increasing personal diminishment and disengagement from life. As an alternative to inevitable senescence, [I want to propose] a new model of late-life development called *sage-ing*, a process that enables older people to become spiritually radiant, physically vital, and socially responsible "elders of the tribe."

Sages draw on growth techniques from modern psychology and contemplative techniques from the world's spiritual traditions to expand their consciousness and develop wisdom. By expressing this wisdom as consecrated service to the community, they endow their lives with meaning and avoid becoming economic and psychological burdens on their loved ones and on society. This ongoing process, which I call *spiritual eldering*, helps us consciously transform the downward arc of aging into the upward arc of expanded consciousness that crowns an elder's life with meaning and purpose.

In putting forth a new model of spiritual elderhood, I am not only reviving an ancient and venerable institution that has enriched civilization since time immemorial, but taking it a step further. As part of the emerging approach to late-life development, the contemporary sage draws on three sources: models of the traditional tribal elder whose wisdom guided the social order for thousands of years; state-of-the-art breakthroughs in brain–mind and consciousness research; and the ecology movement, which urges us to live in harmony with the natural world. These forces converge in the sage, whose explorations in consciousness are giving birth to an elderhood that is appropriate for the modern world.

Throughout most of history, elders occupied honored roles in society as sages and seers, leaders and judges, guardians of the traditions, and instructors of the young. They were revered as gurus, shamans, wise old men and women who helped guide the social order and who initiated spiritual seekers into the mysteries of inner space. Beginning with the Industrial Revolution, with its emphasis on technological knowledge that often was beyond their ken, elders lost their esteemed place in society and fell into the disempowered state that we now ascribe to a "normal" old age. Today, as the Age Wave crests all about us and we confront existential questions about the purpose of our extended longevity, we are searching for new myths and models to ennoble the experience of old age.

The model that I'm proposing does more than restore the elder to a position of honor and dignity based on age and long-life experience. It envisions the elder as an agent of evolution, attracted as much by the future of humanity's expanded brain–mind potential as by the wisdom of the past. With an increased life span and the psycho-technologies to expand the mind's frontiers, the spiritual elder heralds the next phase of human and global development.

Until recently, the techniques for spiritual eldering were unavailable to the public. But as the consciousness movement grew in popularity during the 1960s, 1970s, and 1980s, the once-hidden teachings of yoga, Zen and Tibetan Buddhism, shamanism, Sufism, and Kabbalah entered mainstream Western culture. The same period witnessed the growth of humanistic psychology (with its emphasis on an expanded human potential), transpersonal psychology (which uses meditation as a therapeutic tool), and the brain–mind revolution, which uses contemplative techniques and the latest technology to expand our vast mental potential.

Spiritual elders use the tools from these disciplines to awaken the intuitive capacities of mind associated with inner knowledge, wisdom, and expanded perception. By activating their dormant powers of intuition, they become seers who feed wisdom back into society and who guide the long-term reclamation project of healing our beleaguered planet. Once elders are restored to positions of leadership, they will function as wisdom keepers, inspiring us to live by higher values that will help convert our throwaway lifestyle into a more sustainable, Earth-cherishing one. They also will serve as evolutionary pathfinders offering hope and guidance to all those searching for models of a fulfilled human potential.   —*From Age-ing to Sage-ing, 1–7*

CAN ELDERS SAVE THE WORLD?

I didn't know what was happening to me when I reached my 60s. I wanted to be the same workaholic I had always been, but I couldn't anymore. I couldn't keep up. I was depressed in situations where I had no reason to be. I felt like I had a guilty secret that I couldn't share with others. I kept pretending that I still could do what I used to do.

My inner work involves a mystical form of Judaism called Kabbalah. As part of that work, I do a nightly examination of conscience. I ask myself: what was this day all about? What did I do? How did I feel? How did I relate to people?

It became clear to me as I did this work that the spiritual practices I had been doing up to that time couldn't help me with the new season of life into which I had entered.

It was then that I began to look at life from the point of view of seasons. It seemed to me that the biblical seven years are important time periods, and that each seven-year span could be represented by one month in a hypothetical year. If the Feast of Nativity, December 25, is birth, by the end of January you'd be seven years old. By the end of February, you'd be 14, and by the end of March you would be 21. Then comes the spring of life. By the time you are 42, you are at the end of June, and you're figuring out what you are going to do when you grow up. And you have summer—July, August, and September—to do your life's work.

There is a script for each of these phases. From one to seven, you're a toddler and you start kindergarten. From 14 to 21, you become an adult. You have a script for all of life until you reach retirement age; then *there are no more scripts*. You're no longer a "productive-consuming" adult, so you fall off the perimeters of visibility and must be warehoused until you kick off. From 60 on, when you are in the October and November of your lifetime, there aren't any good models.

It is very difficult to live without a script, so from 65 on, many of us just continue playing the same games we played before.

The Spiritual Eldering theory is this: in the first months—January, February, and March—we are in the world of sensation. In the spring months, we move into the world of feeling. We are in the world of reason in the summer months. But in the fall, we go to a place of intuition, of spirit, and we need models on how to do this[2] . . .

In our society, we have been given an extended life span, but we don't have the extended consciousness to go with it. We have the largest elderly population ever, and we have a planet that is sick and is trying to heal itself. Do you see why elders are so needed today?

But you don't become an elder unconsciously. Nobody is going to do it for you—not mommy, not a teacher, not rabbis, not priests. You've got to do this work yourself . . .

Why is it that people are often depressed about getting older? One reason is that most people, when they get older, have a long history of plowing and of sowing seeds, but not much history of harvesting.

How do you harvest a lifetime? You need internal tools that add to awareness.

Every day, for example, I walk toward the future. What do I see as I look ahead? The angel of death.

Oy! I don't want to look.

So, I back into the future. But what happens if I back into the future? I see the past.

Oy! I remember what I did wrong, and I remember the disappointments.

So, I cut myself off from the past. As to the present, I don't want to think about the diminishments, so I have little awareness of the present either.

When you don't look at the future or at the past, and you don't pay much attention to the present, you're in a box of

---

2. Here, Reb Zalman is adapting the Kabbalistic schema of the Four Worlds in his description of the life cycle. See Chapter 2 of this volume to learn more about this mystical mapping.

crunched, narrow consciousness. This is the psychic field of Alz-
heimer's. No future, no past, very little of the present. Intentional non-consciousness. Invincible ignorance.

When I stretch my awareness of time, I get in touch with an
aspect of God that is called the "Ancient of Days,"[3] which is
witness to everything that has ever happened and ever will happen. That's my companion for eldering. This kind of meditative
work is what needs to be learned in October. When I go inside
myself and start checking the past, I come to things that I don't
want to look at—the file in which I keep my failures, the things
I don't like, the things that are not yet reconciled. Anxiety keeps
me away from there. But in that file may be treasures. Imagine I
had some stocks from before the Depression that I thought were
worthless and I put them in a file of failures. And then one day I
see in the *New York Times* a name that sounds familiar. I go to
the filing cabinet and pull out the stock certificate, and by now it
has become very valuable. So it is with failures. What I felt at the
time was a failure may be what moved me in a new direction;
the fallout of my failures may be where my successes are.

Letting go of vindictiveness and forgiving are other parts of
the harvest work of October. To give you an illustration, the
prisoner does his time in prison, but the warden does time in
prison, too.

Every time you hold somebody in the prison of your anger,
you tie up vital energy in the grudge.

Remember the phrase from the Psalms (23:5) that goes, "You
prepare a table before me in the presence of my enemies?" This is
often interpreted as vindictive: I'm going to have a good dinner,
and you're not. Instead, in this October work I hold (imaginary)

---

3. An appellation for the Divine found several times in Chapter 7 of
the book of Daniel (but nowhere else in the Hebrew Bible), and which is
elaborated on in Kabbalistic sources along the lines Reb Zalman sketches
here. An important text for this later development is the section of the
Zohar known as the *Idra Rabbah*, printed in *Zohar* III:127b-145a. See the
translation by Daniel C. Matt, *The Zohar: Pritzker Edition* (Stanford, CA:
Stanford University Press, 2014), 8:318–46, and ns.11 and 14.

testimonial dinners for the people who did me wrong: because you did this nasty thing to me, you turned me away from a routine life to an extraordinary life. You didn't know you did it for my good, but you did it anyway. Today I honor you for having been a difficult teacher, and I let you go free.[4]

The more energy we can recover from the past, the more life comes back to us and the more energy we have for the present. That's why we say, "Teach us to number our days that we may get at the heart of wisdom" (Psalms 90:12).

If you don't recover the past, you won't get to the wisdom. Wisdom comes from having learned from experience.

How do we expand awareness of the present? There is a kind of conversation that I call "spiritual intimacy" that many of us crave more than any other form of intimacy. It sometimes happens when you sit on an airplane next to a stranger and have a conversation that doesn't require you to tiptoe around the landmines of everyday relationships. It feels so good to be heard and be understood.

You can consciously initiate a conversation of this kind with a trusted confidant. Take turns asking each other questions such as these:

- What are my questions?
- How do I perceive my problems?
- What troubles me?

One Hasidic master said, "When someone comes to me with their problems, I listen to their Higher Self give me the solution. Then I offer the solution that they have brought to me."[5]

4. This also calls to mind the statement by the biblical figure, Joseph, after reuniting with his brothers in Egypt: "Although you intended me harm, God intended it for good, to bring about the present reality—to give life to many people" (Genesis 50:20).

5. Rabbi Pinhas of Koretz, *Midrash Pinhas* (Lemberg, Ukraine: U. W. Salat, 5634 [1873–1874]), 3b-4a, 11. Quoted and discussed in Reb Zalman's *Spiritual Intimacy* (Lanham, MD: Jason Aronson, 1990), 237.

Finally, in opening up to our higher capacities, we need to bring in the body's contribution to extended awareness, keeping in mind the old Hermetic axiom, "As above, so below." This means, among other things, that the brain/mind and body are mirror images of each other, reflecting and intensifying the capacities of each.

Imagine for a moment you've done the October work and become an elder.

To understand what it means to be an elder, recall that God told Moses, "Speak to the elders." The elders of the church serve as mentors and guides. The Russians call their spiritual director *staretz*, which means an "elder." The Sufis call their teacher a *sheikh*, which means an "elder." There is work for the elders to do at this time to give over to the next generation and to help heal the planet.

So you could do what Jimmy Carter did. As an elder citizen of the planet, you could do conflict resolution or build affordable housing for Habitat for Humanity. I'm thinking of an elder corps. Instead of sending young soldiers into the world's trouble spots, we would send in elders. They would meet with those who had lost grandchildren on both sides of the conflict and grieve with them. I think that with such conversations, the aggravated political climate would yield to wisdom and compassion. What if we are caught in the crossfire? It's better than dying from emphysema . . .

Dr. Martin Luther King, Jr., said, "I've been to the mountaintop."[6] I have a contribution to make that is made deeper and richer by my witness at the painful spots on the planet. This is

---

6. This is a reference to Dr. King's final speech delivered in Memphis, Tennessee, on April 3, 1968. Drawing on the biblical scene of Moses overlooking the Promised Land (see Deuteronomy 34:1–4), MLK speaks with great passion about the privilege of living in the current historical moment and contributing to the sacred (and unfinished) work of civil rights. In prophetic-like terms, he expresses contentment for glimpsing a future of racial justice, even if he would not live to see the "promise" of the movement fulfilled. Tragically, the next day he was

my work now. Within the context of eons, our personal lives and actions are both meaningless and intensely meaningful. On the one hand, we're specks of dust on a little planet in an obscure corner of the Milky Way. On the other hand, we're inhabitants of a planet that is trying to save its life. Earth needs a cadre of conscious elders who are aware of their task for healing the planet.

The December work is preparing for the passage from life in such a way that a child can come to the bedside of a dying grandparent and say, "Oh, wow, so that's how it goes."

A good completion would take away much of the fear associated with death, which, in our culture, is often translated to "Eat and drink and take drugs, for tomorrow we shall die."

The work of December is also to leave a moral legacy. This means deputizing the next generation: this is what is unfinished; would you continue that for me?

Can you imagine if people who are not afraid of dying would tell the truth to their children and grandchildren and work with them consciously when a will is written?

When I would ask my dad (God rest his soul) what he wanted to have done with his remains, he would give me a sort of nasty rebuke like, "You can't wait until I die?"

Then one day I said to him while taking a walk, "Dad, the following are the arrangements I've made for my remains."

He listened and wanted to correct me a little bit, but then he got to talk about what he wanted for himself. And it was a relief for him to be able to talk about that because he couldn't talk to his own father about death.

Do you see what intergenerational healing has to be done so that people are not so afraid of dying?

I would like to see an elders' *ashram* where people wouldn't try and cheer us up with old television reruns, but would let us

murdered. See https://kinginstitute.stanford.edu/king-papers/documents/ive-been-mountaintop-address-delivered-bishop-charles-mason-temple.

do the serious work that we want to do. It's so much easier to do this work with other people; the atmosphere gets filled with that electric, shared wave of people doing their inner work.

A good death would be one that says, "I'm not hungry for more life, and I don't think I've over-stayed my time here."

It used to be that life began and ended at home. Then we took it to the hospital, and now birth and death have become pathologies. Instead of being in intensive care, with tubes in you, strapped to the bed, can you imagine being surrounded by loving people as you prepare to die? Can you imagine having a chance to once again glimpse what life is about and to give thanks for the privilege of having had the chance to live?

You begin to appreciate what those last rites are all about, where somebody says, "Taste it once again, a taste of salt. Feel again a soft and gentle touch with oil." All of these things are a way of saying, "Go out in a nice way."

If the right December work is done, the work of grieving for those left behind is easier. Taking the sting from death would help us to live in greater harmony with the process in which life recycles itself for further growth and consciousness.

—"Respecting Elders, Becoming Elders: Can Elders Save the World?"

HOT-HOUSING CONSCIOUSNESS

When my daughter, Shalvi, was eight years old, she asked me, "*Abba*, when you're asleep, you can wake up, right? When you are awake, can you wake up even more?"

It is this issue that made the Buddha become the Buddha—the word Buddha meaning, "the awakened one." Every spiritual technology has been working on this issue and, as you know from my teaching about spiritual eldering, I've often pointed to the opportunities for extended awareness to match our extended life span.

Much of what I am to suggest below will be more delightful if you don't do it alone, but instead do it with a trusted friend in spiritual intimacy. It is then that you can designate a day or a weekend for the two of you in which you decide to pamper your souls. I don't want to call this a "retreat" or a "spiritual practice" because these words tend to tighten us up as if we had to produce something rather than nourish our spirit. Such days will be a matrix for the expansion of awareness.

As I say during From Age-ing to Sage-ing seminars, "If we don't have extended consciousness to match our life span, we are dying longer instead of living longer."

Here are several helpful activities to practice in expanding your consciousness.

1. Learn a new language or a new skill if possible, not only with your mind, but also with your body. If you learn a new language, for instance, learn to write in that language and in that script. If you learn a new skill, practice it for about 40 days [a key biblical number, e.g., Genesis 7, Exodus 24] until you find that your body has integrated it into its habit pattern. That will result in more of the synapses of the brain to be connected and accessed which equals some extension of consciousness.

2. Each time you read something in a book, magazine, or see something on video, set the source of your information aside and, relaxing and closing your eyes, imagine what happened before, what is likely to happen afterwards, picture the setting and characters in your mind's eye so that you almost feel it. The more you are able to do this, the larger your awareness will have expanded.

3. Make an inventory of as many of the experiences that you have had that gave you pleasure and made you feel right about yourself as you can remember. Order them from the mildest to the strongest. In your mind, construct a "rosary" that you can "tell" at will so that whenever you wish to change your attitude and mood you can consult that "album" of peak experiences. This will refresh your mind and your body, and will have the result that even

your T-cells (immune-related cells) will increase, and thus, the vigor with which you face even your diminishments.

4. Study the contemplative teachings of world wisdom traditions. Many a time you have had moments of inspiration and ecstasy which, alas, disappeared from your memory. While they are difficult to access, often because you don't have good concepts for them, studying one form of inner teachings as can be found in the Kabbalah, Christian mysticism, Sufism, the Vedanta, and Buddhism, will give you a grid with which you can better recall those experiences. Then, using your imagination, paint on the inner canvas of thought and feeling, a scene on which you are experiencing that ecstatic moment, that revelation, that theophany. Then, make for yourself a marker, a motto, or a gate which you can re-enter that experience at will.

5. Before you go to sleep, recall some of these ecstatic experiences and fall asleep as you hug them, expecting to have good dreams. If you remember your dreams upon waking, record them in your journal.

6. Mentoring and oral history. If there are some people in your family, or friends who would be interested in some of your reminiscences, if they are younger and have a different map of reality than you, then communicating with them is bound to expand your mind in their direction. Consider how the young ones can handle things of complexity like the Rubik's Cube and the esoteric parts of computer use with ease. Communicating with them will also help you expand in that direction.

7. Find a piece of music you are fond of, and then, when no one else is in the room, as you play it, dance to it in free-form. Visualize yourself, on the inside, as a great ballet dancer so even if you cannot fully execute the movements that you imagine, your imagination and what you *can* do will provide you with a way of expanding your consciousness, not only in your head and your heart, but

also in your thighs and toes so that they, too, will become awakened.

8. When you enter the "December" period of your life, it pays to recall loved ones who have passed on in the most vivid way you can. This will open entrance for you into the regions you are bound to inhabit after you drop your body.

—"Expanded Awareness: Hot-Housing Consciousness"

DECEMBER DAYS

Recently I had a conversation with someone who said to me, "You wrote a very beautiful book [*From Age-ing to Sage-ing*]; it's very uplifting and encouraging. However, isn't there a dark side to aging?" And he is right, there is a more somber side.

I find myself now in my December days. In my book I spent a lot of time on October, becoming an elder, and November, serving as an elder. I was much skimpier on December. The reason is clear: I wasn't there yet. Now I am.

Now is one of the best periods of my life. I'm harvesting so much of what I sowed in the world.

And yet, when I look in the mirror before I put on my public face, I view this slightly stooped old man with wrinkles. The business that I describe as coming to terms with one's mortality has since become coming to terms with actually dying. And there is a tiredness that feels chronic. Thank God sometimes I feel less tired and readier to anticipate and enjoy the good things in my life. Still, it's only a distraction from the pervasive tiredness.

I'm sharing this with you, not because I want to discourage you. On the contrary, I want you to know that from "age-ing to sage-ing" is a positive journey, optimistic and full of sunshine. But I also need to correct the beautiful high notes by playing some somber bass notes to balance and strengthen the truth of what we present.

I do not feel a pang of unlived life. I handled my life repair for much that needed *tikkun* (repair). I believe I have mostly done

the *tikkun* needed. I bear witness to you that the eldering work is real.[7]
— "Reb Zalman's Jewel of Elul: December Days"-

SCRIPTING OUR LAST MOMENTS ON EARTH

A major task of living fully, as we have seen, involves coming to terms with our mortality. One way we can reduce our fear of dying is by rehearsing our own physical death. When we courageously confront the reality of our finitude, we convert the energy that normally goes into repressing death into an increased appreciation for the richness of our life. In the following practice, we will attempt to familiarize ourselves with the reality of physical death by envisioning our final moments on Earth. As we rehearse our deathbed scenario, we not only take steps to reduce the terror associated with death, but we enhance our capacity to experience vitality and joy in the present moment.

1. Prepare to write in your journal by getting comfortable, relaxing your body, and taking several long, deep breaths.
2. Using your imagination, experience your final moments on Earth in the most ideal manner possible:
   a. What music would you like to hear as you are dying? What poems, prayers, or sacred texts would you like recited?
   b. What would you like to taste? What scents would you like to smell? What objects would you like to have near you to touch and appreciate?
   c. What kind of physical surroundings would you like?
   d. Whom would you like to be present?
   e. Whom would you definitely not invite to celebrate your departure from the Earth?

---

7. For more on Reb Zalman's December work, see Sara Davidson, *The December Project: An Extraordinary Rabbi and a Skeptical Seeker Confront Life's Greatest Mystery* (New York: HarperOne, 2014).

f. What would you like to say to those who have assembled around your deathbed? What would you like to have them say to you?

g. How do you imagine the moment of your actual death?

h. How would you like to have your body disposed of?

3. Record your responses in your journal. Read over what you have written several days later and then write a follow-up entry to see whether this exercise has made you more accepting and less squeamish about the reality of your physical demise.

4. As another follow-up exercise, you may want to write your own epitaph or obituary. By increasing your familiarity with the reality of physical death, exercises like these will put you on better terms with *thanatos,* the completing instinct, and facilitate the process of life harvesting.   —*Living Fully, Dying Well,* 164–66

A REHEARSAL PRAYER

God . . . you made me;
From before I was born,
You took me through my life,
You supported me,
You were there with me . . .
Even when I wasn't there with You.

There were times I was sick
And you healed me;
There were times I was in despair
And you gave me hope;
There were times when I felt betrayed
And I could still turn to You;
It was a wonderful life.
I loved
And I was loved;

I sang,
I heard music,
I saw flowers,
I saw sunrises . . .
And sunsets.

Even in places when I was alone,
You, in my heart,
Helped me turn loneliness
Into precious solitude.

I look back over the panorama of my life . . .
What a wonderful privilege this was.

I still have some concerns
For people in the family,
For the world,
For the planet;
I put them in Your blessed hands.

I trust that
Whatever in the Web of Life
That needed me to be there
Is now completed.
I thank You
For taking the burden from me . . .
I thank You
For keeping me in the light . . .
As I let go,
And let go,
And let go,
And let go.

            —*Living Fully, Dying Well*, 140–42

Prayer for Peace (September 11)

May the Holy One who blessed our ancestors
and us over these many centuries,
helping us to get through the many tragedies
and the great pain we have known,
bless all those whose lives
have been changed by this violence.
May those who witnessed these events
find reconciliation and an inner peace
which allows them to live without fear.
May those who suffered injury
find healing and recovery.
And may those who have lost loved ones
find comfort and consolation
in the presence of family, friends, and community.
Our Mother, who is the source of our very being,
please gather the souls of those who passed on
in this tragedy under Your wings[1]
and close to Your heart.
Keep them close to us who live on,
that they inspire us to seek peace,
to be peace, and to end the curse of killing,
hatred, and fear which blocks us
from becoming the compassionate beings

---

1. This language is taken from the traditional prayer *El Maleh Rahamim* ("God Full of Compassion") recited for the dead. See *Hadesh Yameinu—Renew Our Days: A Book of Jewish Prayer and Meditation*, edited and translated by Rabbi Ronald Aigen (Hampstead, Quebec, CA: Congregation Dorshei Emet—The Reconstructionist Synagogue of Montreal, 1996), 547.

which You created us to be.
May the souls of those who were lost today
be bound up with those who live on
that we not forget the love they shared
and the love we all need to share.
May they rest in peace.
Amen.

—All Breathing Life Adores Your Name, 125

Closing Reflections

Acharya Judith Simmer-Brown, Ph.D.

On this Rosh Ha-Shanah day, September 30, 2019, I find myself a few blocks from my home in Boulder, Colorado, at the grave of my friend and colleague, Reb Zalman. His grave is on the wild, steep edge of a historic cemetery, surrounded by natural prairie grasses climbing up the slope of Enchanted Mesa. The gravestone, a large charcoal engraved granite slab, is inscribed with the words, "He loved us to God." This makes me smile as I remember him, during his ten years teaching at my little Buddhist-inspired university. In the early 1990s, Rabbi David Cooper negotiated to bring Reb Zalman to Naropa University from Philadelphia in order to lengthen his life, because we "didn't have so many Jews here in Colorado." Little did he know that the *Rebbe*'s charisma would bring a large community right into the Rockies to be close to their beloved teacher. Boulder's Renewal community has developed the kind of vibrancy befitting the *Rebbe*.

Reb Zalman was one of the most alive humans I have ever known. A whirlwind of joyful activity, he embraced everyone and everything with infectious warmth and enthusiasm. He came to teach during a summer session at Naropa in 1975 with engaged curiosity in the spiritual experimentation that characterized our little university. He loved dialoguing with the Hindus, Buddhists, and Sufis of our little school, vibrantly sharing his own spirituality and tradition. He magnetized many, including Jews who had lost connection with their tradition or who were dual belongers like "JewBus."

When he came back to Naropa in 1995 as a full-time faculty member, holding the World Wisdom Chair, he taught in our Religious Studies department, sharing an office with Dzogchen Ponlop Rinpoche, the magnetic Tibetan lama half the *Rebbe*'s age. One year, Reb Zalman and his wife Eve hosted a special *seder* in their home to which he invited Rinpoche and my husband and me and a few JewBu guests. It was my first experience of a *seder*, as it was for Rinpoche. That evening we engaged in conversations about diaspora, Buddhist–Jewish dialogue, nostalgia and memory, and the future of religion and spirituality. He was always eager to find out how we Buddhists understand community, ritual, meditation, social engagement, and aging, and he quickly put whatever we said in the context of his own rich perspectives. He was a natural dialogue partner.

This beautiful book brings Reb Zalman's voice forward with all its freshness, brilliance, and vitality. Here we see his passion for tradition, his love of community, his realism about social change and the challenges religious communities face in the future. We see his humor and love, and we see his fierce intellect in service of the heart. He speaks here as pastor, mentor, and fellow pilgrim, and the charisma of this work carries us on to look more deeply at our lives and communities, to strengthen their resilience and love as we face the challenges ahead. Even for me as a Buddhist teacher who does not speak this way, I can feel how he "loved us to God."

Father Matthew Fox, Ph.D.

I am honored to offer a few reflections, snapshots really, on my friend, Reb Zalman.

While co-leading a retreat with Rabbi Arthur Green at Elat Chayyim in upstate New York, Reb Zalman showed up near the end, saying, "Looks like you've had a fine retreat; let's end it with a ritual." "What kind of ritual should we do?" I asked. "A Mass," he said. "What? Everyone here is Jewish except me!" I responded. "Let's at least take a vote." All but one older man approved and so we held a Mass, which I co-celebrated with a

dozen rabbis! Little did I know that this would be the last Mass
I would celebrate as a Roman Catholic priest. My letter of dis-
missal from the Dominican Order arrived from the Vatican just
ten days later. A sixty-five-year-old man told me afterwards, "It
was a healing event of a lifetime."[1]

It was Reb Zalman who took up my cause with the Church,
writing the Master General of the Dominican Order on my
behalf, saying, "We Jews are dealing with some of these issues in
our own domain. This is why I am involved in Jewish Renewal."
He also offered to come to Rome to "plead in person and at
greater length," saying, "Fox is the current voice of Vatican II"
and that "there is an abyss between St. Dominic and Tomas
Torquemada (both Dominicans) just as there is between Fox and
Ratzinger."[2]

When Reb Zalman learned that my mother was living in a
retirement home in Boulder, Colorado, he insisted on meeting
her. On encountering her in the lobby, he immediately asked her:
"Will you give me your blessing?" My mother, who had lived
as an Episcopalian for twenty-five years, and a Roman Catholic
for another fifty, had never, I am sure, been asked for a blessing
from a clergy person. Surprised at first, she gave Reb Zalman a
blessing. I then asked him to respond in kind.

I still pray with Reb Zalman regularly, as I prefer his translation of the psalms to any other. Reb Zalman also gifted me
with a prayer shawl and told me that it was a way to enter the
"Via Negativa" in prayer, to wrap myself in God's multicolored
mystery.

I was once invited to a *Shabbat* with Reb Zalman and his
wife, Eve, while visiting Boulder. Following the meal, Reb Zalman took me downstairs to a special room where his papers and
recordings were being processed for archiving. "You are getting
older too," he said. "You must start gathering your talks and

---

1. Matthew Fox, *Confessions: The Making of a Post-Denominational Priest* (San Francisco, CA, 1996), 208.
2. The full letter is found in ibid., 217–18.

papers and the rest to leave your legacy behind. This is part of preparing for death. Don't forget, and don't delay!"

On the occasion of my sixtieth birthday, Reb Zalman offered a beautiful reflection of his own for a volume on my work and contributions, saying:

> It was a privilege to "assist" at your last Mass as a Roman Catholic. . . . Yours were not "venial" sins that upset the hierarchs. Yours were more dangerous by far. You grafted your vision to the conclusions of Vatican II. You derived from Meister Eckhart and the mystics of the Church. You considered the lilies and intuited why it was possible for Mary Magdalene to turn, having loved so much, to be closer to the Master than the right-thinking scribes. So you had moved from the fear of the powers and principalities to the love for Earth and the Flesh of the sacred incarnation of God's original goodness.[33]

I was, and continue to be, so moved by these words.

What can I say of a man so wise, so humorous, so aware, so intellectually curious and busy giving birth to so many works of the Spirit as was Reb Zalman? Thank you, of course.

Rabbi Dr. Tirzah Firestone, Ph.D.

It was November 1992, the eve of my rabbinic ordination. Reb Zalman had arrived in Boulder to confer the honors, and other rabbis, interfaith clergy, and friends from near and far were converging to witness what was in those days still an unusual event: the ordination of a female rabbi. The energy was frenetic.

"Reb Zalman, this whole event is getting so big—too big for me."

"Tirzah," he replied sternly yet lovingly, "it will be as big as the *Shekhinah* needs it to be."

---

3. Mary Ford-Grabowsky, ed., *The Unfolding of a Prophet: Matthew Fox at 60* (Berkeley, CA, 2000), 130f.

With that one comment, Reb Zalman turned my world around. He was telling me that my ordination, indeed my life, was a stage for a much larger purpose than my own. It wasn't about me. It was about a *tzorekh Gavohah* (supernal need), a divine purpose that required me, and all of us, to bring it to fruition. He was also reminding me to let go of my ego's tight grip and allow a force greater than me to handle things. I think back to his words frequently.

Reb Zalman could see clearly that the *Shekhinah*, the powerful but long-obscured feminine facet of Divinity, was reemerging—not only in Judaism, but in all traditions. Sensing the egregious effects of a hyper-masculinized world and an urgency to bring more balance to it, he promoted women's leadership and encouraged women's unique gifts and influence in the Jewish world and beyond.

In later years, Reb Zalman used the term *tzorekh Gavohah* to refer to the tribulations of our imperiled planet, which he believed was the locus and manifestation of the *Shekhinah* herself. He could hear her, Mother Earth (or Gaia), crying out in her present suffering and taught that our active responses to nature and the environment are the *tzorekh Gavohah,* the "big work" of our day. He continuously urged us to consider the good of the Whole—the suffering of God's creatures everywhere. In so doing, he taught, we are attending to the *Shekhinah* and the need on High.

But Reb Zalman was not only focused on global issues; he was also keenly aware of his personal relationships. In his private prayer room he had a basket filled with the names of those for whom he was praying, and he checked on his students regularly, making himself available to us by phone and video conferencing. It was in his students that Reb Zalman's love for the small and the large converged.

"What happens to the accumulated awareness of a lifetime?" Reb Zalman would often ask his students. He fretted that our work innovating Judaism and the burgeoning shoots of a new paradigm might get lost. He urged us to "save" our lives—meaning, to integrate, publish, and pass on our spiritual revelations so that the fruits of our life labors might nourish the world. Even in his loving care of the particulars of life, Reb Zalman was looking out for the *tzorekh Gavohah*.

In this rich and comprehensive treasury lie the holy sparks of Reb Zalman's own luminous life that has been saved. May they illuminate our way forward, and may we continue to do the big work that is upon us.

Glossary

Abba—Father, Dad, Papa

ada'ata d'nafshei—("with the self in mind," Aramaic) situational thinking

Adon Olam—("Eternal Lord") a prayer often chanted at the beginning or end of Jewish prayer services

Adonai—("My Lord") a common name for God in Jewish devotional contexts

Aleinu—("It is our duty") a concluding prayer at Jewish prayer services; originally designed for Rosh Ha-Shanah

Arba Olamot—("Four Worlds") the Four Worlds or levels of existence and experience in Kabbalistic discourse

Assiyah—("Doing") the World of Action in Kabbalistic discourse (the lowest of four)

atarah—("crown") the embroidered strip at the neck of the *tallit* (prayer shawl); synonym for *malkhut* or the lower crown in *Kabbalah*

Atzilut—("Emanation") the World of undifferentiated being in Kabbalistic discourse (the highest of the four worlds)

avodah—("service") a synonym for prayer in Jewish devotional contexts

Ayin—("No-thingness") Primordial Being, the most recondite aspect of Divinity; also described as *Ein Sof*, "Infinity"

ba'al teshuvah—(pl. *ba'alei teshuvah*) one who has re/turned to God and Torah; a common term for "returnees" to traditional Jewish life

Ba'al Shem Tov—("Master of the Good Name") Yisra'el ben Eliezer (1700–60), first great Hasidic personality

Barukh Ha-Shem—("Blessed be the Name") a statement of gratitude to God

beit midrash—informal Jewish study hall

bentshen—(Yiddish) grace after meals, saying grace

berakhah—(pl. *berakhot*) blessing

Beri'ah—("Creation") the World of Knowing and Expression in Kabbalistic discourse (third world in ascending order)

233

binah—("understanding") one of the upper *sefirot* or divine emanations; the Upper Mother, Womb, Palace, etc.

da'at—("knowledge") intimate knowledge; an intermediary *sefirah* situated between *hokhmah* and *binah* (fundamental to *HaBaD* thought)

davvenen—("prayer," "praying," Yiddish) a colloquial way to speak of *tefillah* (prayer in Hebrew) that emphasizes heartfelt worship

deveikut—("adhering," "clinging") intimate connection with God, including peak experiences of absorption or unification

emunah—faith, trust in God

eitzah—("advice" or "suggestion") in the context of *Yehidut* it refers to the rebbe's prescription for the hasid

farbrengen—("time spent together," Yiddish) a session of Hasidic fellowship (with a *rebbe* and/or *mashpiah*), including song, storytelling, and drink; a vital social convention in HaBaD

farginnen—(Yiddish) open-hearted blessing or good wishes

gabbai—attendant or personal assistant to a Hasidic *rebbe*

gartel—(Yiddish) prayer sash

gevurah—("strength," severity, limitation) one of the ten *sefirot*, also commonly referred to as *din* (judgment); paired with *hesed* (loving-kindness)

guf—("body") human body

HaBaD—("Wisdom" [H] / "Understanding" [B] / "Knowledge" [D]), an acronym for three *sefirot*: *hokhmah*, *binah*, *da'at*; the name of the Hasidic sect founded by Rabbi Shneur Zalman of Liadi (1745–1813)

halakhah—("way of walking") the unfolding process of sacred practice, Jewish law

hallah—braided bread traditionally eaten on *Shabbat* and holidays

Ha-Shem—("The Name") a term used in place of the unpronounceable name of God (*Y-H-W-H*)

hashpa'ah—guidance (from Hebrew root for "flow")

Hasid—("devotee," pious one, pl. *hasidim*, derived from *hesed*) a member of the Eastern European Hasidic Movement (also used to describe earlier pietistic groups); a person in relation with a *rebbe*, of the lineage of the Ba'al Shem Tov

Hasidism—Eastern European spiritual revival movement arising in the latter part of the eighteenth-century and continuing today

havdalah—("separation") ritual separating *Shabbat* from the week

hayyah—("life") the level of the soul deeply integrated with God (above *neshamah*) *hazzan*—cantor

heder—("room") traditional Jewish elementary school

heksher—approval, certification

hesed—("loving-kindness") one of the ten *sefirot*, also known as *gedulah* (largesse); paired with *gevurah*—strength

hevrah—companions

heymishe shul—warm and friendly synagogue (Yiddish)

hitbodedut—("aloneness") a term for private meditation; a practice developed in Bratzlav Hasidim (with emphasis on speaking aloud to God in the vernacular)

hitbonenut—("contemplation") a term for meditation; a practice in HaBaD Hasidism (with emphasis on reflection on sublime ideas and concrete life circumstances)

hod—("glory") one of the lower *sefirot* or divine emanations, paired with *netzah* ("victory")

hokhmah—("wisdom") one of the upper *sefirot* or divine emanations, paired with *binah* ("understanding")

Imma—Mother, Mom, Mama

Kabbalah—("Received Tradition," "The Receiving") medieval Jewish mysticism, Jewish mystical tradition in general

Kaddish—(derived from *kaddosh*, "holy" or "separate") public declaration of praise for God, a doxology separating parts of a service (or recited after study); the most well-known form is the mourner's *Kaddish*

kashrut—("fitness") rules defining what is fit and suitable for consumption or other sacred acts (kosher), as opposed to *treif* (unfit, unkosher)

kavvanah—("intention," "aim"; pl. *kavvanot*) focus, concentration invested in specific holy acts and the spiritual life as a whole

keter—("crown") the uppermost *sefirah* or divine emanations; associated with *Ayin*, No-thing

kvittel—("note," Yiddish) the brief written request a Hasid submits to the rebbe for assistance or intervention

Lubavitch—synonym for HaBaD Hasidism; name of the town in White Russia in which this dynasty flourished for a century

malkhut—("kingdom," "sovereignty") the final of the ten *sefirot* or divine emanations; the feminine indwelling presence; *Shekhinah*, Lower Mother, Vagina, etc.

mammash—("so-being-ness") real, palpable

mashgiah—("supervisor") overseeing kosher food preparation and other sacred activities *mashal*—(pl. *meshalim*) parable or analogue

Mashiah—("Anointed One") Messiah

matzah—unleavened bread, traditionally eaten on Passover

mehayyeh—("enlivening") refreshing, a delight

mensch—("human being"; pl. *menschen*) good or exemplary person

mesirat nefesh—("self-sacrifice") handing over or surrendering of one's life to God; adaptation of an older rabbinic expression for martyrdom

mezzuzah—small roll of parchment containing passages from Deuteronomy (6:4-9 and 11:13-21) affixed to the doorposts in Jewish spaces (often placed in a decorative case)

midrash—("inquiry," interpretation; pl. *midrashim*) a method of Torah interpretation; a collection of such interpretations; genre as a whole

mikveh—("gathering of water") immersion pool for spiritual cleansing and/or ritual purification

minyan—("quorum") a minimum of ten Jewish adults assembling for group prayer

mitzvah—("commandment," pl. *mitzvot*) sacred deed, God-connecting action, popularly equated with a "good deed"

m'malleh kol almin ("filling all worlds," Aramaic) God's vitalizing presence throughout creation

nefesh—("anima") lowest of five soul levels; the animative function of the spirit

Ne'ilah—("Closing") final prayer service on Yom Kippur

ner tamid—("eternal light") a light found in synagogues above the ark, modeled after the continuous flame in the ancient Temple in Jerusalem

neshamah—(soul; pl. *neshamot*) the soul level coming between *ru'ah* and *hayyah*; the intellective and communicative dimension of the individual

netzah—("victory") one of the lower *sefirot*; denotes effectiveness and longevity; often paired with *hod*—glory

niggun—(melody; pl. *niggunim*) a Hasidic melody, often wordless

nokhah p'nai ha-Shem—("facing the Name") being in the presence of God

nussah—"version" of prayer; applies both to the prayer traditions of a community (text and music) as a whole (German, North African, etc.), and of particular services within that community (weekday, Shabbat, holy days, etc.)

olam—(pl. *olamot*) world, universe (space and time)

Olam ha-Ba—("Coming World") World-to-Come, Afterlife; the *sefirah* of *binah* in Kabbalistic discourse

Pesah—("Passing Over") the spring holiday of liberation and rebirth

pidyon—(or *pidyon ha-nefesh*, "soul redemption") money given by a Hasid to a *rebbe* for assistance and support

rav—"rabbi," Jewish legal authority

reb—("sir") a term of respect and friendly admiration

rebbe—("rabbi," "master," pl. *rebbe'im*, Yiddish) the spiritual leader of a Hasidic community; also known as *tzaddik* ("righteous one")

Ribbono shel Olam—("Master of the Universe") a common appellation for the Divine; synonym for *tiferet* in Kabbalistic discourse

Rosh Ha-Shanah—("Head of the Year") the Jewish New Year

ru'ah—("spirit," "wind") the human spirit; the emotive dimension of the soul in Kabbalistic discourse

Ru'ah Ha-Kodesh—"Holy Spirit," divine inspiration; synonym for *Shekhinah* in Kabbalistic discourse

seder—("order") the traditional Passover evening (*Pesah*) home ritual

sefer—("book," pl. *sefarim*) holy text

sefer Torah—"Torah scroll"

sefirot—("numbers," "expressions," "orbs"; sing. *sefirah*) the ten primal emanations or attributes of the Divine (also present in the human soul)

seudah—("meal," pl. *seudot*) sacred meal

Shabbat—(*Shabbos*) "Sabbath"

shaliah—("emissary") a representative of a *rebbe*

shaliah tzibbur—("communal emissary") prayer leader

shalosh se'udot—"third meal" of *Shabbat* observed late Saturday afternoon/evening

Shavuot—("Weeks") Feast of Weeks, Pentecost, celebration of the late spring harvest and the revelation at Mt. Sinai

shefa—("flow") Divine energy and blessing

Shekhinah—("indwelling presence"), the immanent presence of God in creation; final *sefirah* (*malkhut*, female principality) in Kabbalistic discourse, often paired with *tiferet* ("beauty," male principality)

Shema—("Hear") the biblical and liturgical statement, "Hear O' Israel, *Y-H-V-H* is our God, *Y-H-V-H* is One"; core Jewish prayer and faith statement

sh'leimut ha'avodah—("Complete Service") full and true service to God

shofar—("horn") usually a ram's horn, sounded during the High Holy Day season

shtetl—(Yiddish) small "town" or "village"

shtiebl—("little room," Yiddish) a Hasidic conventicle or prayer space

shtreimel—(Yiddish) festive fur hat worn on *Shabbat* and holidays by many Hasidim

shul—("school") house of worship, synagogue

siddur—("order") Jewish prayer book

semikhah—("laying of hands") rabbinic ordination

sukkah—("booth") temporary hut constructed for *Sukkot*

Sukkot—("Booths") Feast of Booths celebrating the fall harvest

tallit—"prayer shawl"

Talmud—("Study") compilation of early rabbinic discussions conducted in the first centuries of the Common Era (includes both the Mishnah and Gemara)

tefillah—"prayer"

teiku—("Let it Stand") a rabbinic expression for an unresolved debate; also interpreted as an acronym for "Elijah the Prophet will resolve difficulties and questions"

tefillin—("phylacteries") small leather boxes attached to the head and arm for weekday (usually only morning) prayer; boxes contain scrolls with Exodus 13:1–10, 13:11–16, Deuteronomy 6:4–9, 11:13–21

Tehillim—Psalms

teshuvah—("return") repentance

tiferet—("Beauty") one of the ten *sefirot* (centrally located); also known as *Ha-Kadosh Barukh Hu* ("Holy Blessed One"); intimately connected to *malkhut* (male-female love relationship)

tikkun—("repair") act of sacred mending, healing, or reordering

tish—("table," Yiddish) public table of the *rebbe*

Torah—("Instruction") five books of Moses (Pentateuch), sacred Jewish teaching

treif—("unfit," Yiddish) non-kosher food or other unfit item; derived from the biblical term for a mauled animal, which is forbidden to eat *tzaddik*—("righteous one"; pl. *tzaddikim*) a pious and saintly person; Hasidic leader, *rebbe*

tzimtzum—("contraction"; pl. *tzimtzumim*) the self-limitation or concealment of God; the process of the devotee channeling and/or shaping divine energy

tzitzit—("fringes") ritual threads hanging from the corners of the *tallit* or four-cornered garment worn under one's clothing (*tallit katan*) to remind the devotee of her/his commitments to God and Torah

Yah—a shortened form of the Tetragrammaton (*Y-H-V-H*); one of Reb Zalman's preferred terms for God

yahrzeit—("time of year," Yiddish) anniversary of a death; usually observed for a relative, teacher, or other special person

yehidah—("unified") level of soul totally at one with God (above *hayyah*)

yehidut—("one-ing") a private counseling session with a *rebbe*

yesh—(being) manifest reality, corporeality

yeshiva—(pl. *yeshivot*) academy for traditional Jewish study, including the training of rabbis

yesod—("foundation") one of the lower *sefirot*; the channel between *tiferet* and *malkhut*

yetzirah—("formation"), World of Feeling in Kabbalistic discourse

Y-H-V-H—*Yud-Heh-Vav-Heh*, the Tetragramaton, unpronounceable name of God; a term that carries within it the fullness of existence in Kabbalistic discourse

Yiddishkeit—("Judaism," Yiddish) Jewish religion and culture

yirah—"fear" or "awe," often paired with love (*ahavah* or *hesed*) in rabbinic and mystical thought

Yisra'el—("God-wrestler") Israel

Yom Kippur—("Day of Atonement") Jewish sacred day (9 days after Rosh Ha-Shanah), culmination of the High Holy Days

yontif—holiday (Yiddish)

zemirot—(sing. *zemer*) "hymns"

Zohar—("Splendor") *Sefer Ha-Zohar*, "Book of Splendor," the crowning work of medieval Jewish mysticism

Sources

A Heart Afire: Stories and Teachings of Early Hasidic Masters. Revised Edition. With Netanel Miles-Yépez. Rhinebeck, NY: Adam Kadmon Books, 2017.

All Breathing Life Adores Your Name. Edited by Michael L. Kagan. Santa Fe, NM: Gaon Books, 2011.

Credo of a Modern Kabbalist. With Daniel Siegel. Victoria, BC: Trafford Publishing, 2005. Used with permission

Davening: A Guide to Meaningful Jewish Prayer. With Joel Segel. Woodstock, VT: Jewish Lights Publishing, 2012.

Deep Ecumenism. Unpublished manuscript. Edited by Netanel Miles-Yépez.

"Denominationalism and Jewish Renewal," The Reconstructionist 71, no. 2 (Spring 2007).

"Entering Israel's Second Yovel," Tikkun 13, no. 2 (March/April 1998).

"Expanded Awareness: Hot-Housing Consciousness," Spiritual Eldering Newsletter 5, no. 4 (2002).

Foundations of the Fourth Turning of Hasidism: A Manifesto. With Netanel Miles-Yépez. Boulder, CO: Albion-Andalus Books, 2014. Used with permission.

Fragments of a Future Scroll: A Sampler of Radical Hasidism and Kabbalah. Forthcoming revised edition. Edited by Netanel Miles-Yépez.

From Age-ing to Sage-ing: A Revolutionary Approach to Growing Older. With Ronald S. Miller. New York: Grand Central Publishing, 2014.

Gate to the Heart: A Manual of Contemplative Jewish Practice. Edited by Netanel Miles-Yépez and Robert Micha'el Esformes. Boulder, CO: Albion-Andalus Books, 2013.

God Hidden, Whereabouts Unknown: The "Contraction" of God in Different Jewish Paradigms. Second Edition. With Netanel Miles-Yépez. Boulder, CO: Albion-Andalus Books, 2019.

Integral Halachah: Transcending and Including. With Daniel Siegel. Victoria, BC: Trafford Publishing, 2007.

Jewish with Feeling: A Guide to Meaningful Jewish Practice. With Joel Segel. Woodstock, VT: Jewish Lights Publishing, 2013.

Living Fully, Dying Well: Spiritual and Scientific Approaches to the End of Life. Forthcoming revised edition. Edited by Netanel Miles-Yépez.

My Life in Jewish Renewal: A Memoir. With Edward Hoffman. Lanham, MA: Rowman & Littlefield Publishers. Copyright © 2012. Used by permission. All rights reserved.

"Reb Zalman's Jewel of Elul: December Days." *Huffington Post,* August 30, 2012.

"Rebbe-Talk: A Conversation with Reb Zalman Schachter-Shalomi." With Or Rose. *Sh'ma: A Journal of Jewish Ideas,* March 2012.

"Respecting Elders, Becoming Elders: Can Elders Save the World?" *Yes! Magazine* (August 29, 2005).

"Saying *Zikr* with the Sufis: A Trial," *Spectrum: A Journal of Renewal Spirituality* 3, no. 2 (Summer–Fall, 2007).

Sh'ma': A Concise Weekday Siddur for Praying in English. Edited by Netanel Miles-Yépez. Boulder, CO: Albion-Andalus Books, 2010.

Sparks of Light: Counseling in the Hasidic Tradition. With Edward Hoffman. Boulder, CO: Shambhala Publications, 1983.

"*Teiku*—Because Elijah Lives On!" in *Jewish Mysticism and the Spiritual Life: Classic Texts, Contemporary Reflections*. Edited by Lawrence Fine, Eitan Fishbane, and Or Rose. Woodstock, VT: Jewish Lights Publishing, 2010.

The Emerging Cosmology. Unpublished manuscript. Edited by Netanel Miles-Yépez.

The Gates of Prayer: Twelve Talks on Davvenology. Edited by Netanel Miles-Yépez (Boulder, CO: Albion-Andalus Books, 2011.

The Geologist of the Soul: Talks on Rebbe-Craft and Spiritual Leadership. Edited by Netanel Miles-Yépez. Boulder, CO: Albion-Andalus Books, 2012.

"Torah and Dharma: Torah *Hyphen* Dharma." With Bernie Glassman. *Spectrum: A Journal of Renewal Spirituality* 2, no. 1 (Winter–Spring, 2006).

"Trade Secrets from the Monastery: Rev. Howard Thurman and Brother Franciscus," *Delumin/a: Spirituality. Culture. Arts.* March 30, 2015.

"What I Found in the Chapel," in *My Neighbor's Faith: Stories of Interreligious Encounter, Growth, and Transformation*. Edited by Jennifer Howe Peace, Or N. Rose, and Gregory Mobley. Maryknoll, NY: Orbis Books, 2012.

Wrapped in a Holy Flame: Teachings and Tales of the Hasidic Masters. Forthcoming revised edition. With Netanel Miles-Yépez.

About the Editors

Or N. Rose is the director of the Miller Center for Interreligious Learning and Leadership at Hebrew College where he has served in various academic and administrative capacities for many years. Among his publications are two previous volumes with Orbis: *My Neighbor's Faith: Stories of Interreligious Encounter, Growth, and Transformation* and *Words to Live By: Sacred Sources for Interreligious Engagement* (both coedited). He was ordained as a rabbi by his teachers, rabbis Arthur Green, Neal Rose, and Zalman Schachter-Shalomi in 2005.

Netanel Miles-Yépez is a professor in the Department of Religious Studies at Naropa University and cofounder of Charis Foundation for New Monasticism & InterSpirituality. Among his many publications are *A Heart Afire: Stories and Teachings of the Early Hasidic Masters* (with Zalman Schachter-Shalomi) and *My Love Stands Behind a Wall: A Translation of the Song of Songs and Other Poems* (Albion-Andalus Books). On the passing of Zalman Schachter-Shalomi in 2014, he became the *pir* of the Inayati-Maimuni lineage of Sufism, fusing the Hasidic teachings of Judaism with the Sufi teachings of Islam.

MODERN SPIRITUAL MASTERS
Robert Ellsberg, Series Editor

This series introduces the essential writing and vision of some of the great spiritual teachers of our time. While many of these figures are rooted in long-established traditions of spirituality, others have charted new, untested paths. In each case, however, they have engaged in a spiritual journey shaped by the challenges and concerns of our age. Together with the saints and witnesses of previous centuries, these modern spiritual masters may serve as guides and companions to a new generation of seekers.

Already published:

Modern Spiritual Masters (edited by Robert Ellsberg)
Swami Abhishiktananda (edited by Shirley du Boulay)
Metropolitan Anthony of Sourozh (edited by Gillian Crow)
Eberhard Arnold (edited by Johann Christoph Arnold)
Pedro Arrupe (edited by Kevin F. Burke, S.J.)
Daniel Berrigan (edited by John Dear)
Thomas Berry (edited by Mary EvelynTucker and John Grim)
Dietrich Bonhoeffer (edited by Robert Coles)
Robert McAfee Brown (edited by Paul Crowley)
Dom Helder Camara (edited by Francis McDonagh)
Carlo Carretto (edited by Robert Ellsberg)
G. K. Chesterton (edited by William Griffin)
Joan Chittister (edited by Mary Lou Kownacki and Mary Hembrow Snyder)
Yves Congar (edited by Paul Lakeland)
The Dalai Lama (edited by Thomas A. Forsthoefel)
Alfred Delp, S.J. (introduction by Thomas Merton)
Catherine de Hueck Dogerty (edited by David Meconi, S.J.)
Virgilio Elizondo (edited by Timothy Matovina)
Jacques Ellul (edited by Jacob E. Van Vleet)
Ralph Waldo Emerson (edited by Jon M. Sweeney)
Charles de Foucauld (edited by Robert Ellsberg)
Mohandas Gandhi (edited by John Dear)
Bede Griffiths (edited by Thomas Matus)
Romano Guardini (edited by Robert A. Krieg)
Gustavo Gutiérrez (edited by Daniel G. Groody)

Henry David Thoreau (edited by Tim Flinders)
Howard Thurman (edited by Luther E. Smith)
Leo Tolstoy (edited by Charles E. Moore)
Evelyn Underhill (edited by Emilie Griffin)
Vincent Van Gogh (by Carol Berry)
Jean Vanier (edited by Carolyn Whitney-Brown)
Swami Vivekananda (edited by Victor M. Parachin)
Simone Weil (edited by Eric O. Springsted)
John Howard Yoder (edited by Paul Martens and Jenny Howells)